The first Dramatick Rule is, have good Cloaths,
To charm the gay Spectator's gentle Breast,
In Lace and Feather Tragedy's express'd,
And Heroes die unpity'd, if ill-dress'd.

R. Steele, Prologue to Vanbrugh's *The Mistake* (1705)

Costume on the Stage
1600 - 1940

Diana de Marly

BARNES & NOBLE BOOKS   TOTOWA   NEW JERSEY

TO MY TEACHER —
STELLA MARY NEWTON

© Diana de Marly 1982
First published in the USA 1982 by
Barnes & Noble Books
81 Adams Drive
Totowa, New Jersey 07512

ISBN 0 389 20317 3

Printed in Great Britain

Frontispiece

1 'Ye Countess of Bedford Penthesileia Queen
of the Amazons', a design for Ben Jonson's
Masque of Queens 1609, by Inigo Jones.   THE
TRUSTEES OF THE CHATSWORTH SETTLEMENT

Classical themes of ancient queens in classical
costume represent the Roman ideal of the heroic
with the Amazon ruler attired like an imperial
general in Roman helmet and cuirass. The short
overskirt like a Roman tunic became traditional
for female classical roles. Inigo Jones's
instructions to the tailor read 'Depe pink color.
Deep morrey. Skie color.'

8-2-83

Contents

Preface

Acknowledgements

This study is intended to be a general survey of reform movements in modern theatre costume in relation to artistic theory during the period 1600–1940, and tries to show how each age's artistic policy imposed its own views on the theatre of its day. There were repeated calls for more accurate historical costuming, but it is necessary to consider the inhibitions to a perfect recreation of the past, and how far a revival of historical costume is in fact a compromise between the past and the present.

Unless stated otherwise all translations are by the author.

The author and publishers would like gratefully to acknowledge all those who gave their kind permission to reproduce copyright material:

H.M. The Queen 11, 12, 30; Ashmolean Museum, University of Oxford 69, 70, 71, 72, 88; Birmingham City Museum and Art Gallery 37; The British Library 5, 13, 14, 15, 19, 21, 22, 25, 26, 33, 35, 43, 44, 45, 46, 61, 62, 90, 91, 92, 93, 94; The Trustees of the Chatsworth Settlement, photographs the Courtauld Institute of Art 1, 2; Fitzwilliam Museum, University of Cambridge 9; Folger Shakespeare Library, Washington 8, 20, 28; Guildhall Library, London 40; Harvard University Theatre Collection 18, 36, 49; TV Times 87; Iveagh Bequest, Kenwood 7; Museum of London 24, 53, 65, 66, 67, 68, 79, 82, 83, 89; Manchester City Art Gallery 34; National Portrait Gallery 4; National Theatre photographs, Victoria and Albert Museum 23, 31, 32, 42, 48; Mrs S.M. Newton, photographs the Courtauld Institute of Art 95, 96, 97, 98, 99, 100; Tate Gallery 16, 29, 39, 40, 47; Victoria and Albert Museum 3, 6, 41, 50, 51, 52, 54, 55, 56, 58, 59, 60, 63, 64, 73, 74, 75, 76, 77, 78, 80, 81, 84, 85, 86; Wallace Collection 57; Yale University Center for British Art, Paul Mellon Collection 17, 27.

Costume history adviser: Dr Aileen Ribeiro.

List of Illustrations

7

CHAPTER ONE

The Renaissance and Baroque Ideal

SMITH: And pray, Sir, what is your design in this
Scene?
BAYES: Why, Sir, my design is Roman Cloaths.

George Duke of Buckingham, *The Rehearsal* (1671)

Perhaps the best-known fact about Baroque theatre costume is that actors often wore Roman armour together with seventeenth-century periwigs. Nowadays this is looked upon as a ridiculous mistake, mixing the clothes of antiquity with contemporary garments and accessories, as if Baroque theatre designers did not know what they were doing. Yet our ancestors were not all fools, by any means. There were reasons for what they did, so the question that should be asked is, why did they approach theatre costume in this manner? Was it due to carelessness or was it due to policy? The answer lies in the ideals of the Renaissance period which were inherited by the Baroque era. Starting in Italy, these beliefs spread to France and then to England, and the form of drama which was most affected by these new concepts was tragedy.

The Renaissance and Baroque eras were both very visual, theatrical times. The majority of the population could neither read nor write so the monarchy, the church, parliament, and the livery companies advertised and illustrated their power, authority or wealth in visual and theatrical terms. Public show was the way to let the public know. There was far more celebration of events than there is today, while anyone who was important would ensure that everyone could *see* just how grand he was. A new ambassador would arrive in a foreign capital with a train of coaches; and a duke would visit a town surrounded by scores of his followers and tenants all wearing his family colours; a prince of the church would travel with an equal number of attendants; and members of the craft guilds would honour their patron saint with magnificent processions on land or water. Of course the greatest displays were made by the crown, so every royal birthday, anniversary, arrival, departure, recovery from illness, wedding, or funeral was honoured with appropriate glory. Such festivities with their casts of hundreds in different costumes, their

towering set-pieces, their arches and gateways festooned with garlands and statues, and their odes and speeches, had to be designed with a particular theme in mind. They were productions in the theatrical sense, and even an artist of the standing of Sir Peter Paul Rubens would be called upon to design a state entry, while his pupil Sir Anthony van Dyck was asked to design the decorative programme for Charles I's flagship *The Sovereign of the Seas*. It was only a small step for such artists to be involved also in designing plays for the court or public theatres, and the relation between the state, the fine arts and the stage was much closer than it is today. It was so close that what happened in stage design was a close reflection of the attitudes and theories which were promoted in the world of fine arts, and an imitation of the visual glories to be found outside the theatre.

The principal artistic ideal of the period was to look Roman. Ever since the early Renaissance in Italy scholars and painters had concentrated their attention on the antique world as the perfect model upon which to base their own creative activity. Roman ruins were examined, classical sculpture was unearthed, ancient inscriptions were studied, and the copies of Latin and Greek books in monastic libraries were read with great application. The Gothic world with its myriad feudal states was being replaced by that of the nation state, with the king striving to attain a monopoly of power, so here too for political ideals people looked to the most powerful state Europe had known: Rome. The achievements of that ancient empire were seen as the most suitable precedent to follow, in the hope that by so doing the modern state might achieve similar triumphs in art and power. Culture was part of national glory, so it was important that the classical ideal should be active as much in art as in political ambitions. State processions were redesigned to look like Roman triumphs, the Hapsburg Emperor

2 Final dress for Oberon in Ben Jonson's Christmas masque *Oberon the Fairy Prince*, 1611, by Inigo Jones. THE TRUSTEES OF THE CHATSWORTH SETTLEMENT

Despite the fairy theme the Prince of Wales is presented as an imperial Roman hero, crowned with laurels, although his trunkhose, despite being striped to resemble a Roman leather overskirt, are a compromise between contemporary fashion and historical accuracy.

OPPOSITE PAGE
3 'The Arrival of Juno in her Chariot', from Act IV of Corneille's *Andromède*, Théâtre Royal de Bourbon, Paris, 1650, by F. Chauveau after G. Torrelli.

Roman armour in the theatre was often in fabric as in these examples with pleated skirts. The high waistline instead of a low classical one is due to contemporary fashion preventing accuracy. The production was mounted to display the machines designed by Torrelli now that the theatre was coming indoors, which allowed a lot of pulleys and wheels to be installed in the roof for elevations, descents and heavenly appearances.

Charles V ordered a suit of Roman armour to wear in parades, and plays were expected to imitate classical prototypes. Every activity had to justify itself in Roman terms.

Ancient writers such as Aristotle had laid down rules about drama, the texts of some Greek and Roman plays survived, and some Roman theatres were still standing in Italy and France; so scholars busied themselves working out rules for modern drama based upon classical concepts. Of course the true home of classical drama had been ancient Greece, not Rome; but in the sixteenth century Greece was part of the brutal Turkish empire, and any western Christian scholar who wanted to investigate ancient Greek theatres in that region might end up as a Turkish galley slave. It was too dangerous a place to visit, so scholars based their knowledge of Greek plays upon Roman copies and discourses, which led to the confusion of Greek works with Roman; so long as the play was ancient it did not matter if it came from Rome or Athens.

The ancients had divided drama into comedy and tragedy, ruling that comedy was about ordinary people of humble degree, while tragedy concerned itself with noble themes and characters. This distinction had important consequences for stage costume – comedy and tragedy had to be dressed differently. The first Renaissance scholar to write a book on the production of plays was Geraldi Cinthio whose *Discurso sulle Tragedie* came out in Venice in 1554; he stated that comedies should use ordinary clothes but tragedies must be dressed in an aristocratic and magnificent manner. These ideas were further developed by the Jewish playwright Leone de' Sommi of Mantua who wrote his *Quattro Dialoghi in Materia di Rappresentazione Sceniche* in about 1565. As a practical man of the theatre he did not think that every aspect of the ancient classical theatre should be copied down to the last detail. The clothing traditions of the Roman stage with white costumes for old men, colourful garments for young characters, yellow clothes for prostitutes, and twisted cloaks for pimps and parasites seemed too restrictive to his mind and did not allow for enough variety. He thought it important that each character should be different and individual in his costume so that the audience could recognize him without trouble. Where the ancients had stressed

character types, Leone stressed individual beings. His principal ideal was that the theatre should look magnificent, so he wanted all actors to *vestir nobilmente*, and to be as fine as money could buy. A comedy could have velvet and satin garments provided that tragedy was still better dressed in cloth-of-gold or silver with rich embroidery. The distinction must be kept. It was an absolute rule, but comedy did not have to be shabby in comparison. Comedy might have elegant, fashionable clothes in good materials, but on no account should tragedy ever be dressed in contemporary costumes. Tragedy must be Roman. The theatre costume designer must study antique sculpture and recreate Roman togas and Roman armour.[1]

Such attire was not that of common man, for ancient peasants could not have commissioned statues of themselves; it was the official dress of Roman senators, generals and emperors, the only class of persons in whose honour statues were erected. Thus the Roman attire recommended for stage use was of high social status, and that was very much what tragedies were all about. They did not touch the fate of ordinary man; tragedies dealt with

heroes, kings, princes and even gods. The fate of a great man and the battle of heroic virtue against vice concerned tragedians, not the downfall of a peasant who was too lowly to be worthy of aristocratic attention. The most famous theatrical productions in Renaissance Italy were court presentations, staged during a royal visit, a ducal marriage or a papal celebration, so the characters in the tragedy were of the same social rank as the nobles who sat in the audience. Most of the plots of tragedies were now based on classical mythology; the myths were Roman so the costume had to be Roman too. A stage hero ought to look like an ancient Roman conqueror, so the ancient armour was the only possible costume. One exception was allowed, however. In view of the threat to Western Europe from the Turkish Empire, this contemporary menace to Christendom could not be excluded from the Renaissance mind, for all its concentration on ancient Rome, so some tragedies were written on Turkish themes, such as the battles for power within a sultan's family, or the struggles of Christian forces against Turkish oppression. So strong was the image of the Turk that he could only be conceived in Turkish costume. Accordingly Turks on stage wore turbans and robes, and the women veils, although any Christians in the cast would have worn Roman heroic costume, standing as they did for the fate of western civilization.

There was a strong element of propaganda in the tragedies of the period. They were performed before princes and they honoured princes, so that a play about the clemency and wisdom of a mythological ruler was praising the clemency and wisdom of the current ruler watching the performance. In the days before mass communications the theatre acted as a state propaganda machine, impressing foreign ambassadors, illustrating royal policy, advertising royal attributes. The most brilliant productions were those produced at a court, so the drama had to flatter the patron. Indeed the possession of a royal or aristocratic patron was essential to the survival of a company of actors, for officially the Protestant and Catholic churches condemned actors as vagabonds and damned their souls for eternity by not allowing them to be buried in consecrated ground. Consequently powerful patrons like the Duke of Mantua or Queen Elizabeth I of England were necessary to protect the theatre against the church. Fortunately the clerical attacks on the stage went in phases. Actresses were not allowed to perform in papal Rome, but some cardinals did finance the production of tragedies with all-male casts, in order to honour themselves with a glorious theme. The stage was too powerful a propaganda machine for the church to ignore it completely, and the Jesuit order in particular was to be very active in the seventeenth century in producing dramas with high moral themes as a way of instructing the audiences in Christian virtues.

The idea that the stage could carry a moral message was very important to those trying to protect the theatre against puritanical attacks. Both tragedy and ballet could be used to convey a message, argued the Jesuit father Jouvancy in his *Ratio Discendi et Docendi* in 1685. He believed that a noble tragedy could be accompanied by a dramatic ballet, linked to the main plot, where a martial dance could carry the same theme, the victory of religion over idolatry. Many Jesuit colleges for boys taught dancing, one of the social graces for young gentlemen, so many of them adopted Jouvancy's ideas. The college at Clermont presented a grand tragedy at its annual prizegivings to which it now added a serious ballet, all performed by the pupils, with the text and plot written by the teachers of rhetoric. Only serious subjects were employed, and comedy was not regarded as suitable. The Collège Louis le Grand performed such works up to 1762 when the Jesuit order in France was dissolved.[2]

The French crown was very well aware that the

4 William III as Mercury in the masque *Le Ballet de la Paix*, The Hague, 1678, by J. de Buen. NATIONAL PORTRAIT GALLERY

Every Western European ruler from Sweden to Austria was presented as an imperial Roman idol in Roman armour, helmet topped with ostrich plumes and the marshall's baton, if he could afford it. The ballet was a political gesture to celebrate a peace treaty.

OPPOSITE PAGE
5 Troilus and Cressida from *The works of Mr. William Shakespear, in Six Volumes*, ed. N. Rowe, 1709, by J. van der Gucht. THE BRITISH LIBRARY

The subject may be Trojan but the dress is Roman for that was applied to any ancient subject, armour for the hero, classical overskirt for the heroine although her costume is mainly a fashionable dress of 1709. The tasselled sleeve became a stock theatrical feature and was taken from the mediaeval Fool's costume.

Fortunately the king did not oblige and the theatre stayed, because the king enjoyed it. This illustrates how vital royal support was, for without it, an energetic bishop might have closed every theatre down. The one thing the theatre could not do was annoy its principal patron, and the Italian comedians in Paris, the Commedia dell'Arte, made this mistake with a comedy called *La Fausse Prude* in 1697. Louis XIV's second wife regarded this as a reference to herself, and the king banished the Italians, who did not return to Paris until 1716, after he had died. For the theatre to defy the king was suicide.

In England the involvement of the crown with the stage for political and propaganda motives can be seen clearly in the court masques mounted for Queen Elizabeth I, James I & VI, and Charles I. Elizabeth I was not a lavish sponsor of the arts and in her case the payment for entertaining and glorifying the queen fell on her courtiers and hosts. The mediaeval joust survived in the Accession Day Tilts, when elaborately costumed knights paid homage to their sovereign and offered her shields bearing emblems symbolic of loyalty. The armour of the champions was strictly contemporary, and their lances were mediaeval in pattern, but the classical influence from Italy was beginning to creep in, most notably in the knights' surcoats embroidered with olive branches, and the shields with their classical motifs. A very influential book on the subject of images and the correct attributes for deities and personifications was Cesare Ripa's *Iconologia* of 1593, published in Padua, which was considered such a useful work that editions were still being printed two hundred years later. It was the reference book for anyone faced with the task of designing an emblem or symbol, and was much appreciated at the English court. The whole celebration of Elizabeth was based on classical imagery: she was Gloriana, she was the Vestal Virgin as symbolized by the ermine and the white rose, she was piety symbolized by the pelican feeding its young on its own blood, she was the phoenix, eternally chaste, she was the goddess Iris of the rainbow bringing peace after the storm. The English defeat of the Spanish Armada was a manifestation of her magical powers.

The gradual appearance of classical dress in England happened during Queen Elizabeth I's summer progresses around her kingdom, when she would be fêted by her favourites. The Elizabethan fashion in clothes was very formal and stiff, but they understood that classical dress had been loose and white, so the queen would be greeted by nymphs attired in white silk shifts.[4] When Lord Hertford received the queen at Elvetham in 1591 he provided classical Graces and Hours to scatter flowers in her

theatre could convey a message, and many royal ballets were related to political events such as Louis XIV's marriage in 1660, the birth of the Dauphin in 1662; the king's victories were celebrated by the ballet *Cyrus* in 1673, and the Peace of Nimègue by the *Ballet de la Paix* of 1679. When the king's grandson was 15 in 1697 this was marked by the *Ballet de la Jeunesse*. The crown was thus an active exploiter of the stage for political reasons. Nevertheless clerical criticism could flare up. In December 1694 Louis XIV's sister-in-law Elisabeth Charlotte Duchesse d'Orléans reported:

We hear that all operas and plays are to be abolished. The Sorbonne had instructions to take the matter in hand. What seems so astonishing to me is that they concentrate on such innocent things while all the vices are in full swing. No one says a word against poisoning, violence, and that horrible sodomy [her husband was homosexual]; all the clergy preach against the poor theatre, which does nobody any harm, and where vice is punished and virtue is rewarded. It makes me furious.[3]

path. A fiery monster symbolized the queen's enemies, but he was vanquished by the arrival of the queen, representing as she did peace. It appears that this classical introduction concerned women most to begin with, for nymphs and personifications such as the Graces were female characters; they danced around in their shifts, but one does not find English courtiers stripping down to their shirts. Moreover it would not have been very politic to promote the Roman concept of the hero when the sovereign was a lady. All this changed in the next reign. While James I & VI was so uncouth that it would be difficult to see him as a hero, his heir Henry Prince of Wales had all the heroic attributes; he was an excellent horseman, slim, learned, and a patron of art, so he could fulfil the Roman role. The designer who brought the Italian ideal of the Roman hero to the British court was Inigo Jones.

Born in London in 1573, Jones was the son of a clothworker. This background probably gave him an early interest in fabrics, costume and design. He entered the service of a nobleman in 1598 who took him on a tour of France, Germany, and Italy. Jones spent some time in Italy, returning to London in 1604, and was considered sufficiently learned in Italian style to be engaged by the king. In 1613 he paid another visit to Italy. Each time he brought back Italian books and engravings, and throughout his designing career he was to order prints of the latest productions in Florence and elsewhere, so he had the new ideals of the Renaissance theatre at his finger tips. He used Ripa's *Iconologia*, and Cesare Vecellio's costume history *Habiti antichi et moderni di tutto il mondo* of 1598, which had some engravings of Roman armour, and copied designs by Italian theatre designers like Alfonso Parigi. As Prince Henry was the hope for the future of the realm, when Jones designed his costume for the masque *Oberon, The Fairy Prince* in 1611 it was not a mediaeval prince but a Roman emperor who rode forth. His helmet was plumed and crowned with laurels, his cuirass imitated a Roman one, and he had Roman boots. He did not have a Roman tunic skirt, but wore normal trunkhose; but they were striped to give the impression of the leather strips on the Roman skirt. An introduction is a gradual step, and no doubt there was some hesitation about short skirts which might reveal the prince's drawers, which would explain the retention of trunks.

This promotion of the young heir collapsed in 1612 when Henry died suddenly at 18, so the use of the stage as a royal propaganda machine had to be turned to the next-in-line, Prince Charles, who proved to be an enthusiastic masquer. As King Charles I from 1625 he participated in many a masque, while his French wife Henrietta Maria

acted in pastoral plays as well. The new king was very conscious of the masque as a symbolic justification of his policy and a magnificent illustration of the imperial prestige of a firm believer in Divine Right. *Chloridia*, written by Ben Jonson and performed in 1631, celebrated the happiness of the royal marriage, with the queen appearing as Chloris. Inigo Jones designed the costume to be trimmed round the waist and sleeves with leaves, and with the skirt in tiers like those of a Roman woman's dress, as she represented rural calm. Jones corrected his version of Roman heroic dress for the king in the masque *Albion's Triumph*, which he wrote with Aurelian Townshend in 1632. It showed the king as an autocrat, cast as the Roman Emperor Albanactus, and dressed him in a helmet with ostrich plumes and laurels, a correct cuirass or *lorica*, and most important the correct Roman tunic with skirts and an overskirt of leather strips, the *pteruges*, abandoning the trunkhose retained for Prince Henry 21 years before. There were two errors due to contemporary fashion. The king kept his hair shoulder length and did not have it chopped short like an ancient Roman, and the sleeves were wider at the top than those any Roman wore, but this was the fashionable size in 1632.

Here was the most fundamental problem in theatrical costume: the limitations on purity imposed by contemporary taste. All the enthusiasm for Roman dress displayed by scholars and designers was inhibited by the standards of the age in which they lived, and this inhibition has affected every attempt to revive a costume from the past, as will be seen throughout this book. No matter how much an ancient form of costume may be admired and idolized, when it comes to recreating that form for the stage, contemporary considerations keep intruding. People who grow up in a period of wide clothes will object to a narrow look, and likewise those conditioned by an age of slim modes will look askance at anything wide. This applied in particular to an intimate part of the body like hair, and actors both professional and amateur would object to doing anything to the person which would fundamentally alter their normal appearance, the look they were used to, the look they regarded as the essential part of their identity. It is one thing to use make-up and wigs on stage, for they are temporary adoptions and can be removed after the performance. But to shave off one's hair or eyebrows, and to change one's shape on a permanent basis, touches a very sensitive area, the concept of self. 'What is me' is affected by the period one grows up in, and the contemporary definition of what personalities are socially acceptable. Consequently the monarch or actor in 1632 putting on Roman clothes was a very different type from the actual Romans who used to wear those garments as part of their everyday life. Contemporary politics affected Charles I and his hair; he and the cavaliers of his court grew their hair long, but the political opposition included fanatical Puritans who cropped their hair extremely short. Charles I had no wish to look like a Puritan, even if ancient Romans had done so, so he kept his usual style. *Albion's Triumph* included a Roman Imperial Triumph, with all the cast suitably attired, but this Roman magnificence did not turn Charles I and his court into Romans. Charles I might have wished to be as powerful as a Roman emperor, and so did most of his contemporary kings, but it was on modern terms, with the latest equipment, and all modern conveniences. It was not physically possible to go back to Roman culture in its entirety because other circumstances had come onto the world scene, from Christianity to gunpowder. Consequently the adoption of Roman clothes was for propaganda purposes at court, but come the Civil War in 1642 both sides, royalist or parliamentarian, wore the buff coats and breastplates of contemporary military attire. Roman dress was an illustration of imperial ambitions but it could not bring that empire about, because contemporary considerations got in the way, both fashionable and political. The theatre could not exist in a vacuum, untouched by outside influences, no matter how pure the ideal.

The ancients of the classical world would have recoiled at another event in Renaissance and Baroque theatre, the introduction of actresses. The ancient Greeks had banned actresses completely, expecting all their women except whores to live in harem-like seclusion, while the few women who appeared on Roman stages were classified as the lowest of the low. In the Middle Ages some amateur actresses performed in the mystery plays but the Roman Catholic church was intensely opposed to the idea of a woman having a career in which she exposed herself to public gaze. The church held that women should be modest, obedient and domestic. Eve must be kept down because she had led Adam into a state of sin. The attacks on women made by clerics read nowdays like insane ravings. The more peaceful sex was condemned if it tried to make the tiniest step outside the church's definition of womanhood, and this attitude was also taken up by the Protestant churches. The Puritans attacked worldly entertainment and they disliked the theatre in all its aspects, but for a woman to enter that corrupt world was the height of immodesty, a dance with the Devil. Nevertheless a few women dared to do so, and it took a very bold spirit indeed to fly in the face of ecclesiastical damnation. One of the earliest professional actresses was the Italian Isabella Andreini, wife of an actor in the Commedia

dell'Arte whom she married in 1578. She was the leading lady in the Gelosi troupe and she and her husband went to Paris with the troupe in 1600. This led to a few Frenchwomen daring to imitate her, and when a French troupe paid a visit to London in November 1629 it took some actresses with it. When the girls appeared onstage at the Blackfriars Theatre there was a near riot and they were pelted off the boards. The Protestant audience objected to Roman Catholic whores, for all actresses were branded by that insult. But at court ladies of high estate were appearing in the masques, while the queen herself acted. They were amateurs of course, not professionals with a career to sustain, but they too came under attack for their brazen behaviour. The Puritan barrister William Prynne published a ferocious attack on the stage in his *Histrio-Mastix, or The Scourge of Players* (1633), which classified women actors as notorious whores. This infuriated Charles I, who considered it a personal insult to his queen Henrietta Maria. He had Prynne arrested for high treason, and the barrister was sentenced to life imprisonment, fined £5000, deprived of his degree, and had his ears cut off.[5] A royal actress was above reproach, but lesser mortals did not have such state protection.

The English public theatre continued to use boys in female roles, which was in keeping with ancient Greek precedents, and the outbreak of the Civil War prevented the court masque from exerting a powerful influence which might have led to the introduction of actresses. The first English troupe to have actresses was one in exile. Several actors fled to the Continent during the fighting, and one George Jolly formed an English troupe to perform in Germany and Austria, where he introduced actresses in 1654. Back in London the Puritans had closed the theatres down, but when Cromwell died in 1658, the playhouses began to re-open, and stuck to the pre-war tradition of boys in female roles. This changed with the Restoration of the monarchy in 1660. Charles II had spent his exile in Paris and at The Hague, so he was used to seeing actresses on the public stage and insisted on their appearance in his capital.

The first London actress to be trained appeared as Desdemona in *Othello* on 8 December 1660, although exactly who she was is uncertain. As public theatres were licensed by the crown, the royal taste for actresses ensured their survival, court and city flocked to see them, and no amount of Puritan criticism has yet succeeded in driving women actors from the London theatre since. The arrival of professional actresses inspired playwrights to write roles for them. Thomas Otway was so besotted with Elizabeth Barry that his tragedies were written with her in mind. Her first appearances were failures but her lover the Earl of Rochester coached her and she matured into an actress of great power and dignity. Offstage she was notorious for selling herself to the highest bidder, and the contradiction between stage presence and personal immorality fascinated her contemporaries. Yet there were many actresses against whom the charge of whore could not be levelled. Mary Sanderson was one of the first professional actresses in England and was famous for such roles as Lady Macbeth. She married the most distinguished actor of the Restoration period Thomas Betterton, and they were a couple of the highest reputation. In the eighteenth century Hannah Pritchard, Garrick's leading lady, was an actress of whom no ill could be spoken. She married one of the staff at Drury Lane. To marry somebody in the business was probably about the best thing an actress could do, for if she married a man from outside he would pressurize her to abandon anything so unfeminine as a professional career. If she did not marry the actress still needed some kind of protector, as women had so little legal rights to their own money. One of the most loved actresses was Ann Bracegirdle; trained by Betterton, she lived with the playwright Congreve, and created the first performances in his comedies, being particularly famed for her appearance as Millamant in *The Way of the World* in 1700. Her private life did not prevent her from being buried in Westminster Abbey. Similarly Anne Oldfield, who made her name in the comedies of Farquhar, was accorded burial in Westminster Abbey when she died, despite having been the mistress of the author Arthur Mainwaring and the mother of two illegitimate sons. The church did stipulate that she could not have a memorial over her grave, but it did allow her to have an epitaph written by the playwrights she had worked with, Congreve and Savage. This very enlightened attitude of the church of England towards actresses contrasted strongly with the Catholic church's refusal to grant them Christian burial. In France Voltaire was very bitter when an actress who appeared in his plays and was celebrated in Paris, Adrienne Lecouvreur, had to be buried in marshy ground because no Catholic cemetery would admit her. She died in exactly the same year as Anne Oldfield, 1730, so the two churches could not have been more different in their attitudes. Lecouvreur had had a lover, like Oldfield, but one could guarantee that he, the Maréchal de Saxe, was not refused Christian burial for having kept a mistress, nor were cardinals who had mistresses. The Catholic church had one law for actresses and another one for male lovers.

The theatre historian Allardyce Nicoll did accuse actresses of dragging the playhouse down because they did not all have chaste private lives, but he failed to query how far actors' personal conduct had done the same before the appearance of actresses.[6] Undoubtedly some actresses were brazen creatures, but given the fact that the theatre was condemned by Puritans and popes, and its participants branded as vagabonds, the woman who was prepared to defy such condemnation had to be pretty brazen to tread the boards in the first place. If not immoral she still needed to be thick-skinned, for there was no other activity in society where a woman was so exposed before an audience, except at fairs. Apart from shopgirls and private governesses, or nurses and nuns, there were no other careers for women in any case, so the actress was a pioneer in undertaking such a prominent role for women. The woman actor could become a leading lady, with the audience and town opinion at her feet, and no other woman could attract such critical attention and examination of her individual abilities, except perhaps lady novelists later. Every performance is a trial followed by a judgement, and the theatre was one place where no man could maintain that women were incapable of intelligent and penetrating analysis of character or text. Every generation of actresses has proved that point time and time again. In the theatre women had to be taken seriously.

The interest of scholars, artists and designers in the world of antiquity was to be responsible for the birth of a new art form. It was known that classical poets had chanted or sung their odes to the accompaniment of harps, and it was also established that ancient dramas had used choruses. Roman theatres still standing had an open space in front of the stage, so scholars argued that this area had been used for dancing by the chorus, and as poets had sung their works perhaps the choruses had sung or chanted too. Ancient texts were very uninformative as to exactly how a play should be staged, so scholars had to come up with their own interpretations based on what facts were available. Some went so far as to say that the whole of an ancient play had been sung and danced, while others argued that only the most important speeches should be sung; but they were agreed that for a production to be truely Roman and antique it ought to contain some singing. A classical drama was seen as combining all the arts, for it contained poetry, music, singing, dancing, and scenic and costume design. An individual work of art was known by the Latin word *opus* (a work), so a drama which contained all the works of art should not be called an *opus*, but should use the plural form of that noun, *opera* (works). Thus opera was born, not because everyone was trying to invent a new form, but because they were striving to get back to the true nature of ancient plays. There was the same distinction between comic opera and tragic opera as there was between

Seconde Journée
Theatre fait dans la mesme allée, sur lequel la Comédye, et le Ballet
de la Princesse d'Elide furent representéz.

Jsrael Siluestre, delineauit.   *et excudit. Cum Privilegio Regis.*

spoken comedy and tragedy, so it followed that dress in opera was the same as dress in the rest of the theatre. Tragedy still came first where nobility was concerned, and the Roman themes and the Roman costume dominated operatic productions for the next two centuries, up to 1800.

Musical interludes were a regular feature of the festivities at the Florentine court in the sixteenth century, such as *Apollo's Combat against the Python*, one of six musical episodes in the play *La Pellegrina* which was presented in honour of the wedding of Ferdinando de'Medici to Christine of Lorraine in 1589. What marked this interlude out however was the fact that the poet Rinuccini decided to expand it and renamed it *Dafne*. This meant that the enlarged musical interlude had to have more music, so Jacopo Peri wrote some, and the work, a little opera in essence, was produced at the Florence carnival in 1594/5. In 1600 there was another state wedding when Maria de'Medici married Henri IV of France,

6   The second day of the celebrations at Versailles in 1664 when Molière's comedy *Les Plaisirs de l'Isle Enchantée* and the ballet *La Princesse d'Elide* were presented before Louis XIV. By I. Silvestre.   VICTORIA AND ALBERT MUSEUM

Costly plumes and trains mark out the leading characters; all are crowned with ostrich plumes and all the leading ladies have pageboys to carry their trains.

7 Act III Scene X of Metastasio's *Nitteti*, with
music by Nicolo Conforto, Buen Retiro Palace,
Madrid, 1756. By F. Battaglioli. THE IVEAGH
BEQUEST, KENWOOD

By the mid-eighteenth century opera has taken
the attendants of leading ladies to an extreme
and the prima donnas now have three pages. The
men's coats are flared to match the women's
hoops. The setting of the opera was Ethiopia
and Egypt, which was expressed by the partial
use of Turkish trousers.

so Rinuccini wrote another piece relating the story
of *Euridice*, with music by Jacopo Peri and Giulio
Caccini, which like its predecessor was sung throughout. These three, the poet and the two composers,
were all members of an intellectual salon held by
Count Bardi, which was called the Florentine
Camerata. Another member was the composer
Vicenzo Gallilei, father of the famous astronomer.
All of them gave considerable thought to how an
ancient drama was performed, how far it was sung,
how far it was danced. They concluded that the
popular madrigal style which was now normal was
too complicated a medium, and it did not allow the

poetry of the text to be heard, because of the many layers of sound. For an ancient speech to be sung clearly, they came to the conclusion that one voice would be best, singing in a declamatory manner to convey the dramatic intensity, over a simple orchestral accompaniment. It was a sung recital, which they called *recitativo*. The use of choruses and large ensembles of musicians should be reserved for certain climaxes. Thus the idea of the star singer was promoted, shining in a new work, an opera.[7]

The first genius to elevate this new form was Claudio Monteverdi, court musician to the Duke of Mantua between 1602 and 1612. As many intellectuals were excited by the development, believing that the glory of ancient theatre had been recaptured, the Accademia degl'Invaghiti in Mantua decided to stage one of these new operas itself, so it invited Monteverdi to write the music and the court Chancellor Striggio wrote the poem. *Orfeo* was created in 1607, and it complied with all the artistic ideals; it was a classical story, combining music, dancing, singing, poetry and design in the Roman way. But to these were added Monteverdi's dramatic power, his use of a wide range of instruments to convey a variety of colour, and the way he balanced the new monody or single theme against old madrigal style, for richness of sound and contrast. The new style of music spread rapidly to Rome and Venice in the 1620s and 30s, and the 1640s saw Italian opera in Paris. England first tried an opera in 1656. All Western Europe was influenced, and scholars and musicians could congratulate themselves, they had 'recreated' a Roman masterpiece.

Consequently the Baroque period opened with the guide lines already laid down. The theories had been constructed, so what artists and playwrights now had to do was to put the theories into practice, and to build on those foundations, and if possible to improve on them by advancing art to new heights. However, the arts could still not be divided from politics. The Catholic church had lost northern Europe to the Protestant revolution, so in order to compensate for this disaster and to show that the church still meant something, the popes embarked upon a policy of glorification with new churches, new palaces, new paintings and sculpture, and lavish theatrical spectaculars. In France the theatre, poetry, sculpture, painting and architecture were all ordered to glorify the king, for Louis XIV embarked upon a policy of absolute monarchy with relentless vigour. Paris had an Academy of Art founded in 1648, but under Louis XIV the arts were organized into a state system. The academy was changed into the Académie Royale de Peinture et Sculpture in 1661, while ballet came under royal control in the same year with the foundation of the Académie de Danse. The Académie des Inscriptions

et Belles Lettres followed in 1663, the Académie des Sciences in 1666, the Académie de Musique in 1669, and the Académie d'Architecture in 1671.[8] It was a sub-committee of the Académie des Inscriptions et Belles Lettres which was given responsibility for defining the themes of royal festivities and dramatic productions, while the painter Charles Le Brun was the ultimate authority over painting and the sort of costume which could be allowed in pictures and on the stage.

Le Brun ruled that artists must be accurate in their use of costume, and that they must show the decorum (status) and the quality of characters by giving them correct clothing. When Le Brun painted Louis XIV's campaigns on the ceilings of the Galerie des Glaces at the Palace of Versailles he showed what correct costume was. It was not the king dressed in the actual clothes and contemporary armour he had worn during the battles, it was the king portrayed in ancient Roman armour. Similarly when Coysevox and Bernini sculpted statues of Louis XIV it was again in Roman armour. Louis XIV did not want to look like a king; he wished to resemble an ancient emperor. It was, as we have seen, the imperial connotations of Roman armour which appealed most to the Baroque period. When that king celebrated the birth of his heir the Dauphin, he presented an enormous ballet on horseback, with companies of riders performing elaborate arabesques, and Louis XIV of course dressed as a Roman emperor. The artistic ideal of the Renaissance that Roman dress was appropriate for noble themes was now taken up, organized and established as official government policy in France.

Furthermore Roman dress had another quality. It was an established form of attire, and had not changed its composition since the days of the Roman empire. It was constant, which fashionable clothes, with their changes every season, were not. Fashion made styles go in and out of popularity so that a gown bought one year was démodé the next. Baroque artists loathed this changeability because a portrait of a sitter wearing the height of fashion started to look dated as soon as the clothes went out of fashion. It did not matter how excellent the painting was – twenty years after it was painted people would be laughing at the clothes in it. Consequently artists gave their full backing to having sitters wear Roman dress, because that was unchangeable, relatively timeless and dateless.

Thus in the seventeenth century Roman dress expanded its role. Not only was it suitable for tragedy and state triumphal processions, but it was also the best costume to convey the image of the monarchy, and it was the most changeless costume that could be worn in portraiture.[9] André Félibien, historiographer to Louis XIV and secretary of the

Académie d'Architecture stated, '. . . it is certain that the antique habits have much more grace and beauty than those of the present, where one sees changes every day.' Similar views were expressed by Father Menestrier, who was much involved in the production of triumphs and parades. In his book on ballet (1682) he said that Roman armour was also practical:

That of the Ancient Romans is the most august of all, and there is no costume which leaves the legs so free. It was composed of a cuirass with its pteruges [metal strips over the arms and hips]. It must have short sleeves over the upper arm, and it is accompanied by a silk tunic pleated all round the skirt which makes the coat of arms. The helmet has an aigrette and plumes, and as this habit only represents heroic characters, the only hairstyle must consist of laurel crowns.[10]

It was the august nature of the costume which mattered. Kings posed for their statues and portraits in Roman armour, and stage kings paraded in the same attire. Of course monarchs and actors did not wear Roman dress in their ordinary lives, where they wore the normal fashion of the day. But where an image was concerned, the concept of the monarchy, the status of a stage hero, the personification of noble virtues, then only Roman dress would do. It was the costume for the great.

Accuracy was called for, as the art historian Roland Fréart de Chambray pointed out in his *Idée de la Perfection de la Peinture* (1662). 'It is necessary that any artist who aspires to some degree of glory in his profession, must be very accurate over costume'. For example Julius Caesar should be drawn properly: 'it is necessary to know that he was bald and that he shaved his chin; consequently don't depict him with a beautiful coiffure or give him a long beard, as happens with Pompey and some other Emperors'.

The stage had been reached when the audience expected to see tragic heroes in Roman attire, and could protest when they did not. When an English translation of Pierre Corneille's *Pompey the Great* was produced at Charles II's court theatre in Whitehall Palace in January 1663, it was acted in English clothes and when Julius Caesar appeared carrying a muff he was hissed off the stage for such inaccuracy.[11] The producer was the playwright and master of the king's comedians (actors) Sir William D'Avenant who quickly sought to remedy this failing. When he presented Corneille's *Heraclius or the Emperor of East* later that year Samuel Pepys observed more accurate costuming: 'The garments like Romans very well. . . . But at the beginning, at the drawing up of the curtain, there was the finest scene of the Emperor, and his people about him,

standing in their fixed and different postures in their Roman habits, above all that ever I saw at any of the theatres'.[12] It was a tableau showing the same grouping of the figures that could be seen in an academic painting of a scene from Roman history. The play began as a picture, and conformed to the artistic principles laid down by the French academies. Art and the stage were working hand in hand, for they shared the same ideals.

A breaking-in period was necessary of course before the Roman style became fully established in the theatre. At the end of the sixteenth century an illustration of a performance of Shakespeare's *Titus Andronicus* only shows four characters in Roman armour, the other actors being dressed in ordinary contemporary military attire, as if the company only possessed four Roman suits to begin with. By the 1620s and 30s however Inigo Jones used scores of Roman outfits in the masques he designed for Charles I. Playwrights even came to state that Roman costume must be used in their dramatic works. Richard Flecknoe prefaced his tragicomedy *Erminia; or, The Fair and Vertuous Lady* of 1661 with the requirement, 'The Habits, the ancient *Military Attire* for the more Heroick parts: for the rest, the Toga or *Civil Vest*, wide sleev'd and loosely flowing to the knees, silver'd Buskins, &c.' His description of the toga was wrong, for ancient togae reached down to the ankles; his version resembles the Roman tunic rather than a toga. All the same these tunic-like vests did become popular for non-heroic roles; for they were the same length as fashionable coats and so suited contemporary taste.

Inevitably the use of Roman dress onstage was in time taken to an extreme as managers vied to outdo each other in the splendour of their productions. The heroic nature of Roman armour was emphasized until the poor actor was swamped. As he was the leading character and always a person of high social status in the play, he had to wear the best. Ostrich plumes were expensive so the hero's helmet was crowned with several. Lesser roles in a tragedy were given fewer feathers, so that the audience could tell at one glance as soon as the actors walked onto the stage that the one with the most plumes was the star of the piece. Those wearing three, two or one plume were ranked accordingly in declining order of importance. The status of the heroine was shown in the same way; she was the one crowned with the most plumes, while her companions and attendants had diminishing numbers. Another identity statement concerned the wearing of trains. Kings and queens wore trains which were carried by pages. It followed therefore that heroes and heroines on stage should have trains too since they were noble beings, and that they should be attended by pages. Such accoutrements could in the end

actually handicap a performer, as Addison observed in 1711:

The ordinary method of making an hero, is to clap a huge plume of feathers upon his head, which rises so very high, that there is often a greater length from his chin to the top of his head, than to the sole of his foot. One would believe, that we thought a great man and a tall man the same thing. This very much embarasses the actor, who is forced to hold his neck extremely stiff and steady all the while he speaks; and, not withstanding any anxieties which he pretends for his mistress, his country, or his friends, one may see by his action, that his greatest care and concern is to keep the plume of feathers from falling off his head.

Equally the long train could present problems for a heroine.

. . . a princess generally receives her grandeur from those additional encumbrances that fall into her tail: I mean the broad sweeping train that follows her in all her motions, and finds constant employment for a boy who stands behind her to

8 Mrs Ward as Valeria, Mrs Pritchard kneeling as Horatia, Spranger Barry as Plobius and David Garrick as Horatius in W. Whitehead's *The Roman Father*, 1750. British School. THE FOLGER SHAKESPEARE LIBRARY

Eighteenth-century fashion added long cuffed sleeves and hoops to Roman armour, although kneebreeches were worn underneath the hoop for decency's sake. The plumes and trains remain constant. The tasselled lappets on the women's costumes are another version of the Roman overskirt. Garrick was credited with abolishing the hoop for male characters but it looks as if this only applied to himself, as Barry has kept his.

9 The crowning of the bust of Voltaire, after the sixth performance of his *Irène*, Comédie Française, 30 March 1778. By Moreau le Jeune. THE FITZWILLIAM MUSEUM, CAMBRIDGE

The Roman heroic manner continues to dominate serious works. The leading men have about one dozen ostrich plumes each. The heroines' hoops are draped to give them a classical touch. The shepherdesses on the left in short skirts are dancers. Voltaire himself is in the top box on the left. The set represents the new monumental simplicity of Neo-Classical taste.

open and spread it to advantage. I do not know how others are affected at this sight, but I must confess, my eyes are wholly taken up with the page's part; and as for the queen, I am not so attentive to anything she speaks, as to the right adjusting of her train, lest it should chance to trip up her heels, or incommode her, as she walks to and fro upon the stage. It is, in my opinion, a very odd spectacle, to see a queen venting her passion in a disordered motion, and a little boy taking care all the while that they do not ruffle the tail of her gown.[13]

Addison wished that the nobility of the language, rather than plumes and trains, might illustrate the social dignity of the characters, but the theatre was copying the status symbols used in the world outside. Moreover these symbols were understood immediately by the audience. As only a minority of the population had had an education, simple visual symbols made it easy for the audience to understand who the characters in a drama were. The Baroque theatre made characters obvious, in the same way that persons of high degree demonstrated their rank in the world outside.

Given that the theatre had to keep up with the symbols of status for its leading characters, it was no surprise that when periwigs became highly fashionable in the 1650s the theatre adopted them too. Wigs were expensive, extremely so, and cost more than a working man earned in a whole year, so only the upper classes could afford them. From the middle of the seventeenth century and throughout the greater part of the eighteenth the periwig distinguished gentlemen from artisans and farm labourers. It was an instant badge of social identity, which could be read at a glance. Strictly speaking of course Roman heroes had not worn periwigs in antiquity, but in the Baroque period an actor in a heroic role had to show that he was a gentleman, and in contemporary terms this automatically meant wearing a periwig. It was the influence of fashion, but before the twentieth century fashion was one of the arts the upper classes used to distinguish themselves from the lower orders, so in following fashion the theatre was keeping up with the developments in social discrimination. Similarly when hoops became fashionable after 1708, heroines onstage had to have hoops too; ladies wore hoops, and tragic heroines were ladies of quality. Fashion followed the idea of hoops to the absolute limit, making them wider every season until the point was reached when skirts had become too wide to be manageable. Stage heroines therefore grew wider in sympathy, and the more impractical the costume became the more it emphasized the point that the wearer did not have to do manual labour in order to earn a living. The tails of men's coats flared out to follow the wide fashion, and to keep in some proportion with the width of fashionable women. Therefore stage heroes grew wider too, and the leading man would now be the one with the widest skirt as well as the most plumes, and the longest train or cloak. Anything which emphasized the social superiority of a person could be adopted by the theatre to underline the rank of tragedy. Fashion was all about group identity, high fashion was for high society, so the stage employed its symbols. Accordingly Roman costume was modified to harmonize with the latest ideas on status and display. This may have been inaccurate so far as historical models were concerned, but the audience would not have understood ancient Roman symbols of social superiority since they were not all classical scholars, and so the theatre used such marks of rank as were familiar at the time of the performance. Any revived costume is a compromise between the original look and the vision of the period which restores it. Consequently each generation imposed its own look on Roman dress, be it Charles I with his cavalier locks, or Molière in 1659 playing Julius Caesar in a periwig, and Spranger Barry sporting a paniered skirt in 1750. Each was using his own period's vocabulary of fashionable superiority, to re-emphasize in contemporary terms that the Roman hero was an exalted character.

Magnificence was also important. Royal courts spent fortunes on striving to look breathtaking so it behoved theatrical courts to do the same. Real gold and silver lace was used in some productions, together with velvet, brocade and ermine. Where a company could not afford real gold then copper was much employed. Copper suits of Roman armour, and heroines' gowns heavy with copper embroidery were popular, while rock crystal would do if they could not afford diamonds. If sometimes the theatre had to compromise between its budget and the attempt to look magnificent, the intention remained the same, to present the impression of astounding wealth, luxury, and elevated splendour as gods and goddesses, heroes and heroines paraded and gestured with noble expressions as they related a tale of high tragedy, of lofty endeavour and virtuous devotion to supreme principles. If the hero had to die then he subsided like the setting sun, gleaming and glittering with gold or copper, while ostrich plumes trembled and his train collapsed beside him. He was sublime; Roman in his costume and Roman in his valour.

The glitter was very important because the theatre was coming indoors. When Shakespeare's actors were appearing outdoors at The Globe, in Italy covered theatres were erected in imitation of the old Roman amphitheatre with the seats in tiers facing a permanent set of columns and arches. Palladio designed the Teatro Olimpico at Vicenza in 1585, Scamozzi designed the little theatre at Sabbionetta, and Aleotti was responsible for the big Teatro Farnese at Parma in 1619. Inigo Jones brought this pattern of theatre back to London, and his masques were performed indoors. The English public theatres were slow to follow this example, but by the Restoration all theatres were being built with roofs on, so that performances had to take place by candlelight. This meant that lighting effects such as flares could be tried, and moving scenery could be installed. Costume was less visible than outdoors because candlelight is soft and imprecise, and it deadens some colours. Blue looks black, green darkens to brown, so it was important to use

10 Male tragedy costume, *c* 1750.
DROTTNINGHOLMS TEATERMUSEUM, SWEDEN

The importance of theatrical glitter is shown by the copper embroidery and sequins which cover the costume, to reflect the candlelight. The fin shapes on the costume suggest that it was for a marine character like Neptune or Oceanus.

strong, bright colours in theatre costume such as white, yellow, and scarlet or orange. Moreover costumes could help to increase the amount of light if they acted as reflectors, so that gold and copper had a practical application. Alongside the ideal that the theatre should be richly costumed was the assistance clothes could give as another source of light. Gold, silver, copper, jewels and crystal all sparkle, which was appropriate for the social status of heroes and heroines, but it would also increase the illumination available. The result was that costumes were covered in spangles and sequins to make them shine all over, and the few examples of

Baroque theatre costumes which still survive are so thick with copper embroidery, sequins, braid, spangles and loops, that the underlying material is invisible. The whole costume became an illumination. So much metal made the clothes very heavy although the weight was distributed all over the body. It would be worst for the dancer, who at the end of an entrée would be smothered in perspiration and sinking at the knees. A heroine could claim that her pageboys were an absolute necessity for the weight of her sequined train would have pulled her over. The more glorious and resplendent a costume is, the more the actor needs some assistance in supporting it. The picture was summed up by Mr Webster of Christ Church, Oxford in his poem *The Stage* of 1713:

Beads, Plumes, and Spangles, in Profusion rise,
While Rocks of Cornish Diamonds reach the skies.
Crests, Corslets, all the Pomp of Battle join,
In one Effulgence, one promiscuous Shine.

CHAPTER TWO

The Clothing System

In both the seventeenth and the eighteenth centuries actors were responsible for providing the whole or some part of their costumes. This pattern became firmly established in France from 1600 to the Revolution in 1789, and given the difference between tragic and comic plays the cost hit the serious actor most. The Commedia dell'Arte actor Luigi Riccoboni, who went on the stage in Paris in the 1690s, explained the French system:

The Actors who play Tragedy furnish their Theatrical Habits out of their own Pockets. Those Habits which are commonly in the *Greek* or the *Roman* Fashion, are very expensive, being all finely embroidered with Gold and Silver: Those of the Women especially cost vast Sums. The Players of Comedy are obliged to do the same, but the Expences among them are very unequal.[1]

For the comic actor a simple part could allow for a simple costume, but if he had to perform the role of an extravagant fool or eccentric peer he could well face the same sort of bills as a tragedian. Some help from the French company would be forthcoming if it could be proved that the costume required for a particular play was so extraordinary and unusual that it could not be used by the actor in other plays, in which circumstances the manager would pay for the costume out of the company's budget. Given the cost of theatre costume it is not surprising that French actors tried to make the same costume do for several productions, and they greeted the idea of a new play with new clothes with black looks. The French theatre historian Chappuzeau observed in 1674:

This question of expense for Actors is more considerable than one can imagine. There are few new plays which do not involve them in new alterations, and as artificial gold and silver, which shines quite well, was not then used, a

single Roman habit could cost 500 escus. In order to please the Public they like to employ the best in everything, and there is a certain Actor whose outfit is worth 10,000 francs.[2]

Not surprisingly the actors of the Comédie Française pleaded in 1688 that while they would pledge themselves to continue to furnish their own habits, they wished that where new plays were concerned, they might ask the company to relieve them of part of the expense. On 3 May 1700 the actors again pledged to supply their own costumes, so the fact that actors had to repeat this promise suggests that there were times when they tried to evade the responsibility.[3] No doubt old costumes which had been refurbished were sometimes passed off as being brand-new, and alterations were preferred to outright replacement.

There was a different system in French opera, where the management paid for all the costumes. Writing of the period 1695–1740 Riccoboni recorded that:

The Opera is surprizingly magnificent in the Number and Quality of its Dresses; the Embroidery is but Tinsel, yet it is of an excellent Taste, and makes as fine a Shew as the best dresses in the Play-house. The Diversity and Gallantry of the Dancing-Dresses is very magnificent and peculiar to *France*, and is all provided at the Expence of the Undertakers.[4]

It was a different story when the management had to foot the whole bill, so in opera imitation gold and silver was allowed, while the poor tragic actor at the Comédie Française, the French national theatre, had to pay for real gold himself. The system was different because opera could claim that all its costumes were extraordinary, particularly where the dancers were concerned. Father Menestrier had insisted that for ballet the dancers' costumes must have variety – dancers were dumb actors so their

clothes had to speak for them. Opera, that union of all the arts, used many balletic interludes and *divertissements*, both to give the singers a rest, and to keep the audience amused. Menestrier ruled that dancers should not appear twice in the same costume. He recommended that an entrée danced by soldiers should be followed by an entrée of shepherds, after which could come a dance of gods from ancient legend, then a dance of thieves, followed by one of animals, then some genii, some American Indians, some Persians and finally a dance of Moors.[5] This was the number of dances he expected in one production, so of course the ballet dancer could not afford to purchase such a quantity of costumes out of his own pocket. Moreover as it could not be guaranteed that every opera with a ballet would need an entrée of Moors or Indians, the dancer could claim that the costumes were extraordinaries and not regular items, so the company should pay for them, which it did. Thus, in France, there was a major difference in the clothing systems between drama and opera-ballet.

There was one exception for the serious actor where he might be excused payment for stage dress, and this was the summons of the company to court to give a command performance before the king. Chappuzeau wrote:

... when they were performing a play which was only for the pleasure of the King, the Gentlemen of the Chamber had orders to give to each Actor for his necessary adjustments, the sum of one hundred escus or four hundred livres, and, if it happened that an Actor had two or three parts to play, he could claim the money two or three times.[6]

It is clear from the accounts of the Comédie Française however that the money given by the king was not always sufficient to cover the expense of mounting a performance at court. Louis XIV enjoyed the plays of the great actor and playwright Molière, so they were often acted before him; but it left the company in debt as the treasurer recorded:

Memoire. Of the money which I received for the costumes of the plays which were made for the entertainment of the King.

Mariage forcé	100 livres
Princesse d'Elide	200 livres
Medecins	300 livres
Sicilien	100 livres
Pastoralle Corridon	200 livres
Georges Dandin	200 livres
Pourceaugnac	200 livres
Bourg. gentilhom	200 livres
Princes Magnifiques	200 livres
Psyche	200 livres
Escarbaynas	200 livres
	2100 livres

As what the King gave was not sufficient for the expense involved in the necessary making, the costumes cost us another 2000 livres.[7]

Just occasionally French actors might receive a gift from other quarters. In 1642 the minister Cardinal Richelieu gave the actor Bellerose a court dress, in 1645 the Duc de Guise gave gifts to actors in all the Paris troupes, while in 1667 Louis XIV presented two gowns to the actresses Mlle de Brie and Mlle Molière to wear in M. Molière's *Le Sicilien*. Nevertheless when the Duc de Saint-Aignan gave the company of the Palais Royal 100 gold louis to cover the cost of the costumes in *La Bradamante Ridicule* it was considered an act of extraordinary generosity to pay for the whole wardrobe.[8]

Molière was an actor who ran his own company, and who starred in his own plays. He was active in Paris between 1658 and his death in 1673, and was protected against church attacks by Louis XIV. The inventory of Molière's effects made after his death shows the size of wardrobe which a leading actor could build up. There were the clothes he had worn in *Monsieur Pourceaugnac*, red damask breeches garnished with lace, a coat of blue velvet decorated with artificial gold, a fringed sash, green garters, a grey hat decked with a green plume, a scarf of green taffeta, a pair of gloves, a skirt of green taffeta trimmed with lace, and a cloak of black taffeta, and a pair of slippers, valued at 30 livres. Molière's costume in *Le Sicilien* consisted of breeches and cloak of violet satin, embroidered with gold and silver, and lined with green silk, the skirt of golden moiré, the sleeves of silver stuff, decorated with embroidery and silver, a night cap, a periwig and a

---

11 John Lacy in three of his roles, *c* 1667, by John Michael Wright. REPRODUCED BY GRACIOUS PERMISSION OF H.M. THE QUEEN

On the left Lacy wears Highland bonnet, plaid and trews as *Sauny the Scot* in his own version of Shakespeare's *The Taming of the Shrew*, Theatre Royal 1667; in the centre he wears the height of fashion as the dancing master Monsieur Galliard with periwig, striped coat and enormous shoe roses in the Duke of Newcastle's *The Variety* of 1662, and on the right the sober black costume of a clerk Scruple in Wilson's *The Cheats* of 1663. The painting was commissioned by one of Lacy's greatest fans, Charles II. The Theatre Royal paid for the costumes, Lacy only had to provide the accessories.

sword, valued at 65 livres. His costume for the part of Clitidas in *Les Amants Magnifiques* was a tonnelet of green moiré, decorated with two laces of gold and silver, a bodice of velvet with a gold ground, and the shoes, garters and stockings, all garnished with fine silver, and valued at 60 livres. 'Tonnelet' was the term used to describe the skirt part of a Roman habit. Molière was primarily a comic actor but his wardrobe shows that his costumes were just as fine as Leone de'Sommi had wished a hundred years before, for they glittered with gold and silver, both real and imitation, and were made of fine materials, of silks, satins, velvet, damask, and even cloth of silver.

Even more magnificent clothes could be found in the wardrobe of his wife, the actress Armande Béjart, for she performed in opera and ballets as well. For the opera *Psyché* she had a skirt of cloth of gold decorated with silver laces, over which went a short tonnelet skirt in the Roman style of gold and silver material, the bodice was embroidered, and the sleeves were in the same cloth as the tonnelet. For the same part she also had a skirt of cloth of silver, worn with a sleeveless tunic of crêpe, both decorated with silver lace; and a skirt of green and black moiré garnished with imitation lace, and with a bodice covered with embroidery, the tonnelet and sleeves decorated with fine gold and silver; and a skirt of blue English taffeta decorated with four rows of fine silver lace. In all her costumes for that opera were valued at 250 livres, considerably more than the cost of clothes for one of Molière's roles, showing that opera like tragedy was more magnificent than comedy, with gold and silver used in abundance.[9]

The Comédie Française came into existence in 1680 when Louis XIV ordered the troupe of the late Molière to merge with the other Paris troupe of players to form a national theatre, thereby bringing that aspect of art under state control as he had already with painting, sculpture, music, dancing and architecture. As the Comédie Française performed tragedies and comedies, it did not pay for actors' costumes except when they were unusual kinds. Thus if a drama had a scene in which one of the noble characters was holding a celebration and so a ballet was called for, then the company would pay for the dancers' costumes under 'extraordinaries'. For example, for a performance of Molière's *Le Malade Imaginaire* the Comédie Française paid out 1139 livres for 'habits de ballet', while it ordered dancers' costumes at 77 livres per man for another production. The supplier of such balletic costumes was Jean Baraillon, tailor-in-ordinary to the king's ballets. Baraillon was one of the dominant theatrical tailors in Paris, as he also worked for the Théâtre du Palais Royal and the Théâtre de Guénégaud.[10] Not surprisingly French actors resented the privilege enjoyed by singers and dancers in not having to provide their own costumes, and whilst they could not stop it, they did attempt to lighten their own load by hiring stage costumes. By this method they could have a 'new' costume in a play which they had not had to pay for in full. By 1661 a Monsieur Bourgeois was known in Paris as a hirer of habits for tragedies, in which year he supplied all the wardrobe for a private production of Colletet's tragicomedy *La Révolte de Jupiter contre Saturne*. The Comédie Française itself hired a Jupiter costume in 1697, so it is certain that the theatrical tailor who hired costumes became an established figure in capital cities.[11] He was able to rely on a wide clientèle, not only actors who could not afford cloth of gold for a tragedy costume, but amateur performers among the aristocracy, and the new fashion for masquerade parties which began to flourish from the 1680s brought in another type of customer eager to hire fancy dress and disguises. For one night the masquerader could wear the same costume as an actor or dancer, and be a Roman hero, a sultan, a Turk, or a robber, or a shepherd. Where amateur court festivities were concerned, the participants paid for their own costumes, or hired them, so that the courtiers who took part in a court ballet, dramatic presentation or festival, did so at their own expense. Similarly the king would order his costume from his own tailor and pay for it himself if performing in a work produced only for the court. Louis XIV was an enthusiastic dancer in his youth in the 1650s so the cost of his costumes had to be met by the royal wardrobe.

In England there was the same distinction between tragic and comic stage costume in that the former had to be richer than the latter, but there was a major difference from the French theatrical system in that English companies paid for most of an actor's costumes, while the performer only had to provide his own linen and accessories. Thus English theatres possessed considerable wardrobes of their own, which belonged to the company. This was like French opera houses, but unlike French theatres. In the days of William Shakespeare no playhouse was allowed within the walls of the City of London, so they were built on the outskirts, such as The Theatre by James Burbage at Shoreditch (1576), and the Globe at Bankside (1599), where many of Shakespeare's works were premièred. The principal owner of theatres was the property developer Philip Henslowe to whom the Hope, Fortune and Rose playhouses belonged. He acted as banker to the actors' companies in those theatres, and his accounts show him buying clothes for the wardrobes. The Admiral's Men, a company so called because it was protected by the Admiral Lord

Howard, occupied the Rose playhouse between 1594 and 1600, and among Henslowe's papers is a bill for the Admiral's Men of clothes bought since 3 April 1598.

Bowght a damaske cassock garded with velvett.	18s.
Bowght a payer of paned rownd hosse of cloth whiped with sylk, drawne out with tafitie. j payer of long black woollen stockens.	8s.
Bowght j black satten dublett. Bowght j payer of rownd howsse paned of velvett	£4.15.0.
Bowght a robe for to goo invisibell Bowght a gown for Nembia	£3.10.0.
Bowght a dublett of whitt satten layd thicke with gowld lace, and a payer of rownde pandes hosse of cloth of sylver, the panes layd with gowld lace.	£7.
Bowght of my sonne v sewtes	£20.
Bowght of my sonne iiij sewtes	£17.

The company's wardrobe contained the satin doublet, decked with gold lace, and the velvet gown for King Henry V in Shakespeare's play, a green gown for Maid Marion and six green coats for Robin Hood and his men, and the coat decorated with copper lace and the crimson velvet breeches worn by Tamburlaine in Marlowe's play. An inventory of the company's wardrobe was taken by its most famous actor Edward Alleyn, and it shows just how rich an English theatrical wardrobe could be. Among the cloaks were one of scarlet decorated with silver lace and silver buttons, a short velvet cape cloak embroidered with gold and gold spangles, a damask cloak faced with velvet, a scarlet cloak faced with blue velvet and trimmed with golden buttons, one of scarlet faced with black velvet, and one of worsted decorated with gold lace. Among the gowns was 'Harry yᵉ VIII gowne'. As Shakespeare's play of this name was not written until 1612/13, this gown could have belonged to that king, for several of his garments were still in existence. As late as 1649 the royal Great Wardrobe still possessed Henry VIII's clothes in some number but they were sold off by Cromwell. The Admiral's Men also owned a black velvet gown trimmed with white fur, one of crimson striped with gold and faced with ermine, one of cloth of gold, one of red silk with golden buttons, a cardinal's red gown, several women's gowns, a black velvet gown embroidered with gold, another of cloth of gold for actor Cavendish and one of cloth of silver for W. Parr. There were also a number of 'Antik sutes', meaning old clothes not ancient ones, among which were a coat of crimson velvet paned and em-

broidered with gold, a coat of cloth of gold with green skirts, another also of gold with tawny orange skirts, a coat of cloth of silver with blue silk and tinsel skirts, one of blue damask, a horseman's coat of cloth of gold, a gilded leather coat, and 17 headdresses set with jewels. Among the jerkins and doublets were such splendours as a crimson satin doublet entirely covered with gold lace, and a black velvet doublet cut over a silver tinsel ground, while a doublet of carnation velvet was laced with silver, and a velvet doublet was cut in diamond shapes trimmed with gold lace and spangles. Thus the London stage in the Elizabethan and Jacobean periods could equal France or Italy in the magnificence and costliness of its theatre costume, but it was all owned by the company, not by the individual actors.[12]

The famous masques which Inigo Jones designed, and which were written by Ben Jonson and William D'Avenant, to entertain James I and Charles I in the period 1605–40, were different. These were not public performances in a playhouse, but private productions at court, in which Charles I and Queen Henrietta Maria took part. Consequently they were paid for by the crown. Charles I's costumes were made by his own tailor Patrick Black and came under the accounts of the Gentleman of the Robes as extraordinaries, additional to the king's everyday wardrobe, and were not obtained from a theatrical tailor.

When the Puritans defeated Charles I in the Civil War, theatres were closed down. Some actors had joined the army, on the king's side of course as the court was in favour of theatres, while some went abroad, such as George Jolly who ran a troupe of English actors in Germany and Austria. For nearly 20 years there were no public performances in England. There were a few private productions in great houses, after Cromwell's guards had been bribed to look the other way, and in 1656 Sir William D'Avenant was able to persuade Cromwell to allow him to stage a few performances of his opera *The Seige of Rhodes* on the grounds that it was sung and so escaped the ban on plays, but this was all.

When Cromwell died in 1658 old actors flocked back to London and set about restoring old theatre buildings and re-opening. After the Civil War and puritan gloom people were thirsting for some entertainment. The restoration of the monarchy in 1660 ensured the survival of the theatre, for Charles II was a king who believed in enjoying himself to excess, and he wanted playhouses to go to and actresses to seduce. Theatrical life however was firmly placed under royal control. Only two companies were to be allowed in London, both under royal patronage, the King's Company of Comedians

12 King Charles II in his coronation clothes, 1661, by John Michael Wright. REPRODUCED BY GRACIOUS PERMISSION OF H.M. THE QUEEN

The royal coronation suit, consisting of sixteenth-century-pattern doublet and trunkhose, in cloth of silver, was lent to the public playhouse on two occasions.

13 *King Lear*, by J. van der Gucht, from *The Works of Mr. William Shakespear*, 1709. THE BRITISH LIBRARY

Those plays by Shakespeare which were not Roman subjects would have been performed in contemporary clothes, and such costumes formed the bulk of the wardrobe.

and the Duke of York's players. For Charles II's reign the actors in the two companies were termed royal servants and were granted royal livery, a scarlet cloak with a crimson velvet cape.[13] Thus England had a state theatre before the French. Nevertheless both companies were expected to be self-supporting, and did not receive a royal subsidy. Sir William D'Avenant was put in charge of the Duke of York's company in 1660, and the agreement drawn up at the time makes it very clear what costumes he would pay for and what the actor had to supply:

That the said Sir William Davenant, his executors, administrators, or assignes, shall not be obliged out of the shares or proporcions allowed to him for the Supplyeinge of the Cloathes, Habits, and Scenes, to prouide eyther Hattes, feathers, Gloues, ribbons, sword belts, bandes, stockinges, or shoes, for any of the men Actors foresaid Vnless it be to Properties.[14]

Thus the company would have a budget to buy theatrical costume, but the actor had to pay for the linen and accessories. This still involved him in some expense, for silk stockings, plumed hats, fine lace collars, good swords and perfumed gloves were not cheap by any means. Nevertheless he did not have to worry about trying to afford gold or silver cloth or lace; that the company would pay for. Where the company did pay for accessories it was for stock.

English theatrical costume was just as splendid as the French, and the English system meant that the two royal playhouses in London had wardrobes full of expensive clothes. Inevitably this offered temptation to some. The master of the king's actors Thomas Killigrew had to charge the actor Griffin with stealing a French habit, a laced coat and breeches, a nightgown, hats, shoes, stockings, periwigs and trimmings to the sum of £60, all property of the new Theatre Royal, in Bridges St, Drury Lane. In June 1695 the Duke of York's Playhouse at Dorset Garden by the Thames was robbed of costumes worth £300. A dancer named Phillips was arrested for the crime, and most of the costumes were recovered, but all the gold and silver lace and fringes had been stripped off.[15] It goes without saying that the royal companies were dressed in the genuine article, and not tinsel.

As the companies paid for the main part of the costume, this involved them in considerable expense. To begin with both playhouses had to build up wardrobes from scratch, so in 1661/2 the Theatre Royal, which housed the king's actors, spent £100 on Roman habits. Mounting Purcell's opera *The Fairy Queen* in 1692 cost £3000 for costumes, music and scenery altogether. For a revival of Dryden's tragedy *All for Love* in 1718, nearly £600 was spent on costume alone. Accordingly the company would not spend lavishly on each new production. For the sake of economy and balancing the books, old stock would be re-used, to the great disappointment of the authors of new plays. This happened particularly when plays touched the same or similar themes. Dryden's *The Indian Queen* at the Theatre Royal in 1664 had feathered armlets and skirts presented to the theatre by the playwright Mrs Aphra Behn who had visited South America, so when Dryden wrote a sequel *The Indian Emperour* in 1665, the prologue explained:

The Scenes are old, the Habits are the same
We wore last year, before the Spaniards came.

The anonymous author of *The Constant Nymph* in 1678 prefaced his work with the complaint, 'As for the Adornments, in Habit, Musick, and Scene-Worke, it was Vacation-time, and the Company would not venture the Charge.' The theatre would not risk much money on a new production at the end of the season, and would only be extravagant when the court was in town.

A record of the occasions when a production had new clothes was kept by John Downes, the prompter at the Duke of York's company and later at the Lincoln's Inn Fields theatre, between c 1660 and 1705. At the start of the Restoration he noted that D'Avenant's *Love and Honour* was 'Richly Cloath'd', and D'Avenant's production of Shakespeare's *Henry the VIII* was at his orders 'all new Cloath'd in proper Habits'. Lord Orrery's *Mustapha* had 'All the Parts being new Cloath'd', while the production of Lord Orrery's *Henry V* was 'Splendidly Cloath'd' and D'Avenant's conversion of *Macbeth* into an 'opera' in 1672 had 'new Cloaths' to provide suitable operatic glitter. *King Charles VIII* of France was 'all new Cloath'd', as was the English production of the French opera *Psyché*. Betterton's opera *The Prophetess* (1690) was considered to have costly clothes, and *The Fairy Queen* was very superior, 'especially in Cloaths'. '*Iphigenia* a Tragedy, wrote by Mr. Dennis, a good Tragedy and well Acted: but answer'd not the Expences they were at in Cloathing it'. Rowe's *Ulysses* in 1705 was 'all new Cloath'd', and the only comedy which Downes included was Etherege's *The Man of Mode* in 1676 which was 'well Cloath'd'. Thus for a period of 45 years Downes listed only 12 productions as having new wardrobes for the event; but his notes only concerned the companies he worked with, and did not include productions at the Theatre Royal given by the King's Comedians. If the figures are doubled to cover both troupes that still only results in a small total. It is probable that Downes commented only on those tragedies and operas which caught his eye. Nevertheless his figures do suggest that the theatres limited the number of productions which would have new wardrobes. When a brand new opera house was opened in the Haymarket in 1705/6, the Lincoln's Inn company, founded by the actor Thomas Betterton in 1695, moved in with 'half a Score of their Old Plays, Acted in old Cloaths' from their old playhouse.[16] Sensible economy was essential, given the high cost of tragic and operatic costumes. In the eighteenth century it became common for companies to only buy a handful of new costumes per annum for the leading actors, clothing the rest of the cast in what older stock was held in the wardrobe. Leading ladies were allowed to choose their own garments on these occasions.

A wardrobe could contain quite a range of costume types as dancers in particular were decked out as anything from Indians to Chinese. It was not only a question of Roman dress and contemporary wear. An inventory of old stock from Drury Lane, taken in 1714, makes this very clear. As the costumes were old, their value was low. Ten Roman shapes and Persian vests were priced at £15. Fifty very old Roman, Persian, Chinese and Shepherds'

14 *Hamlet*, by J. van der Gucht, from *The Works of Mr. William Shakespear*, 1709. THE BRITISH LIBRARY

Betterton played Hamlet in contemporary mourning clothes, as it was not a Roman play. The queen wears a royal cast-off, a coronation gown and petticoat. The ghost's armour, painted white, was a genuine suit about 100 years old. Hamlet's ungartered stocking and the fallen chair were two traditional actions in that role.

15 *Othello*, by J. van der Gucht, from *The Works of Mr. William Shakespear*, 1709. THE BRITISH LIBRARY

As Roman suits were expensive, other tragedies were dressed on the cheap in contemporary suits. Othello was a general so he was given a contemporary officer's suit, not a Venetian costume.

dresses were 5 shillings each. Twenty-four Spanish dresses were valued at £5. Five feather shapes were 5 shillings each. Eighteen singers' and dancers' costumes from Purcell's opera *King Arthur* of 1691 were put at 2/6 each. Fourteen costumes for *The Emperor of the Moon* in 1686 were valued at £3. A set of woman's clothes of copper and silk was also £3, so it must have been in better condition than the preceding entry. Three suits of dancing clothes trimmed with copper and oddments were 6 shillings. What had been a magnificent modern costume probably for a fashionable comedy was a white flowered silk manteau embroidered with gold and cherry-coloured silk, which had a petticoat of scarlet stuff trimmed with black-and-white gymp lace, priced at 10 shillings. Lastly there was a parcel of old feathers, which must have graced some heroic heads, now valued at £6.8.6. In contrast to old stock being written off and sold for what it could get, a wardrobe would still be ordering some new garments. In 1735/6 the Theatre Royal, Covent Garden, settled some bills for actors' clothes:

For a Coat & Breech's of Cloth laced with Gold & a Green Silk Wastcoat trim'd the same for Mr. Bridgwater[sic] £15.
Mr. Smart for a Suit of Crimson Velvet trimmed with Gold Shape Lace, £16.11.0.
A blew Cloth Coat faced with Scarlet & a Wastcoat ditto trimmed with Gold, & a dark brown Velvet Coat embroidered with Silver and an Orange col'd Wastcoat embroidered with Silk, Silver, £43.
Paid to Mr. Ryan for a Brocade Wastcoat he bought of Anne Taylor, £6.16.6.

These were highly fashionable suits of the quality being worn by the aristocracy, and would have been intended for elegant comedies of manners, but their theatrical use is shown by the amount of gold and silver employed for glitter.

The theatre was still obtaining royal cast-offs, for the women's wardrobe at Covent Garden in 1769 had seven coronation gowns valued at £237, with coronation petticoats at £52. There were some black velvet gowns for older female roles at £62, and the wardrobes of leading actresses were put at £56 for Mrs Macklin, £106 for Mrs Bellamy, and £119 for Mrs Yates.[17] Such sums are an indication of considerable embroidery in gold and silver and luxurious fabrics like silks, velvets and brocades. The concept of richness was being well maintained.

One eighteenth century actress with pronounced views on costume was George Anne Bellamy, who insisted that she had not been christened Georgiana. She joined Covent Garden playhouse in 1747 when she was 14, and considered, 'The dresses of the theatrical ladies were at this period very indifferent. The Empresses and Queens were confined to black velvet except on extraordinary occasions, when they put on an embroidered or tissue petticoat. The young ladies generally appeared in a *cast* gown of some person of quality.' According to her, her employer Mr Rich was so impressed by her taste that he took her along to his silk mercer's to select her own costumes. She also ordered two tragedy dresses from Paris, one being of deep yellow which she wore with a purple robe; this is an example of a leading actress being allowed to buy her own clothes while the rest of the company had to wear what they could find in the wardrobe.[18] The term 'tragedy dress' was much employed in the eighteenth century as signifying a very grand and specialized outfit. The Theatre Royal, Norwich, possessed several in its ladies' wardrobe in 1784: 'A Blue Plain Silk Tragedy Dress. A Crimson Sattin Tragedy Dress-plain. A Silver Tissue Brocade a Tragedy Dress – with Furs. A Tragedy Vest Scarlet and Silver. A white silk Tragedy Vest, Petticoat and a Train, Silver and Green Flowers. A Tragedy Train Clean'd – blue.'[19]

The fact that companies spent more on tragic costumes than on comic ones was a bone of contention at times, for it made comic actors jealous and tragic actors touchy about impudence from below. Colley Cibber, the actor, manager and playwright, began acting in 1690, and was best known for his comic role as the fop Lord Foppington in Vanbrugh's *The Relapse* which was written for him. The tragic actor George Powell took exception to Lord Foppington's attire in 1696, and Cibber wrote:

The tragedians seemed to think their rank as much above the comedians as in the characters they severally acted; when the first were in their finery, the latter were impatient at the expense; and looked upon it as rather laid out upon the real, than the fictitious person of the actor; nay, I have known in our company this ridiculous sort of regret arrived so far, that the tragedian has thought himself injured, when the comedian pretended to wear a fine coat. I remember Powel, upon surveying my first dress in the "Relapse" was out of all temper, and reproached our master in very rude terms, that he had not so good a suit to play *Caesar Borgia* in, though he knew, at the same time, my *Lord Foppington* filled the house, when his bouncing Borgia would do little more, than pay fiddles and candles to it; and though a character of vanity might be supposed more expensive in dress, than possibly one of ambition, yet the high heart of this heroical actor could not bear that a comedian should ever pretend to be well dressed as himself.[20]

The script does require the foppish lord to be an extravagant dresser, with a coat worth £80, but such a price is worthy of a tragedy costume. Thomas Doggett, for whom Congreve wrote the role of Ben in *Love for Love* in 1695, was a comic performer who was very outspoken on the subject. In his view comedy was closer to nature than grand tragedy, and he considered the 'costly trains and plumes of tragedy' to be a vain extravagance; but even today a tragedy can involve some trains and plumes because it deals with historical and aristocratic characters, and so it still often costs more than a comedy.

No doubt Dogget would have been annoyed by the fact that tragic heroes were also expected to be taller than comedians. They wore boots termed buskins in imitation of ancient Roman boots, and if the actor lacked sufficient heroic height, then his boots could be built up, as an exchange in *The Stage Mutineers* (1733) makes clear:

WARDROBE-KEEPER: A new Plume of the largest Size, with a Pair of Buskins higher than ordinary.

16 *The Beggar's Opera*, Lincoln's Inn Fields
Theatre, 1728, by W. Hogarth. THE TATE
GALLERY
John Gay's ballad opera with music arranged
from traditional tunes by Dr Pepusch, was a
tremendous success. As the scene is
contemporary there is no need for operatic
splendour in the Roman manner, so it was
dressed on the cheap in ordinary clothes without
spangles. Mrs Egleton played Lucy, Mr Hale
with the keys was Lockit the jailor, Mr Walker
in irons was Macheath the highwayman, and
Lavinia Fenton was Polly with Mr Hippisley as
her father Mr Peacham. Their clothes are street
wear. Miss Fenton eloped with the Duke of
Bolton who is shown in the stage box wearing
the garter.

SECOND MANAGER: Who was that for?
WARDROBE-KEEPER: Mr. *Pistol* – We were
obliged to give him a little Assistance; for, by
the stated Rules of the Theatre, a Hero shou'd
be at least Five Foot Three Quarters.

The combination of buskins and helmet of heroic
plumes could result in a hero seven feet high, a
visual symbol of superiority.

As not every production got a new wardrobe
there could be arguments among the cast as to who
should get the best costume in the playhouse's
collection. One such dispute happened when Mrs
Barry was playing Roxana and Mrs Boutel Statira in
Lee's *Alexander the Great; or, The Rival Queens*, when
the rivalry was very real:

It happened these Two Persons before they
appeared to the Audience, unfortunately had

34

some Dispute about a *Veil*, which Mrs. Boutel by the Partiality of the Property-Man obtained; this offending the haughty *Roxana*, they had warm Dispute behind the Scenes, which spirited the Rivals with such a natural resentment of each other, they were so violent in performing their Parts, and acted with such Vivacity, that *Statira*, on hearing the King was nigh, *begs the Gods to help her for that Moment*; on which *Roxana* hastening the design'd Blow, struck with such Force, that tho' the Point of the Dagger was blunted, it made through Mrs. *Boutel's* Stayes, and entered about a Quarter of an Inch of Flesh.[21]

The nervous tension before a performance could result in many outbursts of jealousy, but fortunately bloodshed was rare on the boards. One way the management could get an actor to take on a role at short notice was to offer him a new costume for the part. This happened with George Frederick Cooke when he made his first appearance at the Theatre Royal, Dublin. In March 1795 the manager asked him to take over as Don Felix in *The Wonder*, and agreed that he could have a new costume. Come the night, no costume had arrived, the manager could not be found, and the theatre tailor would not make the costume without an order from the manager, so Cooke, deeply offended, stormed out of the theatre and refused to perform for that company again.[22] New clothes were part of the star's superior rank.

There was one method the theatre used to obtain costumes without having to buy new ones, and this was to borrow or purchase cheaply the cast-offs of the nobility, as Mrs Bellamy mentioned. During the reigns of Charles II and James II when the London stage was part of the royal household and wore its livery (a relationship lost under William III and later kings), the loans and gifts could be surprisingly rich. When Downes admired the production of *Love and Honour* it was because Charles II allowed Betterton to wear his coronation suit to act Prince Alvaro, the Duke of York let Harris wear his suit to play Prince Prospero, and the Earl of Oxford gave his suit to Price to perform the Duke of Parma's son. These same coronation suits were also used in Lord Orrey's *King Henry V*, both performances being at the public playhouse but in the king's presence. As the coronation suit consisted of a sixteenth-century-type doublet and trunkhose this represented an attempt at historical costuming. The king's coronation clothes cost £2027 in 1661 so they were probably one of the most expensive tragedy costumes to grace the public stage. Similar generosity was displayed by James II's second wife, Mary of Modena, who presented her wedding dress and her coronation dress to Elisabeth Barry.

This custom of presenting clothes to leading actors continued until the mid-eighteenth century, after which the companies had to buy them, second-hand. Mr Rich of Covent Garden purchased a gown of Augusta Princess Dowager of Wales for Peg Woffington to wear, at which Mrs Bellamy mewed, 'It was not in the least soiled, and looked very beautiful by day-light, but being a straw colour, it seemed to be dirty white, by candle-light; specially when my splendid yellow was by it.' Mrs Bellamy got a royal cast-off herself, when Rich bought a birthday gown of silver tissue that had belonged to the Princess of Wales, in which she was to act Cleopatra in a revival of Dryden's *All for Love*. Her costume became a talking point as several ladies lent her diamonds to sew onto the dress, and attended the performance expecting to see their jewels; but a rival actress Mrs Furnival so envied the royal garment that she stole it from Mrs Bellamy's dressing room and wore it herself, so Mrs Bellamy had to enter in plain white satin. The leading patroness exclaimed of Furnival, 'Good Heaven, the woman has got on my diamonds', and the act ended with Furnival being shouted off.[23] Such gifts and loans did inhibit the actor in that the benefactor expected to see his generosity worn on the stage whenever he came to see a play, no matter what the play might be. The actor John Thurmond was given a court suit, but found himself in a predicament when his patron made an unexpected appearance at the theatre at the moment when the suit was reposing in a pawnshop.[24]

In the nineteenth century the theatre still tried to obtain royal and aristocratic cast-offs. James Winston, acting manager at the Theatre Royal, Drury Lane in 1820–27, noted on 20 July 1821 that the lessee of the theatre, the actor-manager Robert Elliston, was trying to borrow the clothes worn in the spectacular and extravagant coronation of George IV. In the event he was only allowed to have drawings made of the costumes, from which to make imitations. The coronation was in July, but this prohibition meant that Elliston's production could not open until August.[25] It was usual then for the theatre to stage events which the general public could not see for itself, such as royal festivals, or important naval or military battles against Napoleon, as a form of illustrated history cum 'television' reportage. The fact that Elliston failed to obtain these coronation clothes had a good result in the long run as George IV's coronation dress – doublet and trunk-hose of cloth of silver, lavishly bedecked with gold lace and gold braid, and a surcoat of crimson velvet faced with silver and embroidered in gold – still survives in the Museum of London, and has not been worn to pieces at Drury Lane. Less specialized gowns however continued to be available from courts, because women courtiers were not allowed to wear the same clothes twice, so there was a supply of rich evening gowns available after every major court event. This system was still operating in Paris under the lavish Second Empire, with the cast-offs of Empress Eugénie ending up on the stage, as *Punch* reported in 1856:

The guests are all expected to change their costume twice a day; and no lady is allowed to appear at the Château twice in the same dress; the Empress setting the example by giving every robe once worn to her attendants. As these are of course sold again, all Paris overflows with the Imperial *défroque*, and a few nights ago on the boards of one of the theatres was recognized a brocade that had lately figured on the throne.

The Second Empire collapsed in 1870, but the clothes worn in Parisian high society were still available at the end of the season, as were garments from foreign courts, until the Great War brought a serious reduction in the number of monarchies, and the supply of aristocratic and royal second-hand clothes began to dwindle. After the war surviving courts simplified their regulations and there were fewer receptions at which full evening dress had to be worn, so here too the supply of gowns was reduced. However the use of old clothes by the theatre has not died out yet. For a provincial company with a small budget second-hand garments are a necessity, and there are still rich women with dresses to dispose of when they have tired of them.

Stars in the nineteenth century still expected to get new clothes, leaving the cast-offs to the lesser members of the company, and when Charles Frederick Worth opened the first *haute couture* house in Paris in 1858 and became Empress Eugénie's couturier in 1860, many actresses and singers rushed to be dressed by him. Adelina Patti, Emma Albani and Dame Nellie Melba were all operatic prima donnas who placed themselves in Worth's hands, while the playwrights Alexandre Dumas *fils* and Victorien Sardou used to take actresses along to the rue de la Paix to be improved by the couturier; among them was Mlle Delaporte, and Eugénie Doch, the first Marguerite in Dumas' *Dame aux Camélias*, and Mlle Antoine. The Comédie Française sent Maria Favart, Sophie Croizette and Sarah Bernhardt.[26] This new pattern of going to a couturier for theatrical costume continued for the next hundred years, and has not vanished completely yet.

There was less need for a theatrical hiring costumier in England than in France, but there were some, supplying the masquerade market in the main. Actress Hannah Pritchard lent her name to a clothing warehouse run by her son-in-law James Spilbury, which sold masquerade costume alongside robes and court dress. In 1761 it made the clothes for the wedding of Princess Charlotte to George III, and Mrs Pritchard was so highly esteemed for her elegance on stage that she was appointed Charlotte's dresser for both her wedding and her coronation.[27] This establishment was in Tavistock Street; other masquerade or hiring agencies were in Monmouth Street. When Tate Wilkinson made his first appearance on the London stage he found that the wardrobe had no costume suitable for his part, so he went to Monmouth Street and hired a 'heavy, rich glaring, spangled and embroidered velvet suit of clothes'.[28]

The most famous hiring firm in London opened its doors in 1790 and is still going strong nearly 200 years later. Lewis Nathan was a gentleman's tailor at 24 Tichborne Street, making beautifully embroidered suits, a few of which are still in the company's collection. No documents survive to say precisely when the tailor's business expanded into lending theatrical costume, but the firm thrived well enough to open other premises at 94 Berwick Street in Soho. This was opened by Lewis's son Jacob and bore the name 'Masquerade Warehouse and Fancy Costumes'. The firm started calling itself Nathan's when the next generation Lewis and Henry took over further premises, 44 Tichborne Street, under the title 'Court and Theatrical Costumiers and Fancy Dress Makers' in 1845. This means that they were selling and hiring out official court uniforms, and court evening dress which consisted of a black tail coat, white waistcoat, black kneebreeches, black silk stocking and buckled pumps for civilian males. The theatrical and fancy dress would have overlapped in character, for masquerades and amateur dramatics were both very fashionable in high society. A very enthusiastic amateur actor and masquerader was the novelist Charles Dickens who wrote to Nathan's in 1844 that he would like a costume for Twelfth Night festivities, and fancied himself in the role of a magician with a black cloak covered with hieroglyphics, a doublet to go underneath, a fierce black beard, a sugar-loaf hat and a wand with a snake on it. His friend Mr Forster wanted to go as a Mephistopheles so a similar costume but in flaming red was requested. Unfortunately Dickens only gave Nathan's 48 hours to find and make these outfits, so the order had to be declined. The rest of their relationship was better organized, and Dickens could rely on Nathan's to dress his amateur productions which were a great success. In 1846 it was seventeenth-century-type costumes for Jonson's *Every Man in Humour*, in which Dickens played Captain Bobadil, which was so well received the amateur troupe took it to

17 Susanna Cibber as Cordelia in *King Lear*, painted by P. van Bleek. YALE CENTER FOR BRITISH ART, PAUL MELLON COLLECTION

As Cordelia was of royal birth she was costumed in velvet lined with ermine, a satin petticoat, and high-heeled shoes despite her distressed situation, for leading actors would insist on the best costumes for themselves. Her collar is the only indication that the play was set in the remote past.

Manchester and Liverpool on tour. In 1848 it was Shakespearian costume when Dickens produced *The Merry Wives of Windsor* at the Haymarket Theatre, London, with a tour round Manchester, Birmingham, Edinburgh and Glasgow. This enterprise was devoted to raising money to endow a curatorship at Shakespeare's birthplace at Stratford-on-Avon. Another member of Dickens's circle, the illustrator George Cruickshank, went to Nathan's in 1850 to borrow an eighteenth-century-type suit to wear at a country dance. The firm was always on the look-out for new possibilities and when in 1846 persons in artisan dress were banned from walking in St James's Park, Nathans advertised a stock of second-hand liveries from the best families, much bedecked with gold and silver lace, which could be hired by any working-class person who wished to stroll in the royal parks.

Royal recognition of the hiring house was a result of its supplying costumes for the *tableaux vivants* which were now highly popular in aristocratic circles. These were posed scenes representing a famous painting, an incident from history, or a scene from a play. The artist David Wilkie promoted these entertainments in England after seeing such a presentation in Dresden in 1826, and they became firmly established. In 1870 Nathan's supplied the clothes for the *tableaux* mounted during a house party at Kimbolton Castle, the seat of the Duke of Manchester, in which the Prince and Princess of Wales took part. This led to more orders from the royal set, and in 1888 an order from Queen Victoria herself to dress the *tableaux* to be held at Osborne House on the Isle of Wight. This required classical draperies for the queen's ladies when they posed around her bust, bearing garlands, in a scene entitled 'Homage to Queen Victoria', and Spanish costumes for *Carmen*, which was posed by Prince Henry of Battenberg as Don Escamillo and Minnie Cochrane as Carmen herself. Queen Victoria also liked *tableaux* to be organized at Balmoral. This set Nathan's a problem as that Scottish castle was remote from express railway systems, so the subjects to be performed had to be decided well in advance to allow plenty of time for the costumes to be despatched north. The sort of scenes presented there were 'Prince Charles Edward' in 1888 with Prince Albert representing Bonnie Prince Charlie and Princess Victoria of Wales as Flora Macdonald, all draped in tartans, and *The Sleeping Beauty* in 1890 with Lord William Cecil in tights as the prince, and Princess Alexandra of Edinburgh as the heroine in a sleeveless white gown, and with her hair crowned by flowers. As a result of these costuming triumphs Nathan's was granted the royal warrant so that they could now style themselves costumiers by appointment to Her Majesty Queen Victoria. In 1897 the

firm made the costumes for the Prince and Princess of Wales in the Devonshire House Fancy Dress Ball, given by the Duke of Devonshire to celebrate Queen Victoria's Diamond Jubilee. Nathan dressed the prince in a sixteenth-century outfit representing the Grand Prior of the Order of St John of Jerusalem, and the princess as Marguerite de Valois, but of course the result still looked 1897 for the princess kept to her fashionable corset underneath, and did not change her hairstyle either. The personal identity always intrudes.

The first definite evidence of theatrical costuming came in 1848–50 when Nathan's supplied the costumes for *Othello* at the Olympic Theatre; an unreliable actor, G. V. Brooke, was performing there. Brooke never paid bills so Nathan's had to sue him for £123, and eventually recouped £100 out of the sum owed. Relations were much more reliable with William and Madge Kendall, the actor managers who ran the St James's Theatre between 1879 and 1888. The Kendalls were sticklers for accuracy so when in 1880 they produced *William and Susan*, which had a large cast of sailors, naval officers, and royal marines, Nathan's had to ensure that each costume constructed was correct down to the last button. The uniforms might be contemporary, but this meant even more research and accuracy because there would be service personnel in the audience who would explode at any slips, whereas with historical costume not every spectator knew the clothes inside out. In 1881 the professional beauty Lillie Langtry took up acting, being tutored by Squire and Mrs Bancroft at the Haymarket. She organized her own company and produced Sheridan's *The School for Scandal* in 1883–5, and ordered the costumes from Nathan's: 18 gentlemen's outfits and three ladies' costumes in eighteenth-century pattern, but she exercised the star's right to something superior for herself and ordered her gowns from Maison Worth in Paris. Nathan's also dressed her company for *The Hunchback*, *The Lady of Lyons* and *Pauline*.

The theatrical company with which Nathan's has been involved longest is the D'Oyly Carte, for it was Richard D'Oyly Carte the impresario who encouraged Gilbert and Sullivan to collaborate on their light operas. These works were so successful that the impresario built the Savoy Theatre, the first London house to have electrical lighting onstage, on the proceeds. It opened with *Patience* in 1881 and costumes by Nathan's who supplied 16 Dragoon officers' uniforms at £12.10.0 each. The male tailoring origin of the firm had not been forgotten. Nathan's went on to dress *Ruddigore* and *Iolanthe*, and continued costuming D'Oyly Carte, in what must be something of a record, the same theatrical tailor supplying the same company for 100 years.

By the turn of the century Nathan's could number George Alexander, who took over the St James's theatre in 1891, as a star customer, who had his greatest success in the dual role in *The Prisoner of Zenda* which called for invented uniforms for an imaginary state. Another client was Lewis Waller who like Alexander was dubbed a matinée idol, the term now coined for the most romantic and dashing actors. Waller was famed as Monsieur Beaucaire, so required eighteenth-century suits from Nathan, then mediaeval ones for *Henry V*, and seventeenth-century types in which to play D'Artagnan. Another idol was Martin-Harvey who was so celebrated as Sidney Carton in *The Only Way*, an adaptation of Dickens's *A Tale of Two Cities* that he had to perform it throughout his career, although he was capable of much more dramatic power as shown by his performance of Oedipus Rex for Max Reinhardt in 1912. Sidney Carton of course required more eighteenth-century clothes from Nathan's. By this time the firm had its own designer in the Dutchman Mr Karl, but it would make up designs by other theatre designers such as Percy Anderson. In 1907 came one of the most lavish productions the firm had to costume. Kaiser Wilhelm was in London on a state visit so Beerbohm Tree mounted a spectacular at His Majesty's Theatre. Entitled *A Vision of Delight* it contained most of the leading actors of the day in splendid costumes, but Nathan's clothes were outshone by all the real diamonds in the audience, as it was a gala state occasion with tiaras and orders in plenty. This was a rare contrast to the normal situation where the stage dazzled the audience.[29]

The arrival of electric lighting had important consequences for theatre costume. Being much sharper, clearer and whiter than candlelight or gas, it showed up far more detail and did not kill green or blue. The first result was that white fabrics would shine so much that they had to be replaced by cream. As the light was so strong it ended the need for massive amounts of metal embroidery on costumes. Some glitter remained necessary to indicate a character's wealth and social class, but it was no longer necessary to cover the whole costume with sequins or gold lace. Introductions of new technology were gradual of course. There were gas-lamps outside Covent Garden in 1815, and some indoors on the stairs, and similar arrangements at the Olympic Theatre, before there was stage lighting by gas at the sides of the stage as Drury Lane introduced in 1817. There were experiments with electric arc-lights at the Paris Opéra from 1846, but in Paris too the installation of electricity began outside and on the staircases of theatres before it reached the stage. J.W. Swan's invention of the incandescent lamp bulb was the important step, and the Savoy Theatre was equipped with these and with its own generator by Siemens & Bros. in 1881. Irving at the Lyceum had started lowering the auditorium lights during a performance and this system was now imitated at the electric Savoy, so that the audience was plunged in darkness and the stage alone remained brightly lit.[30] This was a major alteration, for hitherto the stage and audience had both been lit by chandeliers throughout the performance, a tradition started by the need to have as many candles as possible in operation to produce reasonable illumination. This change in lighting separated the actors from the audience, whereas in the past the actor could see the spectators and watch their faces for their reactions to his performance. With the audience now invisible in the blackness actors had to listen for the audience reaction, and could no longer act 'eye to eye'.

CHAPTER THREE

Voices for Reform

'We are to have no manner of relish for *Gothique* Ornaments, as being in effect so many Monsters, which barbarous Ages have produc'd', wrote Du Fresnoy in his *De Arte Graphica*, which was translated into English by the playwright Dryden in 1695. As far as the Baroque period was concerned the period which lay between the fall of the Western Roman Empire and the rise of the modern nation state was an age of blackness, of hideous, clumsy art, of barbaric behaviour and ignorance. Only the ancient world could be admired as a model. The seventeenth century put much emphasis on exquisite good manners, and could only regard the less polite Middle Ages with a shudder. The facts that the Eastern Roman Empire at Constantinople managed to survive as late as 1453, and that Greek scholars from that city had helped to spark off the Renaissance in Italy, were both ignored, for this Byzantine extension of the Roman pattern seemed too far removed from the original model to be worthy of attention. In any case that area had since fallen to the Turks, so any study of Roman survivals in Byzantine art was out of the question. The Baroque scholar looked more to the history of Western Europe and there, could only see a dense fog, since the fall of ancient Rome.

There were a few exceptions to this condemnation of all things mediaeval and Gothic. The herald and scholar Sir William Dugdale spent 1640/41 recording mediaeval church monuments and stained glass in London and the Midlands, because he wisely foresaw on the eve of the Civil War that the Puritan extremists in the Parliamentary party might unleash a campaign of destruction not unlike that perpetrated in the mid-sixteenth century. Dugdale was right, and his record of some of the tombs in Lichfield Cathedral is the only surviving evidence of them, for the tombs were smashed by the Parliamentary troops in 1643 when they sacked the cathedral. Here the hatred of mediaeval art was based on religious reasons not artistic, damning works which survived from a Roman Catholic era. A few institutions founded in the Middle Ages such as abbeys and universities still felt sympathetic towards the Gothic style as their own buildings were in that manner, so that when they had to commission improvements they still considered that the Gothic style should be employed. Thus Sir Christopher Wren's completion of Tom Tower at Christ Church, Oxford in 1681/2 harmonizes with the Tudor Gothic base, and Hawksmoor's towers for Westminster Abbey keep to the original manner, although when he rebuilt All Souls College at Oxford he provided the Gothic exteriors with very classical interiors. Yet such sympathies were defeated in the end as even universities went classical, and Wren won the battle with the clergy to rebuild St Paul's in a classical manner.

Consequently when the Baroque theatre is criticized for not being antiquarian in its approach to plays set in the Middle Ages, and in particular for not using mediaeval costume, the critics overlook the strong artistic and religious pressures placed upon the theatre not to be Gothic. The manager who put on a play dressed in fifteenth-century costume would have been soundly condemned for such barbarism. Unfortunately there were a few mediaeval characters who would not lie down. King Henry V was immortalized by Shakespeare's play and was a national hero, while King Richard III made a fascinating villain. The theatre could not exclude them from its repertoire because they made such good drama, but a way had to be found to remove their Gothic fifteenth-century nature and 'civilize' their appearance to suit Baroque taste. The answer was found in official dress. A monarch's coronation suit, the suits of the Order of the Garter and the Ordre du Saint Esprit, and the livery of page boys, all retained a historical form of dress, the

Hamlet Act 3. Scene 7.
Engraved for y Universal Museum.

doublet and trunkhose of the sixteenth century. Here was an old style which was familiar, which was approved by court and aristocracy, and which avoided the pointed extremes of Gothic dress. The theatre adopted it with relief as the universal answer to any play set in the non-Roman past. King Henry V could be performed in a suit of sixteenth century type.

The best way to avoid the problem of historical costuming was to dress plays in contemporary clothes. After all Shakespeare's dramas were mostly performed in the clothes of his own day, and he himself would not have expected *King Lear* or *Macbeth* to be attired in Saxon or ancient Scottish dress, indeed he would have had no idea what such clothes had looked like. As the majority of the clothes given to the playhouses were contemporary, and the second-hand clothes bought were not antiques, it would be cheaper for the theatre to dress most productions, particularly comedies, in contemporary dress. As tragedy costumes cost so much there was less money available to dress other forms

18 David Garrick in *Hamlet* Act 3 Scene VII, 1769. HARVARD THEATRE COLLECTION

Contemporary clothes for a non-Roman play of indeterminate period, with Garrick leaning against Ophelia's knees; they are in the garb of gentlemen and ladies of quality. The players in the background however are in Van Dyck dress, to give them a historical character, although the murder of Hamlet's father had not taken place very long before.

19 *Macbeth* from *The Works of Mr. William Shakespear*, 1709; by J. van der Gucht. THE BRITISH LIBRARY

Contemporary military attire for General Macbeth, a red coat and gold lace of the officer in the British Army. The three witches were always played by men in shawls, plain dresses and aprons.

20   John Philip Kemble as Macbeth, 1794.
THE FOLGER SHAKESPEARE LIBRARY

Eighty-five years later the policy illustrated in **19**
continues with Macbeth as a contemporary
soldier, now expressed in the slimmer line of
late-eighteenth-century fashion.

OPPOSITE PAGE
21   *The Life and Death of Richard III*, from *The
Works of Mr. William Shakespear*, 1709; by J. van
der Gucht.   THE BRITISH LIBRARY

The costume for Richard III was a firm
tradition, with a fur-edged gown worn over
trunkhose as a sixteenth-century-type
compromise for a fifteenth-century king. The
ghosts, thoroughly whitened with chalk or flour,
are mostly in their nightshirts although two in
the background wear their shrouds, gathered at
the head.

22   'The Play-house Habit of King Richard
the 3.ᵈ', by Thomas Jefferys, from his *Collection
of the Dresses of the Different Nations*, 1757.   THE
BRITISH LIBRARY

The stock costume would be slightly modified
according to the latest fashion so here Richard's
trunkhose have been lengthened to resemble
contemporary kneebreeches, and his pleated
sleeves are a misunderstanding of slashing.

of drama. If Roman heroes had to have ostrich
plumes and gold lace, non-Roman plays had to be
dressed more cheaply. Therefore the stage adopted
a limited policy towards history plays.

It was recognized that a few characters had to
have historical costume as this was part of their
identity, so a sixteenth century pattern doublet and
trunk hose would be made for them; but where
plays were set in the remote and misty past, such as
Lear, Macbeth or *Cymbeline*, it was more economic to
use a contemporary wardrobe. Nobody was likely
to protest, because the Gothic age was out of
fashion. Accordingly the seventeenth century
theatre carried on much as the Shakespearean stage
had done, with Roman costume for obviously
Roman plays, contemporary dress for most other
works, and only a few attempts at historical clothes
for special cases. Shakespeare's leading man Richard Burbage acted Hamlet, Lear and Othello in
contemporary dress, Thomas Betterton played
Hamlet as a contemporary Restoration gentleman,
David Garrick wore typical eighteenth-century

black court suit, ruffles at the wrist, bag wig,
buckled shoes and cravat.[1] Similarly Macbeth was
dressed in contemporary style with this distinction:
as he was a general when the play opened, he was
given military uniform. As the British Army was
famous for its redcoats, General Macbeth wore
scarlet decked with gold, and was so performed by
Garrick, and John Philip Kemble in the 1780s. As
fifteenth-century Italian dress seemed too horrible
to contemplate, and moreover Romeo himself did
not have a strong historical image, there was no
need to give him a doublet and trunkhose. A
fashionable contemporary suit was the answer, as
Romeo was of good family, so Garrick in 1765
performed Romeo in stylish cutaway coat, waistcoat, and kneebreeches, like a contemporary aristocrat. Othello was another example of a soldier,
so the same solution was applied as to Macbeth –
dress him as a general.

To the Baroque mind it was very remiss of
Shakespeare to have written so few Roman plays.
Troilus and Cressida, Timon of Athens, Coriolanus,

Julius Caesar, Titus Andronicus, Antony and Cleopatra,
and *Pericles* were outnumbered by plays dealing
with the Wars of the Roses and even earlier
mediaeval subjects like *King John* which, horror of
horrors, was set in the twelfth century, together
with the comedies of indeterminate period. Playwrights in the next two centuries worked very hard
to produce a body of Roman plays to redress the
balance. At first French plays with a Roman plot
were translated, notably Pierre Corneille's *Horace*
and *Pompée, Héraclius* and *Nicomède*; then from 1660
onwards D'Avenant, Dryden, Otway, Lee, and
Settle wrote heroic tragedies, and in the early
eighteenth century Dennis, Gildon, Mrs Manley,
and Mallet strove to do the same. William
Whitehead's *The Roman Father* of 1749 has the title
of the ideal. As Shakespeare's comedies so rarely
conformed to Roman ideals, *Love's Labour Lost, The
Two Gentlemen of Verona, The Comedy of Errors, All's
Well that Ends Well,* and *As You Like It* were all
banished from the Restoration stage.[2] This act of
artistic policy relieved the wardrobe department of

the problem of dressing these works with their
vague period settings. Of his tragedies the Roman
plays were retained of course, and could be dressed
in the correct plumes and trains, while a work like
Lear, set in such a remote period of British history,
would have to have contemporary dress. Only the
outstanding tragedies with a mediaeval setting were
retained, and here costuming was a special case.

Richard III was highly popular among actors and
audience alike, so it was allowed the doublet and
trunk hose of sixteenth century type together with a
gown trimmed with ermine to clothe that king. This
became the stock costume for that part, from the
Restoration right through to the nineteenth century, and no doubt Shakespeare would have seen it
performed in similar costume at the première.
David Garrick wore this uniform costume when he
made his triumphant London debut as Richard III
in 1741. John Philip Kemble wore the same design
at the turn of the century, as did George Frederick
Cooke for his London debut in the role. The
playbill proclaimed:

THEATRE ROYAL; COVENT GARDEN,
This present FRIDAY, October 31, 1800,
King Richard the Third,
With New and Appropriate Dresses, . . .

The clothes might have been newly made but the
style was the now firmly traditional one, still
deemed appropriate, with the sixteenth century
pattern. When the fiery actor Edmund Kean played
his last role it was Richard III in that same type of
costume in 1833. From Shakespeare to 1833 is a
tremendous run for one pattern of dress.

Henry VIII was another character dressed in this
type of costume. After all he had worn it in his own
lifetime, and sufficient portraits of him by Holbein
and others still survived to maintain his image down
the years. Consequently the theatre dressed him in
doublet, trunkhose and gown. Where historical
costume was allowed, the costume was used for
fifteenth and sixteenth century characters without
discrimination. It was historical, so that was
enough. Precise details from the past were not
required; the general approach dominated.

Burly Falstaff was a much loved character, so

OPPOSITE PAGE
23 George Frederick Cooke as Richard III,
Theatre Royal, Covent Garden, 1801. British
School. THE NATIONAL THEATRE

Still in firm tradition with slight modification,
a frill collar replacing a ruff. Heroic plumes
continue, and so do the marshall's baton, and
gloves. The slashing of the upper sleeve is more
accurate. Cooke's moustache is coming unstuck.

RIGHT
24 The Richard III costume worn by Edmund
Kean, in the last role he played at Drury Lane in
1833. THE MUSEUM OF LONDON

Doublet and trunkhose of black cotton velvet
decorated with spangles, and gown edged with
imitation ermine on crimson velvet. This was the
end of a centuries-old tradition, for the
Victorians put Richard III into mediaeval dress.

25 *King Henry VIII* from *The Works of Mr.
William Shakespear*, 1709, by J. van der
Gucht. THE BRITISH LIBRARY

The Tudor monarch was another example of a
strong historical character being given historical
costume of the sixteenth-century pattern, which
was correct so far as the king's own period was
concerned. Nevertheless only leading characters
were given special clothes, and the rest of the
cast had to make do with the contemporary suits
in the wardrobe.

26 *Henry IV Part I*, from *The Works of Mr. William Shakespear*, 1709, by J. van der Gucht. THE BRITISH LIBRARY

Sir John Falstaff was another character with such strong historical identity that he had a traditional costume of his own of roughly sixteenth-century pattern, because mediaeval dress was unacceptable. It always included a bonnet with heroic plumes, a doublet and a ruff and originally trunkhose.

OPPOSITE PAGE
27 Falstaff in *Henry IV Part I*, 1746. By Marcellus Laroon the Younger. YALE CENTER FOR BRITISH ART, PAUL MELLON COLLECTION

The bonnet, ruff and doublet continue, but the mid-eighteenth century gave Falstaff kneebreeches as it disliked the exposure of the upper leg. The other characters show some historical touches too. The soldier on the right has four vertical pockets *à la* 1680s, and the woman in the background has the hood and pointed hat of 1660.

popular that he was introduced into other plays not written by his creator Shakespeare. Strangely enough he was not given the doublet and trunkhose that one would expect of a fifteenth-century character. His enormous belly meant that the actor in the part had to wear a lot of padding, but this presented a problem with trunkhose because they were very short, and exposed most of the man's legs. A padded actor with bulging stomach above his own skinny legs would have looked ridiculous, so it was more sensible to put Falstaff into breeches. That would allow for even more padding to be stuffed in, and would solve the problem of a matching pair of legs. True padded stockings might have been used, but they would not have looked very convincing and there was a danger of the padded calves and thighs shifting. So it was that Falstaff was not dressed as his period required, but in the doublet and breeches of the 1630s, with a large pair of riding boots to conceal his calves. No part of the actor's anatomy need show other than his face and hands. This became the stock costume for Falstaff throughout the seventeenth and eighteenth centuries and into the nineteenth. One of the earliest attempts to reform the anachronism of a fifteenth-century character in seventeenth-century dress was made by George Frederick Cooke in 1802, when he wore a ruff and trunkhose, albeit with a still very seventeenth century doublet. By this date Cook's own legs were so fat from his excessive fondness for the bottle that they matched the part very well.

Villains were another character type which had a stock appearance. As black represents evil in colour symbolism, villains were identified by having black wigs and black clothes. This made them very easy to recognize, which was important when dealing with an audience which was not sophisticated. The villain did not enter and say that he had evil intentions; as soon as he slid onto the stage his blackness announced his identity, his clothes said who he was. The three evil sisters in *Macbeth*, the witches, were dressed in cloaks and hoods through the seventeenth century and well into the eighteenth. The association of tall pointed hats with witches began in the late eighteenth century. The tall pointed hat had been worn by both sexes in the 1660s, and was still worn among the working class into the 1750s when it began to yield at long last to fashion. Thereafter only very conservative old women wore the hats; so when the theatre started giving a pointed hat to witches it was as the hat of old women, not as a hat peculiar to witches. Real witches in the past did not have a uniform, for that would have betrayed them, and they dressed in the same way as everyone else.

While the theatre did have these stock costumes for particular characters it was not very generous in

their distribution. Obviously to dress the whole cast of *Henry V* or *Henry VIII* in sixteenth century clothes would have cost a lot of money, at a time when most of the costumes in the wardrobe were either Roman or contemporary. Managers evidently writhed at the idea of the expense as they did not equip the whole cast with historical clothes. The company only provided the leading characters, the kings, with appropriate attire, and everybody else had to make do with what was in the wardrobe. Neither of the plays was Roman, so the other actors had to have the contemporary garments. There was nothing else available, apart from the variety of clothes used by dancers, which might be Chinese, or Indian, and they would not do either. In any case the dancers would probably have objected most strongly to straight actors making off with their tinsel glory. Thus the strange situation existed in which only the leads in one of Shakespeare's historical plays had period costume, while the rest of the cast wore contemporary. When a tragedy costume cost scores of pounds, the budget available for other clothes was reduced. This problem persisted in both the seventeenth century and the eighteenth, with Garrick playing Richard III in doublet and trunkhose against a background of actors in contemporary suits, cravats, powdered wigs, and cocked hats.[3] It was historical costuming, but on the cheap.

It was not until 1724 that a voice of criticism was raised. The playwright Aaron Hill had a great interest in those foggy periods of British history which were out of fashion. He even read Richard Verstegan's *Restitution of Decayed Intelligence* of 1605, an extremely unusual work which studied ancient British antiquities. Hill began to think that the theatre ought to have plays set in Saxon times and the like, and that these productions ought to have ancient costume, for all the characters. His thoughts were inspired by the receipt of a playbill on 12 October 1724 announcing a puppet show at the White Hart tavern in St Margaret's Lane, London. The playbill read, 'Every Figure dress'd according to their own Country Habits'. Now this was not an announcement of historical costuming, but of correct national dress; nevertheless it set Hill thinking that it might be a first hint of a change in attitude.

And it will be reasonable to hope, after the Publick Taste has been so refin'd, by these *Chips of a New Block*, that we shall see no more Intermixture of the Ancient, with the modern Dresses: Where the Order of Things is so capriciously revers'd, that the Courtiers of an English Monarch shall stand round him, like *Beaux* of *Yesterday*; and the Sovereign himself strut about, in Trunk Breeches, and be dress'd, as *old* as a Patriarch.

Hill did not stop there, but busied himself writing a play with a Saxon setting and tried to design the costumes himself. He wrote to the manager of Drury Lane, Robert Wilks, on 28 October 1731:

Sir,
    I send you herewith, the shadows of a set of dresses for the *Generous Traitor*. You must not expect *drawings*. They are, however, plainly enough mark'd, to give *Ideas* of their meaning.

He argued that all the costumes were meant to be Saxon, and advocated that each character should be dressed in different colours. He had employed a lot of fur as that was truly Saxon and gave their clothes much grandeur, but if real fur were too expensive, the production could use imitation as the effect would seem the same from a distance. Hill stressed that all the high-ranking characters in the play had to wear their coronets all the time as Saxon nobles did. They could have one feather with it, but not a forest of plumes like a Roman hero. He argued that Saxon dress would have a very novel appeal.

To say nothing as to the *impropriety*, in the custom of dressing characters, *so far back in time*, after the common fashions of our days, it weakens *probability*, and cuts off, in great measure, what *most strikes* an audience; for it relaxes the pomp of Tragedy, and the generality, being led, by the eye, can conceive nothing extraordinary when they *see* nothing uncommon.

Hill was so delighted with Saxon dress he thought it could not fail, and even considered it superior to contemporary dress.

It is, also, worth notice, that a fine, natural *Shape*, receives great *advantage*, from a well-imagined turn of *habit*, and an aukward [sic], unnatural one has an *air*, that *burlesques* dignity without it.[4]

As Aaron Hill was an established playwright, with a number of tragedies having been performed

---

28 Robert Elliston as Falstaff, 1826, by T. Wageman. THE FOLGER SHAKESPEARE LIBRARY

The ruff has turned into a lace collar but otherwise the principal components of the costume are present, the bonnet and plume, the doublet, and the riding boots. Elliston has added a coat, while the baggy breeches allow a lot of padding to be used without showing. This traditional dress was also abolished by the Victorians.

29   Charles Macklin as Shylock in *The Merchant of Venice*, Theatre Royal, Covent Garden, *c* 1768, by Johan Zoffany.   THE TATE GALLERY

Macklin's famous reform of 1741 of playing Shylock in Jewish long coat and beard was repeated throughout his acting career. It was however contemporary Jewish dress, not Shakespearian in period. Macklin's daughter Maria plays Portia in a lawyer's black suit and legal gown, while Matthew Clarke as Antonio bares his chest as Shylock demands his pound of flesh. The Venetian senators are dressed as English judges so the reform was a limited one.

at Drury Lane before, his new play, renamed *Athelwold*, was accepted and presented in December 1731. While Hill was rich enough to have paid for Saxon costumes himself, if Wilks refused to spend company money on such unusual clothes, he does not appear to have done so. The Theatre Royal advertised two performances of the tragedy in *The Daily Post* for Friday 10 and Saturday 11 December 1731 with the claim that it had 'new Habits, Scenes and other Decorations proper to the Play'. This suggests that some effort was made, but no details were given. The play was published on Monday 20 December with an advertisement in *The Daily Post*. Other newspapers of the day, *The Daily Journal* and *The Daily Courant*, make no mention of the performance, so there does not seem to have been a sensation. On the contrary the tragedy was a flop, for a Saxon subject proved to be too outlandish to appeal to the public. If Aaron Hill did succeed in having some Saxon tunics edged with fur, nobody took any notice. It was one of those occasions when an innovation is too far ahead of its time to catch on. There will always be a few original minds which will swim against the tide, but in this case the tide was not yet ready to turn.

Ten years elapsed before someone else in the theatre took positive action towards greater accuracy in stage costume, and this was the actor Charles Macklin in 1741, when he was to play Shylock in *The Merchant of Venice*. Hitherto actors such as Dogget had played Shylock like broad farce, but Macklin saw that the part allowed for dramatic possibilities, so he determined to perform it more powerfully. As part of his thinking about the role he had to consider what his Shylock should look like. A new appearance would suit a new interpretation. All his colleagues were telling him that to attempt a new way of acting the play, and to break with tradition, would prove disastrous, but Macklin persisted. He donned a red hat, a pointed beard, and a loose, black gown, and thus attired faced the suspicious audience. He conserved his forces until Act III where the Jew's scenes of joy and grief allowed him to burst forth, showing his powers in both emotions to the full. The night proved a triumph, the nobility flocked to the green room to congratulate the actor, and a few days later Lord Bolingbroke invited him to dinner. At the party was the poet Alexander Pope, who asked Macklin why he had worn a red hat. Macklin replied that he had read that Jews in Italy had to wear red hats.

'And pray, Mr. Macklin', said Pope, 'do players generally take such pains?'
'I do not know, Sir, that they do, but as I had staked my reputation on the character, I was determined to spare no trouble in getting at the best information.'

Macklin responded. Pope replied that this was 'very laudable'.[5] This was accuracy but in contemporary terms, for Macklin did not perform Shylock as a Jew of Shakespeare's time but as one who might be found in Venice in 1741. It had long been the law in Christian countries that Jews had to wear distinctive dress. When John Evelyn made his European tour in 1644/5 he noticed that Jews in both Italy and France had to wear red hats, except that in Rome they had to wear yellow lest they be mistaken for cardinals.[6]

Macklin's approach to accuracy was not exactly compelling, for it was not until 1772 that he made another innovation. He was to play Macbeth, and as his eye was always on his profession, he thought that he could increase his impact here if he changed the costume. With Macbeth always being dressed as a British general, and the only touch of Scottish

local colour being in the use of claymore and targe, Macklin concluded that the character ought to have more Scottish elements in his dress, particularly as the play was set in pre-Norman times. He introduced his reform, Macbeth in tartan, and it was very successful, other actors like John Philip Kemble taking the idea up; but some felt that Macklin, now rather stout, looked more like a Scottish piper than a Caledonian prince.[7] It is highly debatable as to precisely what form this Scottish dress took, because it was illegal. Following the uprising led by Bonnie Prince Charlie in 1745, the British government had banned Highland dress:

That from and after the first Day of August one thousand seven hundred and forty-seven, no Man or Boy within that part of Great Britain called Scotland, other than such as shall be employed as Officers and Soldiers in his Majesty's Forces, shall, on any Pretence whatsoever, wear or put on the Clothes commonly called Highland Clothes (that is to say) Plaid, Philebeg, or Little Kilt, Trowse, Shoulder Belts, or any Part whatsoever of what peculiarly belongs to the Highland Garb; and that no Tartan or party-coloured Plaid or Stuff shall be used for Great Coats or for Upper Coats.[8]

The penalties were six months in jail for the first offence, and seven years transportation for the second. How could Macklin get round this act when he was performing in London under the nose of the government? Firstly he might argue that the act applied to Scots, but as he was British there was nothing in the act to state that Britons might not wear tartan. Secondly, the act allowed Scottish regiments in the British Army to wear Highland Dress, and Macklin could argue that Macbeth was a Scottish general. Thus it is likely that Macklin wore the contemporary uniform of a Scottish officer, with no attempt to unearth what the original Macbeth might have worn nearly a thousand years before. Of course once the British Army got its hands on Highland Dress it tamed it, and smartened it up, and established a basic pattern, according to the rule book. Macklin probably wore a tartan jacket and trews, or else tartan kneebreeches and stockings – a kilt and bare knees on the London stage in 1772 would have been the height of impropriety.

Macklin's Jewish innovation back in 1741 did not go unnoticed. David Garrick, whose London debut was that very year, became one of the managers of the Theatre Royal, Drury Lane in 1747, and began to show some concern for better, more accurate costuming straight away. In that year he produced *Albumazar* 'New Dress'd after the Manner of the Old English Comedy', and in 1750 clothed the

English characters in *Edward the Black Prince* 'in the Habit of those days'.[9] It is unlikely that these costumes were other than the customary sixteenth century pattern already used for history plays, but Garrick was appreciating that the general public would now be attracted by this claim to authenticity in costume. The fact that he stated that he was putting the English characters into period habits indicates that he was using the costume for a number of players, and not simply for the star actor alone, so that Garrick's innovation was to increase the number of historical garments worn in one production. Aaron Hill's hopes that the public would become more sophisticated in its attitude towards theatre costume seemed to be fulfilled. Novelty is an attraction in itself, so for theatre managers to advertise new and appropriate costumes was a means to stir general interest, and the more they advertised the fact the more the public would come to expect it.

A new form of theatrical historical costume appeared in the eighteenth century which was closely allied to developments in portraiture. Baroque painters had considered Roman dress to be timeless and thus highly suitable for portraits; the artists of the Rococo period now looked for another form of timeless dress, as the feeling had grown that the Baroque Grand Manner of Roman dress and flowing draperies was too grandiose for the new taste, which stressed neatness and small scale, intimacy not grandeur. It seemed to Rococo eyes that the most elegant painter of clothes had been Sir Anthony van Dyck in the 1630s, and his portraits seemed to have a timeless sophistication and grace which might be reproduced in the 1700s, and which might give their paintings the same eternal values. Accordingly Van Dyck dress was approved for portraits, for masquerade parties, where it was worn in abundance, and for the theatre. Not that eighteenth-century Van Dyck dress was perfectly accurate – it could not be, as the fashions had changed. In the 1630s high waists had been in fashion, but in the eighteenth century the stress was on a normal waistline so they made their Van Dycks with *their* waist, not his. Moreover they did not copy Van Dyck's sleeves, which had been very full and round, because their own sleeves were narrow in accordance with the new artistic vogue for neatness, so they gave Van Dyck suits their sleeves. Van Dyck's sitters had worn very wide collars, but these seemed too big to a period which now idolized the small scale, so they reduced the collars. The gentlemen of Van Dyck's day had worn straight breeches reaching down to the top of the calf, but in the eighteenth century the knee breech was now universal in Western Europe, so they gave Van Dyck's suits contemporary knee breeches. Thus the

whole scale of an original Van Dyck was reduced, and the aristocratic height his portraits had conveyed was replaced by the petite person the next century favoured. The eighteenth century retreated on every side from the larger dimensions of Baroque taste, which was the only thing it could do to establish its own identity; it would have been impossible, given the techniques of the day, to have kept on growing ever bigger and grander. The reaction was inevitable.

So it was that the stage acquired another historical costume, albeit in a very eighteenth-century shape. It was seen as the ideal outfit for seventeenth-century plays of course, so when David Garrick revived Ben Jonson's *Every Man in his Humour* on 29 November 1751, and played the role of Kitely 75 times over the next 25 years, at Drury Lane, he donned Van Dyck dress. Strictly speaking he was in error, for Jonson's comedy had been produced first in 1598 with Shakespeare in the cast, so Garrick should have worn sixteenth century doublet and trunkhose, but he had succumbed to the current craze for Van Dyck. As Jonson's works were not printed in folio until the early seventeenth century that was grounds enough in Garrick's eyes to make Jonson contemporary with Van Dyck. He claimed the production was dressed 'in the Old English Manner'.[10]

Garrick did not introduce Van Dyck dress to the stage. It was worn in an amateur performance of Dryden's *The Indian Emperor* at St James's Palace in 1731, when young Lord Fermor acted Cortez. That was correct if one took the date of the play as one's starting point; Dryden wrote it 1665 and so it was seventeenth century, if not early enough for Van Dyck. In fact the action of the play concerned the conquest of Mexico in the sixteenth century, so there should have been trunkhose. Clearly the stage was using Van Dyck dress for a wide range of historical plays and the employment of doublet and trunkhose was being reduced, except for a case of strong identity such as *Richard III*.

---

30 David Garrick as Kitely in Ben Jonson's *Every Man in his Humour*, *c* 1768, by Sir Joshua Reynolds. REPRODUCED BY GRACIOUS PERMISSION OF H.M. THE QUEEN

Van Dyck dress with slashed doublet and breeches and a lace collar was the eighteenth century's answer to historical problems. Garrick called it 'Olde English' and it was often used in Shakespeare's plays. However Garrick has not altered his wig for long Van Dyck curls. A revival is always a compromise between the past and the present.

The precise origin of Van Dyck dress onstage can be traced back to the 1690s, when it was considered to be Spanish. In Spain in 1623 Philip IV had banned French fashion for men from court and insisted on a doublet with short skirts and narrow kneebreeches, as this sort of costume had existed during Spain's earlier glory. The costume was much mocked by the French for its conservativism, but in Spanish eyes it maintained their separate national identity. This particular dress was a gift to the theatre, for it meant that Spanish characters could be easily identified by the use of Spanish court dress for men. In the 1690s it had two slashes on the chest but that was the only historical detail, for the silhouette was sufficiently historical in itself. A doublet reaching only to the top of the hips was highly unusual in an age when the men were wearing knee-length coats. Twenty years later when the eighteenth century first began to illustrate Van Dyck dress, the basic shape was this Spanish suit, the Van Dyck character showing in the increased amount of slashing, on the sleeves and even on the breeches, although there had been no big slashes on breeches in Van Dyck's time. The slash was 'historical' so it was put everywhere regardless of previous practice. It was inevitable that the Spanish suit and the Van Dyck dress should merge into one, so that the eighteenth century actor played a Spaniard in more slashes than he would have had, and used the same suit for a Restoration play. The two costumes were too close in outline to stay independent. The Van Dyck dress became a convention that was still being worn in the Regency period a hundred years later.

How far costume reform in the theatre went is open to some doubt, for the claim that Garrick was a major reformer has been over-emphasized. Thomas Davies claimed that Garrick got rid of heroic plumes from tragedy but they did not disappear from the stage at all and Richard IIIs and Robin Hoods were still wearing heroic plumes in the nineteenth century.[11] All the claim can mean is that Garrick himself stopped wearing them by appearing less in Roman tragedies. Being fairly short he felt that towering plumes made him look ridiculous, so this was a case of individual sensitivity rather than a managerial policy. Garrick did show some interest in costume for his library included some of the most important books on the subject available in his day. He had a 1653 edition of Richard Verstegan's *Restitution of Decayed Intelligence in Antiquities*, Rowe's illustrated edition of Shakespeare (1709), P. Picart's *Cérémonies et Costumes Religieuses du tous les Peuples du Monde* (1723), Thomas Jefferys' *A Collection of Dresses of Different Nations, Antient and Modern, also of the Principal Characters of the English Stage* in four volumes (1757), J.B.

Greuze's *Divers Habillements suivant le Costume d'Italie orné de fonds* (1768), and Strutt's *Manners, Customs, Armour and Habits of the People of England*.[12] The Jefferys was particularly useful for its scores of plates on European, Turkish, Chinese and American dress, as well as its designs for the stage, and Thomas Jefferys was a great admirer of Garrick's costume changes:

As to the Stage Dresses, it is only necessary to remark that they are at once elegant and characteristic, and among many other Regulations of more Importance, for which the Publick is obliged to the Genius and the Judgment of the present manager of our principal Theatre, is that of the Dresses, which are no longer the heterogeneous and absurd Mixtures of foreign and antient Modes, which formerly debased our Tragedies, by Representing a Roman General in a full bottomed Peruke, and the Sovereign of an Eastern Empire in Trunk Hose.

Thus Garrick may have removed the periwig, which by 1757 was long out of fashion, but he always performed in a contemporary wig, for it would have been most ungentlemanly to appear in public without one. He may have ensured that oriental characters got proper trousers and robes, but not everybody shared in Jefferys' opinion. Professor Georg Lichtenberg from Germany was a great admirer of Garrick's acting range, but after seeing several Garrick productions in 1775 he wrote:

It seems to me that, if we are not vastly learned, antient costumes on the stage are too reminiscent of a disguise worn at a masquerade . . .[13]

Research should be done but not by the stage. 'I think, however, that where the public is not yet awake to a certain point of antiquarian interest, the player should not be the first to disturb their

---

31 John Palmer as Don John in Fletcher's *The Chances*, Theatre Royal, Drury Lane, 1791, by Samuel de Wilde. THE NATIONAL THEATRE

Fletcher's play of 1638 was based on Cervantes and set in Spain, which problems were answered by using Van Dyck costume for it was historical and its outline was roughly Spanish. Instead of wearing a doublet however Palmer has a jacket and waistcoat, which are given the Van Dyck look by being slashed. Two heroic plumes denote the leading man. In Act I Scene III Don John was handed a bundle which he thought was treasure but which turns out to be a baby.

slumbers.' Such work should be left to professors. The actor John Philip Kemble was also dissatisfied with Garrick's costuming, for after the 1776 production of *Macbeth* which Garrick considered to be 'dressed in the Habits of the Times', Kemble wrote, 'I have seen some of these Habits, and very paltry and improper they were.' [14]

Professor Lichtenberg was very puzzled by Garrick's performing *Hamlet* in a French suit when Drury Lane surely had plenty of historical costumes *à la* Van Dyck in the wardrobe. He recognized that 'Our French coats have long ago been advanced to the dignity of a tunic, and their creases to the importance of play of the features', but it was not until he had seen Garrick in his French suit that he could tell why. After the duel, Garrick 'partly turned his back on the audience, and I perceived that his exertions had produced that well-known diagonal crease from the shoulder to the opposite hip, it was, in truth, worth the play of facial expression twice over.' The tightness of French cut allowed stress to show in the clothes, so Garrick was too fond of that dramatic effect to abandon it for Van Dyck or doublet and trunk hose. In other words he would not be historical in his dress if it lost him one of the tricks of his craft. Thus Garrick was no purist or revolutionary in his costume reforms.

The lead in reform was taken over by members of the Kemble acting dynasty, who were alive to the new artistic style of Neo-Classicism. From the 1760s people began to feel that the frivolity of Rococo art had gone too far, particularly in France, where it was luxurious, sensuous, and too fussy in its small scale and details. There was a swing to the opposite, to the simple and the dignified. Painters like Wright of Derby and Vien painted quiet scenes, the scholar Wickelmann lauded the white nobility of classical sculpture, the painters Gavin Hamilton, Benjamin West and Mengs sought to express this nobility in their pictures, and the movement found its first great exponent in J.L. David. There was something of a nostalgia for the grandeur of Baroque style after the littleness of Rococo, and for the source of Baroque scale, ancient Rome. This time however it was not imperial Rome which was taken as the ideal model, but republican Rome. In France revolution against the monarchy was to burst forth in 1789, and the principles the revolution fought for were the ancient Roman ones, liberty, the rights of man, the end of dictatorships, and the return to innocent virtue after decades of corruption. Fashion followed this policy by abandoning hair powder so that the natural locks could show unsullied by artifice, and the fashionable shape adopted the high classical waistline. The first French Republic organized enormous festivals, designed by J.L. David who dressed people and senators in Roman togas.

32 Thomas Collins as Slender in *The Merry Wives of Windsor*, Theatre Royal, Drury Lane, 1802, by Samuel de Wilde. THE NATIONAL THEATRE

Van Dyck dress is used here for Shakespeare's comedy but by 1802 the seventeenth-century use of slashing is misunderstood and treated as trimming on top of the suit. The falling ruff is a good historical touch, but Van Dyck dress was abolished by the Victorians as not being accurate enough.

33 Habit of Tancred in the *Tragedy of Tancred and Sigismunda*, from Thomas Jefferys' *Collection of the Dresses of the Different Nations*, 1757. THE BRITISH LIBRARY

Garrick favoured this Hungarian Hussar's costume for the part, although the play was actually set in the Middle Ages, and he did not even use Van Dyck costume as a gesture towards historical character. As a reformer Garrick was no revolutionary.

David also dressed the great French actor of the day, François Joseph Talma who joined the Comédie Française in 1787. Talma agreed fully with David's ideas on the reform of stage dress, so he wore a toga too, with bare legs and arms, which to begin with thoroughly shocked the audiences. Roman purity became the ideal in the theatre too.

In England Sarah Siddons, who acted under the name of her husband although she was the sister of John Philip and a Kemble, became a believer in reformed dress. Although her London debut in 1775 was not a success, after a period acting in Bath she took London by storm in 1782 when she was hailed as the greatest tragic actress England had ever produced. A very dignified woman in herself, she was the new ideal of nobility and purity personified. To begin with she conformed with standing theatrical tradition, acting Lady Macbeth with her brother in 1786, wearing Van Dyck dress which was more accurate than usual with its wide collar and high waist, but as the decade advanced she paid more attention to the new developments in art. Sculpture from Greece and Rome was held up as

34 A Scene in *Twelfth Night* Act 3, 1771, by Francis Wheatley. MANCHESTER CITY ART GALLERY
This cast appeared at Drury Lane in 1771, and the costume was a mixture of historical and modern. Francis Waldron on the left as Fabian had Van Dyck dress, Elizabeth Younge as Viola was attired as a Hussar, James Dodd played Sir Andrew Aguecheek in a contemporary suit albeit in yellow satin, and James Love as Sir Toby Belch wore Falstaff's costume with the bonnet, ruff, doublet and riding boots. It was a case of reform for some but not for all.

35 Habit of Zara in the *Tragedy of the Mourning Bride*, from Thomas Jefferys' *Collection of the Dresses of the Different Nations*, 1757. THE BRITISH LIBRARY
As Congreve's play of 1697 was not exactly ancient it was performed in contemporary dress which by 1757 meant hoops, and the idea of abolishing such width took 30 years to achieve.

Hoops had to go if a slender classical line was to be achieved, but it could not happen overnight. The gradual reduction of female width took 20 years, and Sarah's abandonment was only possible when the movement was well underway. By 1776 the bustle was highly fashionable, a half-way stage between very wide and very slim, but full hoops were still worn with evening dress, and it was not until around 1787 that the fashionable really began to look slender, so only around this date could the theatre do likewise. The British court however still insisted on hoops at the turn of the century, as Sarah Siddons found when invited to Buckingham House to read to George III and Queen Charlotte:

One could not appear in the presence of the Queen except in a Dress, not elsewhere worn, called a Sacque, or Negligée, with a hoop, treble ruffles and Lappets, in which costume I felt not at my ease.[16]

Once the theatre did begin to abandon hoops, every actress liked to think she had had some part in it. Not surprisingly George Ann Bellamy was one who made such a claim, when playing in Dodley's *Cleone*, although she failed to mention the date of course:

The unaffected *naiveté*, which I intended to adopt in the represension, was accompanied by the same simplicity in my dress. This was perfectly *nouvelle*, as I had presumed to leave off that unwieldy part of a lady's habilliments, called a hoop. A decoration which, at that period, professed nuns appeared in; as well with powder in their hair.
Novelty has charms which cannot be resisted. And I succeeded in both points beyond my most sanguine hopes.[17]

As Mrs Bellamy retired in 1785 this can only have been towards the end of her career.
John Philip Kemble made his London debut in *Hamlet* at Drury Lane in 1783, and was as stately and formal in acting style as his sister Sarah. His biographer James Boaden writing in 1825 could not understand why Kemble had not worn Van Dyck dress in the part, but Kemble conformed to tradition for his debut by wearing the normal costume:

. . . a modern court dress of rich black velvet, with a star on the breast, the garter and pendant ribband of an order – mourning sword and buckles, with deep ruffles: the hair in powder, which, in the scenes of feigned distraction, flowed dishevelled in front and over the shoulders.

That is, as a contemporary prince in mourning. Boaden approved of the loose hair, and thought it

Habit of Zara, in the Tragedy of the Mourning Bride.

Habillement de Zara, dans la Tragédie intitulée the Mourning Bride.

perfection, so Sarah Siddons decided to learn from it, studying how the folds fell, and how the drapery was arranged. She was guided in her appreciation by no less than the President of the Royal Academy, Sir Joshua Reynolds, who approved the introduction of classical elements into stage costume.

Sir Joshua often honoured me by his presence at The Theatre. He approved very much of my costumes and my hair *without powder*, which at the time was used in great profusion, with a reddish-brown tint and a great quantity of pomatum, which, well kneaded together, modeled the fair ladies tresses into large curls like demy-cannon. My locks are generally braided into a small compass so as to ascertain the size and shape of my head, which to a Painter's eye was of course an agreable departure from the mode. My short waist too was to him a pleasing contrast to the long stiff stays and hoop petticoats which were then the fashion even on the stage, [and] obtained his unqualified approbation.[15]

36 Hannah Pritchard as Hermione in the statue scene from *The Winter's Tale*, 1765, by Aliamet after R.E. Pine. HARVARD THEATRE COLLECTION

When an actress or ballet dancer appeared as a classical statue, the hoops might be discarded, but not when performing a human character.

37 A Scene from *The Tempest*, 1787, by Francis Wheatley. BIRMINGHAM CITY MUSEUMS AND ART GALLERY

By 1787 Neo-Classical taste was simplifying theatre costume. The hooped skirt for males has gone to be replaced by kneebreeches and only the top of the costume remains heroic Roman armour, although the plumed helmet was retained. Miranda's costume was simplified into white silk without a hoop. It was customary to give Prospero and bards a rough wool robe and beard. It has been argued that the painting might represent Garrick's version of Dryden's *King Arthur*.

38 Sarah Siddons, *c* 1796, by Sir Thomas
Lawrence. THE TATE GALLERY

A leading figure in the abolition of hoops on
stage, and for reducing the size of hairstyles. Her
high classical waistline delighted Sir Joshua
Reynolds.

39 John Philip Kemble as Hamlet, 1801, by Sir Thomas Lawrence. THE TATE GALLERY

Kemble abolished contemporary dress for *Hamlet* in 1793, and thereafter used Van Dyck costume with trunkhose and a ruff-effect collar. His hat is crowned with black plumes for even the mourning hero must look heroic.

40 John Philip Kemble as Coriolanus, *c* 1797, by Sir Thomas Lawrence. THE GUILDHALL LIBRARY, LONDON

The Neo-Classical ideal, Roman armour without any Baroque or Rococo trappings, a black cloak, and the sensational bare feet and sandals. It went a long way towards an accurate revival but Kemble's hairstyle and sideboards are strictly contemporary, for the hair is the last thing to be sacrificed to reform.

had a superior effect to the tight curls of a wig, but he felt that Van Dyck dress would have been a better costume, removing anachronism and inconsistency.[18] This was to think with the attitude of 1825, by which time Van Dyck dress for Hamlets had become standard. Kemble did consider the question of suitable costume later in his career, and in October 1793 performed Hamlet in a Van Dyck costume of black satin. It was after this that Van Dyck dress became the fixed costume for the part. It was in 1793 that Kemble made another move towards historical accuracy in engaging William Capon to design Gothic sets. Like his sister, Kemble followed tradition in the 1780s but turned to new ideas in the 1790s, being determined to make plays perfect in text and set.

To do this, he was first to study the antiquities of his own and other countries, to be acquainted with their architecture, their dress, their weapons, their manners, and he, by degrees, assembled about him the artists who could best carry his designs into effect.[19]

41 James Northcote, Edmund Kean as Brutus in *Julius Caesar*. VICTORIA AND ALBERT MUSEUM

The triumph of Neo-Classical intentions, the toga for Roman plays. Baroque Roman heroes had been military; now the civilian version of Roman dress was idolized. It represented a new look at old Rome, but for all the difference it was still Rome that was admired. Powdering the hair went out in the 1780s as did wigs, except for elderly men. The Titus crop was the latest fashion, for by 1800 fashion and artistic theory were agreed on looking Roman.

It was Kemble who was alive to the developments in France, and learning that the toga was being revived there decided to introduce it himself in England. Under Neo-Classicism it was the republican toga which was the ideal, unlike the Baroque period when it had been imperial Roman armour. With his height and magnificent bearing Kemble could wear togas superbly well.

It would be impossible to conceive anything finer than Kemble's appearance in the Roman costume, as introduced by himself. When he revived 'Coriolanus' and 'Julius Caesar' at Covent Garden, his togas, then for the first time exhibited on the English stage, became the theme of universal admiration. They were pronounced faultless, minutely classical, even to the long disputed *latus clavus*, severely correct, and beautifully graceful beyond precedent.

So enthused another theatrical biographer, John Cole.[20] There were still some however who felt that bare arms and legs on the stage was too indecent for polite taste to approve.

As the Napoleonic War was in full spate it was not possible for anybody in the English theatrical world to cross over to Paris to make a comparison with Talma's togas, and not until Napoleon had been defeated could the English visit France. The frontier opened in 1815, and the first actor to visit Paris from London was Kemble's disciple Charles Young, who hurried back with the news that Talma's togas were much fuller than the English ones. On reconsideration John Philip Kemble decided that perhaps he had underestimated the amount of material in a Roman toga, and resolved that Talma's were more authentic in this respect, so he adopted the French model, originally designed by David. (Exactly how Romans made togas and put them on is a still disputed point of study because no Roman writer left a description.) Charles Young was kept busy instructing his fellow actors how to achieve the fuller drape, from John Philip himself to his brother Charles Kemble. Charles would trot along to Young's dressing room before playing Mark Antony in order to have the folds in his togas checked for accuracy, and it certainly gave actors a new problem – how to get the folds exactly right like a statue. The other acting dynasty in town, Edmund Kean and his son Charles, also took to togas for Roman plays. In 1817 Talma himself visited Covent Garden to perform extracts from his repertoire, and when John Philip Kemble made his farewell performance that year Talma attended both the play and the banquet in Kemble's honour. No doubt he was asked about how he folded his togas, at what was the meeting of the two leading classicists on the European stage. Another artistic ideal had triumphed, and dress was reformed, but only in Roman works, the principal concern at that date.

CHAPTER FOUR

Romantic Abundance

A new movement in art often stresses the opposite of what the previous art policy has admired. The swing from repression to expression and back again, that endless to-and-fro which characterizes Western society, resulted in a reaction against Neo-Classicism at the start of the nineteenth century. Whereas the classicists had favoured nobility, order and serenity in works of monumental stability, the new generation pursued disorder, vitality and change. The eighteenth-century concept that man was a rational creature above all was shaken by the violence and blood-lust of the French Revolution. The succeeding Napoleonic régime stressed an irrational devotion to glory, heroism and triumph, in which the policy of the emperor was not to be questioned. The previous belief that human emotions must be kept under control was discarded for a declaration that they must be unleashed in joyous chaos. The individual human being was elevated to a pinnacle of self-awareness and self-preoccupation. Whereas the eighteenth century had repressed individuality by powdering everyone's hair white to produce a uniform look, the young nineteenth century went to the opposite extreme with the individual hair colour displayed. It was highly appropriate that one of the most romantic composers of the new movement, Hector Berlioz, had bright red hair in flaming individuality.

The new movement called itself Romantic, although this was not a new term. Pepys had used the adjective to describe Margaret Duchess of Newcastle in 1667, an amateur playwright:

The whole story of this lady is a romance, and all she doth is romantic. Her footmen in velvet coats, and herself in an antique dress, as they say;[1]

The duchess loved acting out romantic episodes in which she would be carried off by brigands only to be rescued by the duke galloping up like a portly hero. Thus 'romantic' here is applied to an eccentric but charming creature who liked to be a beautiful heroine even when of mature years. By 1755 the word had taken on a relationship to nature, for Dr Johnson's *Dictionary* defined it as meaning wild and fanciful, like stories set against untamed scenery, and this aspect was emphasized as the period progressed. By 1800 'romantic' evoked Nature in all its towering strength and ferocity. Gales and tempests were now admired, unleashing emotions to the full, whereas the Rococo period had recoiled from such disorderly abandon. Well-mannered parks and gardens were rejected for rocky crags, waterfalls and gorges, preferably topped by a ruined castle occupied by ghosts.

The ideal of the emotions required that all the range of emotional experience be undergone, not only fervour, love, enthusiasm, heroism, but also fear, horror, dismay, terror, grief and despair. Novelists were the first to express the full range of

---

42 Thomas Potter Cooke as Roderick Dhu in *The Lady of the Lake* by Thomas Dibdin after Sir Walter Scott, Surrey Theatre, 1818, by John Boaden. THE NATIONAL THEATRE

The Romantic rebel of Scott's poem epitomizes the wild attractions of the Highlands, and the Romantic fondness for stormy clouds and rocky crags where unbridled Nature seemed to reflect the inner soul of mankind. This interpretation of the Highlander is more Roman than Scottish, for only the bonnet and eagle's feather denote a Highland chief – the tunic with the high waist, the type of armour, the bare legs and the sandals are all Roman. T.P. Cooke is reputed to have performed the part some 250 times. Rossini turned the poem into an opera. Cooke also was famous as Ruthven in *The Vampire* (1820).

feelings, and the theatre was quick to translate such works into action. Sensation was the order of the day, although this could only end in sensationalism as each novel and play sought to be more extreme than its predecessors. The Gothic horror was born where the heroine undergoes every emotion in turn as she is carried off by a wicked count, imprisoned in a terrifyingly gloomy castle, and visited by spectres and visions, and encounters a mysterious monk who turns out to be the rescuing hero in disguise, who guides her out into the light, as a convenient earthquake and landslide hurl the villain into an equally convenient flood. The melodrama emerged, penned by Mrs Radcliffe and Monk Lewis in London, and by Guilbert de Pixérécourt in Paris. Favourite settings, with ample quantities of gloom and mountainous crags, were Scotland and the Rhineland.

No one did more to popularize such a background than Sir Walter Scott, whose historical novels set in the Middle Ages and the sixteenth and seventeenth centuries contained elaborate descriptions of old buildings, past customs, ancient clothes, and wild and tempestuous scenery. His books were read throughout Europe from Edinburgh to Vienna and Rome, and he helped to create a public appetite for historical accuracy on a far wider scale than had existed before. Scott's novels were adapted for the stage, and opera, after two hundred years of Roman themes, took to him too as Italians and French used his plots. Rossini set Scott's *Kenilworth* as *Elisabetta Regina d'Inghilterra* (1815), and his *Lady of the Lake* as *La Donna del Lago* (1819), after which Anglo-Scottish history became a favourite source for Romantic composers and Roman subjects declined. Georges Bizet set *The Fair Maid of Perth* and Boieldieu wrote *La Dame Blanche* (1825), while in Italy, Donizetti's *Alfredo il Grande* (1823), *Anna Bolena* (1830), and *Lucia di Lammermoor* (1835) all followed English and Scottish stories. The playwright, antiquarian, costume designer and Somerset Herald, James Robinson Planché, wrote that Scott kindled the public's interest in historical subjects and archaeological accuracy.[2] Walter Scott made history fashionable. This was reflected in the published versions of plays which began to include descriptions of the clothes and scenes for a public now avid for historical information.

The first Gothic horror tale of note on the English stage was Monk Lewis's *The Castle Spectre*, performed at the Theatre Royal, Drury Lane in December 1797, termed as a dramatic romance. It had the proper ingredients, the fair maid Angela being carried off to his castle by wicked Earl Osmond, and rescued by the hero Earl Percy. The costume was described as follows: Earl Osmond wore a yellow tunic, trimmed with silver spangles, and buttons, a purple velvet belt, white pantaloons spangled, short blue velvet robe trimmed with fur only, open sleeves; second dress, a handsome satin morning gown. Hero Earl Percy had slate-coloured shirt tunic, trimmed with black galloon, and flesh pantaloons for his first dress which was simple before he donned his heroic attire, green old English suit, with puffs trimmed, steel breastplate, long scarlet satin sash, leather belts, black velvet hat, white feathers, gauntlets, russet boots, and a ruff. Osmond's spy Kenric had a brown velvet outfit, puffed with blue, with a brown cloak and stockings. Osmond's three African minions had white coats with the sleeves looped up, white trousers, black leggings and arms for skin, black velvet flies, silver buttons, and sandals. The fool Motley was to be dressed like Shakespeare's Touchstone, while Father Philip was to have Falstaff's belly, a friar's grey gown, with a cord round the waist, flesh-coloured stockings and sandals. The minor character Allan had an old English dress of drab trimmed with black, and the fisherman Edric a blue Flushing great-coat, blue trousers, a striped Guernsey shirt, a blue cap and fishing stockings and boots. Angela's father, Reginald, long held prisoner by wicked Osmond, had a very torn costume of brown tunic and pantaloons, with a torn cloak, flesh-coloured arms and legs, and old sandals, while Angela herself was very elegant in embroidered white satin, the tone of innocent virtue. The old dame Alice had a black gown trimmed with point lace, open to show a red petticoat, a black hood, and high-heeled shoes with buckles. The spectre, Angela's mother murdered by Osmond, rises in ghostly white, a plain white muslin dress, a white head-dress, or binding under the chin, and a light loose gauze drapery. The descriptions were of great assistance to amateur actors, for private theatricals at country houses were now highly fashionable, such as the one organized in Jane Austen's *Mansfield Park*. Nevertheless the clothes were mixed in period, for alongside the old English suits of Van Dyck style are a tunic of early sixteenth-century type for Osmond, and the fisherman has a contemporary pair of trousers where he should have had very full breeches as worn by seafolk in Elizabethan and Jacobean times. The term 'pantaloon' refers to the equivalent of tights, being tight-fitting leggings and trunks. The use of skin covers will be noticed, as the bare flesh could still not be displayed without causing controversy.

The first play to call itself a 'melodrama' was Thomas Holcroft's *A Tale of Mystery*, first performed at the Theatre Royal, Covent Garden on 13 November 1802, with 'new dresses'. Here the villain Count Romaldi had a jacket of purple and gold, with light drab and gold pantaloons, and russet boots. Good uncle Bonamo wore a mantle of purple and gold with black trunks, black silk hose and a sword. The heroine Selina wore white muslin trimmed with blue satin, and her true love Stephano had a drab hat, a green plume of course, as he was a hero, and a blue and gold jacket, with white pantaloons and russet boots. In this work the villain was masquerading as the count, so he wore bright clothes, not conventionally villainous black. The continuance of Baroque splendour will be seen in the gold, the spangles, and the plumes, for after Neo-Classical purity came a return to such glitter and shine. The theatre offered the most breathtaking magnificence the ordinary person was likely to see in an entire lifetime so it could not discard such weapons, even if they were sometimes tinsel.

James Robinson Planché wrote Gothic horrors as best evidenced in *The Vampire*, which he called a romantic melodrama. Produced at the English Opera House in the Strand in August 1820, it was not set in Transylvania but in Scotland, and was sub-titled *The Bride of the Isles*. It began with a vision where the vampire Ruthven, Earl of Marsden, rose from the tomb, watched by Unda Spirit of the Flood attired in a white satin dress trimmed with shells and such, a blue satin robe, with her hair in long ringlets, and a tiara, and carrying a wand. With her is Ariel Spirit of the Air, in a white muslin dress decorated with spangles, a sky-blue robe, wings, a tiara, and a silver wand. The vampire earl, being a Scot, was attired in a silver breastplate studded with steel buttons, a plaid kilt, a cloak, flesh-coloured arms and leggings, with sandals, and a grey cloak to form the drapery as he rose with menace. In the play proper he added a Scotch hat with feathers, and a sword and dagger. The heroine was in the inevitable virtuous white satin but given a touch of local colour in the plaid trimming and the plaid silk sash and the Scotch hat with a feather, which the Scots would have called a bonnet. She was Lady Margaret the Bride of the Isles, whom the vampire wished to make his next victim. Her father Ronald, Baron of the Isles, wore a crimson shirt with large clasps down the front, a plaid cloak, the usual flesh-coloured arms and leggings, sandals, a sword and belt, and the Scotch hat with feathers, which in the Scottish case should be eagle feathers, not ostrich ones. The English character Robert was distinguished by a grey shirt, trimmed with yellow binding, drab pantaloons, a grey hat with black feathers, a sword and belt, russet boots, and a large collar. The term 'shirt' here indicates a tunic to the top of the knee. The baron's henchman M'Swill was Scottish with a red plaid jacket, kilt, flesh-coloured leggings (no bare knees), plaid stockings, black shoes with buckles, and a Scotch cap. The vampire's steward Andrew combined English and Scottish

with an old man's brown coat and breeches, worn with a plaid waistcoat and stockings, old shoes with buckles, grey wig, black kerchief, and the Scotch cap. His daughter Effie displayed her nationality in a black velvet bodice and a plaid petticoat with a plaid sash. The servants were in kilts and jackets. Such a flourish of what is now called tartan was the principal method the theatre employed in identifying Scots during the Romantic period. Scottish peers had managed to get the Act of Dress repealed in 1782, Sir Walter Scott had made Scotland highly fashionable and stage-managed the first visit of a monarch to Edinburgh since the seventeenth century when he persuaded George IV to travel north, and even got the king to don a kilt. The German composer Mendelssohn was moved to visit the country which inspired his Fingal's Cave overture and his Scottish Symphony, while the Frenchman Hector Berlioz wrote a Rob Roy overture. The theatre was participating in and encouraging a mania for things Scottish.

Probably the most famous horror story to come from the Romantic era was Mary Shelley's novel *Frankenstein* (1818) which was adapted for the stage in several versions. H.M. Milner made the adaptation which the Royal Coburg Theatre mounted in 1826, called a peculiar romantic, melodramatic pantomimic spectacle, *Frankenstein; or, The Man and The Monster*. The scene was the estate of Prince del Piombino, who wore a green Italian tunic, richly embroidered with silver as suited his rank, a crimson sash, white pantaloons, yellow boots, and an Italian hat with feathers. The experimenter Frankenstein wore a black velvet vest and trunk breeches, with an open grey tunic over them which had the sleeves slashed over white, and black stockings and shoes. Quadro in the prince's employment wore doublet, trunk breeches and vest, all in blue velvet. The cottager Ritzberg had a dark brown doublet, mantle, and trunk breeches, stockings and a cloth hat, sober colours being correct for a humble person. Frankenstein's servant Strutt had a blue doublet with long skirts, a dark brown vest, tight pantaloons, boots and a three-cornered cloth hat. The monster was supposed to look fairly naked so he had a tight-fitting vest and leggings in very pale yellowish brown, heightened with blue to indicate muscles, his only garment being a Greek shirt or tunic in very dark brown with a broad belt of black leather. The prince's sister Rosaura wore a gown of embroidered pink satin as her virtue was not in danger, and Frankenstein's girl-friend Emmeline appeared in a short German pelisse of dark brown over a slate-coloured petticoat, and a dark brown Polish cap, a mixture presumably designed to show that she was not Italian. The setting was close to Mount Etna, so that there could be a spectacular finale with the monster pursued up the volcano and jumping into the crater as it erupts. The references to trunk breeches, that is trunkhose, show that the period was the sixteenth century as far as the men were concerned but Emmeline's pelisse puts her firmly in 1826.

It was and is always more difficult for an actress to be historical in her looks than for the male actor, because the management and the public would most admire the woman who was fashionable. While a very senior actress might ignore fashion and rely on her acting ability and experience, the young actress would be groomed into the latest look, and was often chosen, like film stars later, because her features came close to the current ideal. She was so conditioned into being beautiful according to the contemporary definition that she would have lost all confidence if told to alter her appearance by shaving off her eyebrows and her hair at the forehead in order to look mediaeval. Society demanded that women be only decorations, not active characters or individuals; and the Romantic period saw women as passive and helpless, heroines who had to be sacrificed or rescued because they had no strength themselves. The actress who criticized this attitude would be told not to bother her pretty head with such matters, only men could take decisions, only men could be heroes. Men wanted women as decorative adjuncts not as rivals, and it was the male managers of theatres, like producers of films, who decided what women would look like, and they wanted the contemporary idea of beauty. The men were conditioned to what they considered attractive in a woman by that self-same idea. Regimentation into a glamorous stereotype has long been, and continues to be, the fate of young women in the world of entertainment. Artistic theory has a sexual character in its different movements. The Rococo style with its curves and small scale was feminine, and that period allowed women to have intellectual interests and to run literary salons. The Romantic movement was a masculine one which replaced feminine sensitivity with violent passion and furious energy and reduced what women were allowed to do. No Romantic playwright wrote a role like Lady Macbeth. When men were men, women were expected to be children.

Melodrama was to have many forms but one of the most popular was the nautical version which replaced ghostly castles with ghostly vessels. Edward Fitzball's *The Flying Dutchman; or, The Phantom Ship* opened at the Adelphi Theatre on Monday 8 January 1827 with 'entirely New Music, Scenes, Dresses, &c.' The first scene was the cavern of Rockalda Evil Spirit of the Deep, played by a man carrying a trident wand, and wearing a sorceress's sea-green dress trimmed with seaweed and shells, a tiara, and a long black veil. Her water imps, eight in number, wore green seaweed dresses and grotesque, nondescript masks. The Flying Dutchman Vanderdecken, already a century old, is granted another hundred years by the sorceress. His costume was suitably dated, a green old-fashioned dress, with white sugar-loaf buttons, a belt, high boots, an old English hat with a red feather, constituting a Van Dyck outfit. The rest of the cast were in contemporary clothes. The rescuing hero, young Lieutenant Mowbray, wore a lieutenant's blue coat, with cassimire waistcoat, blue trousers, boots, and a black stock. The marine painter Varnish was dressed like a sailor in a striped shirt, nankeen jacket, white waistcoat, nankeen trousers, and a straw hat. Later in the play he dons a bearskin to get near his love Lucy, who wore blue muslin. The heroine Estelle Vanhelm had two costumes, an open pink gown trimmed with pink and white sarsnet, and old English stomacher in the manner of a shepherdess; her second costume, when she was near to being sacrificed so that the Flying Dutchman may have his freedom, could only be innocent white muslin and flowing hair. The Dutch sailor von Swiggs had a blue jacket with white sugar-loaf buttons, a belt and large blue trousers, while the ordinary sailors had check shirts with blue jackets and trousers. The comic character von Bummel was given old-fashioned elements: an old brown Dutch suit, red stockings with clocks, square-toed shoes with red roses, an old English high-crowned hat with a red band and a rosette, and a long neckcloth. When faced with danger he tries to escape dressed as a shepherdess in a pink and white gown with a stomacher and large straw hat, which would draw further laughter after his quaint first costume. There were a number of slaves in white calico jackets trimmed with red binding, white vests, white trousers tied below the knee with red binding, dark brown flesh-coloured stockings, and red slippers, while their leader was distinguished by a white hat with red trimming. There were straightforward costumes for straightforward characters, and more picturesque ones for comic roles.

One tradition which emerges clearly from these melodramas is the theatre's continuing use of colour symbolism in its costume. As well as virginal white, there was green for sea creatures, blue for seamen and spirits of the air, cowardly yellow for a villain masquerading as good, earthy brown for country-folk and the poor, while the silver spangles indicate the wealthy roles. It was simple colour symbolism, not the complicated, sophisticated system where every combination of two colours or shades had a special meaning, but this was well suited to an unsophisticated audience. Green, the colour of nature, was often used for nymphs and shepherds and had been so used back in Renaissance Italy.[3] Some colours had two meanings. Black was not only the shade representing evil, but also the mark of sobriety and respectability, so as well as being worn by murderers it was also worn by clergymen and philosophers. Red meant martial bravery so it was correct for soldiers, but its fiery aspect was employed for devils and fiends from hell. The root of colour symbolism was Mother Nature, and in order for some characters to be understood they wore the colours nature used, the light blue of the sky, the deep blue of the sea, the green of leaves, the brown of earth, the red of blood, to identify the role's origins or profession. It is impossible for mankind to invent colours which are not related to nature, for all dyes are made, ultimately, of natural ingredients both vegetable and mineral. It is a very ancient principle that Art must imitate Nature.

As Romanticism had made antiquarian research fashionable, theatre managers now felt compelled to declare an interest in history and accuracy. When Robert Elliston took over Drury Lane the men's clothes were valued at £3133 and the ladies' wardrobe at £807, but as the new actor-manager wished to equal the splendour of one of John Philip Kemble's productions of Shakespeare, he thought there should be more accurately historical clothes. He took himself off to the British Museum and read Strutt's book, which Garrick had owned in his day, and Charles Hamilton Smith's *Ancient Costume of Great Britain and Ireland* (1814), and a work Smith wrote with Samuel Rush Meyrick, *The Costume of the Original Inhabitants of the British Islands* (1815); he also gathered together a collection of engravings. This research was first applied to a production of Shakespeare's *Richard III* on 8 November 1820 with Edmund Kean as Richard, and Elliston himself as Richmond. *The Times* approved of the costume as being of 'superior description', but claiming to be accurate, as Elliston did in the advertisement for the play, could lead to attacks from sharp-eyed enthusiasts. The *Theatrical Inquisitor* sneered at the cast's wearing silk stockings because the first silk stockings in England were worn by Elizabeth I, a century after Richard III.[4] The day had come when many persons were regarding themselves as experts on costume, now that several books on the subject were available, and the stage and the fine arts could both come under criticism for inaccuracy if a production or a painting was not absolutely perfect in their eyes.

Elliston next tried with *King Lear* in February 1821, and resolved to set the play in the early Saxon period, about which actor Kean had considerable reservations. Elliston put him in a crimson Saxon robe and a Saxon cap which was approved by the press, but he was criticized for the large white wig which Lears had worn in the past as it overwhelmed the effect of the rest of the costume, and it was felt that Elliston had been downright mean over the women's clothes. He had kept to the tradition of spending the most on the costumes for the leading characters, but now audiences were beginning to expect every member of the cast to have appropriate and good quality garments.

In the view of James Robinson Planché reform had not gone far enough. While he admired Kemble's classicism in abolishing the barbarisms which Garrick had failed to remove – the bag wig for Brutus, and gold laced waistcoats for Macbeth, there was still one area which cried out for reform, the Middle Ages.[5] Sir Walter Scott's novel *Ivanhoe* of 1819 made chivalry and knighthood a fascinating subject, and when at the extravagant coronation of George IV in 1821 the King's Champion in full armour rode his charger into Westminster Hall, that mediaeval palace, and threw down his steel gauntlet to challenge anyone who dared to dispute the king's right to the throne, many a feminine heart fluttered at the age of chivalry made living. Romantic heroism now donned a mediaeval habit, knights were the champions of Christian virtues, and society began to model itself upon that ideal, with public schools training the future administrators of the Second British Empire to be Christian knights carrying civilization and enlightenment in a noble crusade to the barbarous corners of the world.

The manager who was quick to catch this mood was not Elliston at Drury Lane, but Charles Kemble at Covent Garden. He decided to revive Shakespeare's mediaeval play *King John*, and he invited Planché as a costume authority to design the clothes. It was 1823 and Planché determined that the year would see the most accurate reproduction of mediaeval clothes that the theatre had ever seen; not that the theatre had yet tried to be twelfth century. As a herald and Fellow of the Society of Antiquaries Planché knew which manuscripts to go back to. He knew that King John's tomb was in Worcester Cathedral and wrote in his *History of British Costume*:

We have now arrived at a period when a new and most valuable source of information is opened for our assistance. The monumental effigies of the illustrious dead, sculptured in their habits as they lived, and in a style of art remarkable for so dark an age, many elaborately coloured and gilt, and all of the full size of the figure. . . .[6]

He studied the king's effigy, and for armour looked at the figure of Geoffrey de Magnaville Earl of Essex, in Temple Church, London, and that of William Longespee Earl of Salisbury in Salisbury Cathedral, as well as the figures and coats of arms

43 James R. Planché's design for *King John*, his second dress, Theatre Royal, Covent Garden, 1823. THE BRITISH LIBRARY

Planché brought the twelfth century onto the stage, not only in the plot but in an effort to make the appearance of the production actually resemble the period of the play. Instead of making a few historical gestures over costume as had happened in the previous century, Planché put the whole cast into historical costume.

44 James R. Planché's design for Blanch of Castle, in *King John*, Theatre Royal, Covent Garden, 1823. THE BRITISH LIBRARY

Planché was not so accurate with the women, for he gave them simple gowns with high waists which were very fashionable in 1823 but which lacked the heavy folds of the twelfth century they were supposed to represent.

OPPOSITE PAGE
45 James R. Planché's design for *Hamlet*, 1823. THE BRITISH LIBRARY

This was Planché's idea of eighth century Danish. As the prince was in mourning for his murdered father he had to wear black, but Planché's research revealed that the Danes had all worn black. The hat is odd, a pleated bonnet where a simpler pointed cap would have been more accurate.

46 James R. Planché's design for the Queen of Denmark in *Hamlet*, 1823. THE BRITISH LIBRARY

Inevitably the female characters were the least historical, for they were always presented as the fashionable stereotype, so the queen's high waist, narrow dress, and tiara are in the style of 1823, as if a woman could have no existence outside the fashionable definition dictated by her period.

found on seals. He observed that the tunic worn by John was shorter than those worn by his father and brother Henry II and Richard I, exposing the under-tunic and the ankles, and noticed that men's hair grew longer in the reign of King John and was curled by heating tongs. All these elements he put into his designs, and was so proud of his achievement that he published the drawings along with his designs for *Hamlet* which he dressed in eighth-century Danish style. The production has gone down in history as the first to have truly mediaeval costume; moreover the whole cast was dressed in that way, not just the leads. However, it took a historian to achieve it, not an actor-manager.

A start had been made, but strangely enough Charles Kemble did not apply this policy to all his productions. In 1827 he took his actors over to Paris on the first visit from Covent Garden to that city, presenting Sheridan's comedy *The Rivals*, Otway's tragedy *Venice Preserved*, and Shakespeare's *Hamlet* and *Romeo and Juliet*. Shakespeare was not well known in France and, as his works did not obey the unities of time, place and action instituted by French scholars, he was regarded as barbaric, mixing comedy and tragedy in the same play. The Romantic writers in France, however, were eager to break these formal restraints, and Shakespeare was to them a tremendous revelation, showing how it could be done. The melancholy and the madness in *Hamlet* so affected the French audience that they wept, swooned, and staggered outside while the poetry and intensity in *Romeo and Juliet* reduced men to tears. For a period which put emotional expression at the top of its list of ideals, the range in Shakespeare's emotional content was shattering.

The performances were seen by all the leading French Romantics, the writers Hugo, de Vigny, Dumas *père*, the painter Delacroix, and the composer Berlioz. Victor Hugo was inspired to write a play *Hernani, ou l'honneur castillan*, which the Comédie Française presented on 25 February 1830. It deliberately broke the rules of French drama, Hugo demanding that art should be liberated from the despotism of codes and rules, but the première resulted in a riot as traditionalists shouted their outraged opposition, and the Romantics hurled back counter-arguments. Alfred de Vigny translated both Shakespeare's *Merchant of Venice* and his

Othello in 1828 and 1829 so that they could be produced in Paris, and wrote a play about the English poet Chatterton in 1835, Berlioz composed his versions of Shakespeare, *The Tempest* fantasia, the *King Lear* overture, the funeral march *Hamlet*, the opera *Beatrice and Benedict* after *Much Ado*, and the great choral symphony *Romeo and Juliet*; what's more he married Kemble's leading lady Harriet Smithson who had played Juliet and Ophelia.

The visit of the English actors had an enormous impact on French culture, but the one thing it did not do was to bring reformed theatre costume to Paris. Charles Kemble dressed the cast in the same sort of jumble that had existed in Garrick's day, as if Planché's improvements had not taken place. In *Hamlet* the king wore an outfit that was more Hungarian than old Danish, while Harriet Smithson performed in a contemporary evening gown. His production of *Romeo and Juliet* was no better, for Charles Kemble acted Romeo not in mediaeval Italian dress but in early sixteenth century, and Harriet Smithson as Juliet was again presented as a fashionable young lady, not as a historical character. Thus Planché's designs had been a pioneering attempt, but as with all innovations it took time to catch on, for people are generally conservative in their attitudes. Charles Kemble was 52 in 1827, so having made one outstanding gesture towards authenticity in costume, it looks as if he was content to leave it there.

Whilst French Romantic poets wrote for the theatre and used the stage as part of their artistic manifesto, English poets such as Keats and Wordsworth did not. Firstly they had no French rules to rebel against, and secondly their mood was introspective and contemplative rather than dramatic and active. However the actor William Macready, who became a regular performer at Covent Garden and Drury Lane from 1819, and had been educated at a public school, Rugby, was most anxious that English poets should contribute to the stage. The obvious poet to turn to was one of the committee members at Drury Lane, Lord Byron, already famous as both writer and Romantic hero. Byron responded to the actor's request for poetic parts, writing several tragedies set in the historical past. *Marino Falieri*, set in Venice in 1335, was produced at Drury Lane in 1822, but as Planché was not involved it is unlikely that the clothes were very appropriate. Byron died in 1824 but he left other works which Macready performed. *Werner* was produced at Drury Lane in 1830, and the period of the piece was 1648, so it accorded nicely with all the Van Dyck costumes still in the wardrobe. *Sardanapulus* followed in 1834, but the setting in ancient Assyria was unlikely to have seen anything more historical than Roman in the costume, for archaeol-

ogists had not yet unearthed Nineveh. Macready staged *The Two Foscari* in 1838 at Covent Garden, which was another Venetian subject where accurate clothes cannot be taken for granted. The period and setting of *Manfred*, the Alps in the Middle Ages, presented at Covent Garden in 1834, was probably better for the wardrobe department as some of the clothes for *King John* were still around, aged 11, and even if the moths had taken a few nibbles, they could still serve as an inspiration if not as acting wear. Macready also persuaded other poets and writers of note to offer works to the stage. In 1837 he appeared in Browning's *Strafford*, in 1838 in Bulwer Lytton's *The Lady of Lyons*, and in 1839 in the same author's *Richelieu* which gave him a splendid part as the cardinal. All three works

satisfied Romantic taste by having historical settings, for there was a convention that poetic tragedy could not appear in modern dress or time.

The revival of mediaeval chivalry received an added impulse when Britain acquired a girl queen, Victoria, for whom British knights could fight. Her coronation was more modest than had been George IV's, which disappointed some. The 13th Earl of Eglinton, one of the wealthiest young men in the country, decided he would honour the young queen with a mediaeval tournament at Eglinton Park in Ayrshire in August 1839. In view of the mediaeval craze collecting armour was already fashionable, and the armour dealer Samuel Luke Pratt of Bond Street was called in to oversee the armour for the jousters. He assembled a mixture of genuine

47 The Play Scene from *Hamlet*, 1842, by Daniel Maclise. THE TATE GALLERY

Many an artist painted scenes from Shakespeare's plays, particularly during the Romantic period, but here too fashion intruded. Maclise has put the men in a mixture of fifteenth and sixteenth century costume, but the women with their hair draped over their ears are all strictly early Victorian. No painting, no production, no photograph can escape a period look.

armour, some modern copies, and some fakes, which were put together in composite suits. Over 2000 spectators made the trip to Scotland, many of them travelling by that new and highly unmediaeval form of transport, the railway. They were requested to wear fourteenth- or fifteenth-century dress, but the majority turned up in early Tudor, as did most of the participants in the action. Unfortunately it poured with rain, which resulted in the Marquess of Londonderry, attired in full armour, sitting on his charger, and carrying a very nineteenth-century umbrella. The present will always creep into attempts to be historical. The earl declared that the purpose of the tournament, which cost more than he expected, was to show the true spirit of a better age in a time when society was becoming increasingly utilitarian as the Industrial Revolution raced ahead.[7] When audiences flocked to the theatre to see a mediaeval spectacle they were escaping from the smokey world outside. The young queen herself participated in the movement, for when she gave her first fancy dress ball in 1842 she appeared as Queen Philippa, and Prince Albert as Edward III, both of them in gold brocade and red velvet, designed by Planché, who considered the result highly accurate; the queen, however, was still wearing her 1842 corsets and petticoats underneath so her shape was not period. There are limits to how far people will go in altering their contemporary image, because their appearance is part of their identity.

A major change in the theatre came in 1843 when the 1660 restriction whereby only the Theatres Royal at Drury Lane and Covent Garden could present serious drama was removed. This meant that the secondary theatres, hitherto only allowed to produce burlettas, which had to have five songs in them, could now stage dramas. The actor-manager Samuel Phelps immediately took advantage of the act to turn Sadlers Wells Theatre into a centre for Shakespearian drama, reviving many of the plays which the Theatres Royal had ignored, such as *Pericles*, and giving many future actors an excellent training. Another actor-manager Charles Kean, son of the tragedian Edmund Kean, was able to make the Princess's Theatre the centre for his Shakespearian productions, which were on a considerable scale. Charles Kean took historical authenticity very seriously, and put his ideas into full force when he produced *King John* in February 1852. The accuracy was taken as far as going to Worcester Cathedral and measuring King John's skeleton to find out his exact height, and studying heraldic records to ensure that the individual coats-of-arms of the noblemen in the play were all correct to the last detail. His biographer Cole wrote:

OPPOSITE PAGE

48 William Pleater Davidge as Malvolio in *Twelfth Night*, Theatre Royal, Manchester, 1846, by Harry Andrews. THE NATIONAL THEATRE

To the Victorians this costume was accurate, but it lacks the rigidity of sixteenth-century dress with all its padding and stiff linings. The trunkhose are too long, and the ruff should be starched and there ought to be a codpiece present, but here the Victorian concept of decency forbade accuracy.

ABOVE

49 Mr and Mrs Charles Kean as King John and Lady Constance with Prince John, 1858. HARVARD THEATRE COLLECTION

The leading champion for mediaeval accuracy whose every production would have realistic castles, battlements, halls, flags, shields, and clothes based on research into old manuscripts, tomb effigies, paintings, murals and seals.

50 Charles Kean as Richard II, Princess's
Theatre, 1857. VICTORIA AND ALBERT MUSEUM

The coat-of-arms, the heraldic stripes, the pattern
on the carpet, the throne, the footstools, the
mantle, the houppelande, the crown and jewels
were all based on historical precedents, but
Kean's hairstyle was contemporary with
fashionable curls as Charles Dickens had. The
houppelande ought to have wide sleeves.

OPPOSITE PAGE
51 Ellen Tree, Mrs Charles Kean as the Queen
in *Richard II*, Princess's Theatre, 1857.
VICTORIA AND ALBERT MUSEUM

An attempt to achieve the impossible, combining
mediaeval research and heraldic colour systems
with the width of a Victorian crinoline. There is
an attempt at a low waist, but Mrs Kean and her
ladies are all tightly laced into their Victorian
corsets showing the fashionable small waist as
well. The hairstyles of course are very much
1857. Why Kean gave the women a low waist is
strange because in the reign of Richard II the
waistline went up.

The time had at length arrived when a total purification of Shakespeare, with every accompaniment that refined knowledge, diligent research, and chronological accuracy could supply, was suited to the taste and temper of the age, which had become eminently pictorial and exacting beyond all former precedent.[8]

In May 1855 Kean produced *Henry VIII*, and announced that whereas audiences in the past had only expected a few striking gestures over accuracy in costume and set, this production was to have authentic dress, accessories, and architecture throughout the whole presentation. Kean played Cardinal Wolsey and, as the prelate used to carry a hollow orange containing a sponge dipped in vinegar to ward off smells and plague, Kean did the same. But where Shakespeare would have expected a bare stage Kean virtually rebuilt Hampton Court Palace on stage, with a vast Tudor hall filled with a host of dancers, guards, servants in addition to the principal characters. Kean's sets were so huge they required some 140 stagehands to change them. The wardrobe was under the control of Kean's wife Ellen Tree who was faced with a need for hundreds of historical costumes. Fortunately the sewing machine was now available so the number of seamstresses did not have to equal the numbers in the cast. Tudor costume was fairly simple to reproduce with tunics and hose sufficing for most of the male characters; Holbein's portraits and the drawings at Windsor Castle were conveniently near so research was not difficult. It was the basic shape of the women which failed to achieve real authenticity, for the crinoline was just coming into fashion; a Holbein original was too narrow for contemporary taste, consequently the female costumes were a mid-Victorian shape with Tudor trimmings.

The contemporary definition of what was decent intervened, for when the fashion is growing very wide, a narrow look reflecting the body underneath is regarded as sinful. Concepts of decency had long affected the display of bare limbs on stage by requiring flesh-coloured pantaloons, but the Victorians liked to hide limbs altogether. One thing Henry VIII's costume did not have in 1855 was a prominent codpiece.

In October 1856 Kean followed this with his production of *A Midsummer Night's Dream* in which he rebuilt ancient Athens, and the woods outside, where scores of girls fluttered about as fairies in crinolined fullness. Next year in the March he tackled *Richard II* for which he rebuilt the London of 1399, and it was said that if a citizen of that date had returned to life he would have recognized the scene down to the last brick and plaster. But where Shakespeare had simply directed that the king and Bolingbroke enter the city, Kean seized on the episode to crowd the stage with about 600 performers, dancing, playing music, forming processions, waving from balconies, and ringing church bells. By now his reputation for striving after authenticity stood so high that it had won the respect of scholars, and he was elected a Fellow of the Society of Antiquaries of London, the first actor to be so honoured. The certificate of his election, dated 21 May 1857, gives Kean's qualification as 'a knowledge of the History and Antiquities of this and other countries'.[9]

Twelfth Night was next given the Kean treatment with transformations as trees rose from beneath the stage and fountains gushed forth, and nymphs and naiads dashed about with far more clothes on than classical nymphs would have had. In the eyes of some of his contemporaries Kean was displaying pure taste, but when Charles Dickens took Hans Christian Andersen to see the production they felt the Shakespeare had disappeared beneath the gorgeous trappings. A Kean production lasted five or six hours as it took so long to change the elaborate sets and dress the hundreds of actors. Labour was

extremely cheap and Kean exploited it to the full, but the result was a picture so crowded with details that a strong image did not come across the footlights. It was all very colourful, but it left a blur. It was enough for Shakespeare to direct in *Henry V*: 'France. Before Harfleur. Alarums. Enter King Henry, Exeter, Bedford, Gloster and Soldiers, with scaling ladders', and Kean would inflate the direction to rebuild the city walls of Harfleur, add a few seige towers and several cannon banging away, and flood the stage with enough soldiery to form a regiment. Kean's vision was affected by the Industrial Age and his sets seemed as big as railway stations, which meant that the impact of the costume was reduced. In the end Kean's research was defeated by the scale of the production. For example when he played Hotspur in *King Henry IV Part I* in 1850, his leather armour had a damask surcoat with the arms of Percy of Northumberland, down to the lions and fishes, with across the chest in highly accurate detail the label of three points denoting the eldest son of the House of Percy. All this was perfectly correct, but it was the sort of detail which could not be seen from the back of the pit. The intention was good but there was so much of it that none of it stood out. What was the point in being authentic, in so far as the period permitted, if the result was not visible?

A traditional form of theatre costume came into some criticism as the Romantic period became affected by Victorian views on modesty. This was the wearing of men's breeches by actresses, a custom which had started in the Restoration era, when women first appeared on the English public stage. The tradition of a man playing female roles ended in 1660 with women playing male roles, although the reasons were completely different. Whereas it had been thought too immodest for a woman to appear in public on a stage, so men took their parts, the reason women donned breeches was that a woman's legs could thus be shown at a time when fashionable skirts did not reveal more than the ankle. Of course in the country and in fishing ports working women hitched their skirts up, but such a sight was not to be found in town and still less at court. Consequently Charles II and the rakes around him encouraged the introduction of such glimpses of the female limbs on the stage in London. An immoral court wanted blatant sexuality, so the theatre responded to its customers. Nell Gwyn was one bold hussy who would don the breeches, which showed off her hips and thighs to advantage, and swept her into the royal bed, and the result was a bastard duke. The actress who pandered to that demand was guaranteed a success of sorts, and playwrights busied themselves with plots in which the heroine for some reason has to don male clothes

52 Mr and Mrs Kean in *Macbeth*, Princess's Theatre, 1858. VICTORIA AND ALBERT MUSEUM

This was braver in that Mrs Kean is wearing a smaller crinoline, bell-shaped rather than wide, but she could not appear without a crinoline of some sort for that would have been indecent. Macbeth's cloak with a check pattern shows research into early Celtic plaids although his chain mail, stuck on not interlinked, is Norman and it is arguable whether the real Macbeth would have worn it during his reign (1040–57).

and pretend to be a man, perhaps in order to find her missing brother or lover, as no woman could undertake detective work in her own right. If the play was not one where a breeches role could be fully justified, then the author would put one into the epilogue. It became a stock theatrical tradition, but by the late eighteenth century some doubts began to emerge. Sarah Siddons considered breeches roles beneath her dignity. In 1787 she had to play Imogen in *Cymbeline* but made sure that she did not reveal her limbs. Boaden wrote that taste required 'females, who assume the male habit, for a more complete display of the figure, than suits the decorum of a delicate mind. Mrs Siddons assumed as little of the man as possible.' [10]

In the early nineteenth century one actress and opera singer made her name through breeches roles, Mme Vestris. Born Lucia Elizabetta Bartolozzi, she was the granddaughter of the engraver to George III. At 16 in 1813 she married the Frenchman Armand Vestris, himself the grandson of a very famous French dancer. Trained as a singer Lucia made her debut at the King's Theatre Opera in 1815, where her husband was ballet-master. Vestris soon proved a bad husband and a reckless spender; he was soon declared bankrupt and cleared off to Paris where he abandoned Lucia, and ran away to Naples with a ballet dancer. The unfortunate Mme Vestris had to return to London and look for work. As well as her voice she possessed a good figure so in July 1820 the Haymarket Theatre put her into a revival of Gay's *The Beggar's Opera* with Mme Vestris playing Captain Macheath. Elliston at Drury Lane was so impressed by the sight of the lady in breeches he put her into the trifle *Don Giovanni in London* which proved a towering success and made Mme Vestris famous. A poet enthused:

What a breast – what an eye! What a foot, leg, and thigh!
What wonderful things she has shown us;
Round hips, swelling sides, masculine strides –
Proclaim her the English Adonis! [11]

Her costume was a tunic to just above the knee, short boots, a tight, high waist, slashed sleeves, and a large hat with a dozen heroic ostrich plumes. In view of this success managements were eager to star Mme Vestris in other roles usually played by men, and she appeared as Apollo, and as Don Felix in *The Wonder*, a role Garrick had played; but the lady herself began to feel annoyed that her entire reputation should depend on showing her legs. To show that she had other talents she returned to opera, singing in Rossini's *Barber of Seville* and Mozart's *Cosi Fan Tutte*. In June 1829 *The Morning Chronicle* declared that it was high time that breeches roles for women were abolished, and censured Mme

Vestris for having worn the tightest buckskin possible, as taste began to swing towards greater modesty in women. A period which liked to define women as helpless angels with no minds of their own could not stomach the sight of women striding across the stage in heroic roles, taking decisive action. The custom had to go. To some extent it did, and by the dawn of the Victorian era a distinction came into being, whereby serious actresses in the leading playhouses did not play breeches roles; but in the lesser houses the custom continued, most notably in pantomimes where the hero remained a female in tight breeches, a tradition still alive today. Nevertheless some general covering up took place, and even in the most shocking dance the nineteenth century produced, the Parisian Can Can, the dancers wore thick white drawers down to their knees. Still, when skirts were ground length it was a sensation just to show the knickers.

Mme Vestris herself lessened her appearances in such attire, for in 1829 she took a lease on the Olympic Theatre in Wych Street, and became a theatre manager; she was the first woman to hold such a post. Of course the licence from the Lord Chamberlain still restricted lesser houses to burlettas, but Mme Vestris did not allow this to restrict her principal aim, to be a theatre reformer. She engaged James Robinson Planché to be her costume adviser, and also commissioned him to write numerous musical extravaganzas. When she produced *Mary Queen of Scots* in 1831 she could claim that all the furniture, the clothes, the curtains, the goblets, the carpets were as true to period as the age could make them, and she ransacked antique shops looking for genuine sixteenth-century artifacts. She was an enthusiast for greater realism on the stage, and she dressed a set in the same way that she dressed her own drawing room, an approach only a woman could have conceived. Not for her painted flats and a few gestures towards an interior; she insisted on the real thing, clocks which ticked, lamps which lit, and Kidderminster carpets, the whole surrounded by proper walls. She introduced the box set, with three walls, a ceiling, and working windows and doors, first presented in Bernard's *The Conquering Game* at the Olympic on 28 November 1832. She was equally realistic in her costuming.

Her second husband was the famous comic character actor Charles Matthews, so not surprisingly she improved the dress of comedians. It had formerly consisted of a bright outfit with claret-coloured coat, salmon-pink trousers, with a broad, black stripe, a sky-blue neckcloth with a large paste brooch, and a cut steel eye-glass with a pink ribbon, amounting to a very affected costume, but Mme Vestris changed this and put her light comedy actors into fashionable dress. In 1841 Mme

Vestris produced the first comedy by young Dion Bouccicault, *London Assurance*, which had a tremendous success, and was a triumph for Charles Matthews in the role of Dazzle. In pattern it was a reworking of Restoration comedy, but given an 1841 setting, so Mme Vestris had it dressed in contemporary style. One of her tenets was that everything on the stage should be in the best taste, so the most fashionable role in the play was given suits from the top tailor in London, Stutz. Another example of her historical dressing concerned milkmaids whom she put into seventeenth-century style with red stuff petticoats, white aprons, a white handkerchief around the shoulders, a white cap with lappets, a steeple crowned hat, grey stockings and black shoes.

In the years 1839–42 Mme Vestris managed Covent Garden, where she put Planché in charge of the wardrobe and the scene painting room. He wrote 'There I had the pleasure of continuing my reform of the costume of the national drama'.[12] They produced some very elegant performances of Shakespeare, which Macready felt were too pretty, and when Sir Robert Kerr returned from Persepolis with drawings of the ancient Persian reliefs, Planché and Mme Vestris wasted no time in staging *Artaxerxes* with correct Persian dress and curled beards. They were determined to keep in the vanguard of accurate costume on the stage. Mme Vestris next moved on to manage the Lyceum Theatre, and died still in harness aged 59 in 1856. Although she ruled with a rod of iron, she was recognized as an excellent manager. It was her husbands who let her down, for Charles Matthews went bankrupt just like the first one, and spent some months in jail, which bit into his wife's profits. To the Romantic mind Mme Vestris's insistence on using real everyday or historical objects on stage showed a lack of imagination; to which she would reply that the theatre ought to be realistic, not fantastic. This was an argument which was to rage well into the twentieth century.

The battle for accuracy had been won in so far as mediaeval plays were now given mediaeval costume, and an oriental setting could have appropriate Eastern character, but the limit to accuracy, the

53 Leather armour worn by Charles Kean as Hotspur in *King Henry IV Part I*, Princess's Theatre, 1850. THE MUSEUM OF LONDON

Kean's archaeological approach at its best, with every detail correct but the trouble with keeping the scale of the original is that it cannot be seen clearly from the back of the auditorium. In the theatre a degree of enlargement or exaggeration is necessary for visual detail to get across.

impact of fashionable taste could not be avoided. An absolutely perfect recreation of the past is not possible, but the nineteenth century embarked on enormous research in the happy belief that it was attainable. Thanks to the survival of manuscripts, to all the costume books published, and now to explorers sending home photographs of remote peoples, it was possible to tackle any period anywhere. This can be seen very clearly in the variety of subjects selected for opera.[13] The most famous operatic composer in Italy of the day was Guiseppe Verdi and he took his inspiration from a very wide field indeed. His first international triumph was *Nabucco* (1842) which was set in Biblical times, while *Il Trovatore* was about mediaeval troubadours. *Don Carlos* was set in sixteenth-century Spain, *Les Vêpres Sicilennes* (1855) in thirteenth-century Sicily, while *Aida* of 1871 took place in ancient Egypt. Verdi's two last operas were based on Shakespeare; *Otello* (1887) where the setting was of course Venice in the Jacobean period, and *Falstaff* (1893) that fifteenth-century character. When Verdi tackled a contemporary subject, a love affair of the 1840s, he ran into trouble with the censors who objected to the depiction of modern sin on the stage, so the action of *La Traviata* was set well back in time. The production at Her Majesty's Theatre in London in 1856 dressed the opera in the clothes of the 1630s. Thus the subjects of Verdi's operas ranged over some 4000 years, and thereby required clothing from such a span of history.

A similar policy of 'any subject anywhere' can be seen in the operas of Puccini, which covered Bohemians in the Paris of Louis-Philippe in *La Bohème* (1896), Rome during the Napoleonic period in *Tosca* (1900) while *Madame Butterfly* (1904) occurred in Japan, and *The Girl of the Golden West* (1910) was set in the Californian goldrush. When he died in 1924 Puccini was still working on a Chinese subject *Turandot*. So much material was available that all things were possible. Any culture could be attempted, any period tackled; a relative accuracy of costume was guaranteed, in so far as the period saw it. The principle of accurate research had triumphed but it was now to be swamped by the possibilities, for the choice was virtually infinite. The attempt to discipline the theatre into following a predominant ideal like ancient Rome or the Middle Ages was overwhelmed. An absolute licence now broke forth. It had an ideal, but that ideal was applied to a global range of topics.

In Germany even Wagner, while considering himself a more serious composer than most Italians, was equally happy to tackle themes centuries apart. He looked to the Middle Ages for *Rienzi* (1842), for *Tannhäuser* (Dresden 1845), *Lohengrin* (Weimar 1850), and *Die Meistersinger von Nürnberg* (Munich 1868), which were all staged with an attention to mediaeval detail worthy of Charles Kean FSA. Yet Wagner went even further back in time for his plots, to Celtic myth for *Tristan und Isolde* (Munich 1865) and then back to time before time, to the Teutonic gods for his famous cycle of operas *Der Ring des Nibelungen*, first given over the years 1869–76, starting at Munich and concluding at the Temple of the Arts Wagner built at Bayreuth. Strictly speaking an opera about ancient gods could be clothed in an ancient or approximately timeless manner, but Wagner's productions all stressed the German origin of the myths. Wagner himself sketched winged helmets, tunics to the calf, and elongated shields as his image of the gods, and these costumes became traditional at Bayreuth. The warrior maiden Brünnhilde Wagner dressed in a corselet of chain mail, with flowing hair and that winged helmet. The result was that the casts looked like Vikings, or rather a nineteenth century conception of Vikings, for the winged helmets were a misunderstanding. There was precious little evidence to rely on; the ancient German and Scandinavian tribes left few representations of their deities, so a look had to be more or less invented. When the Swedish sculptor Fogelberg depicted Odin he looked to classical art for his model, as did the Danish sculptor Freund, while artists who painted scenes from *The Ring* such as von Carolsfeld and Hansen selected early mediaeval costume, so that confusion existed as to what constituted a correct look. Wagner's preference was for about the seventh century, when Saxons and Vikings had fought and conquered.

The rise of nationalism is evident in Wagner, a Germanic resistance to centuries of Italian opera, and this nationalism also affected the development of opera in Slavonic countries. Smetana's *The Bartered Bride* concerned peasants in a Czech village in 1866, while in Russia the hitherto Italian and French diet at the Imperial Opera in St Petersburg was now joined by operas based on Russian history. Glinka's *Ivan Susanin* (*A Life for the Czar*, 1836) and *Russlan and Ludmilla* (1842) were followed by Mussorgsky's *Boris Godunov* (1874). These works required Russian peasant dress and Russian historical costume, but as the first productions all took place in Russia such costume was easy to reproduce, and later Western presentations were able to copy the Russian designs, while books written by travellers or artists contained much information on that country. Slavonic opera might be new, but the nineteenth century had no problems over what such works should wear. It was an age of information, so it could pride itself on accuracy. The belief and the intention were genuinely felt, even though unfortunately any presentation dates, and timeless perfection cannot be.

CHAPTER FIVE

Balletic Contrasts

Ballet has grown out of the formal court dances of Renaissance Italy. While dancing dates back to prehistory when it was used as a magic ritual to ensure success in a future hunt or battle, and peasant societies have long had their boisterous rounds and romps, the more that royal and ducal courts wished to appear sophisticated and cultured the more attention had to be devoted to civilizing the dance. The first books to regulate court dances appeared in Italy. Domenico da Piacenza's *De Arte Saltandi et Choreas Ducendi* (On the Art of Dancing and Conducting Dances) appeared *c* 1400, and his pupil Guglielmo Ebreo, dancing master at the court of Milan, followed it with his *Treatise on the Art of Dancing* of 1463.

These works made Italian choreography famous throughout Europe, and in the fifteenth and sixteenth centuries the demand was for Italian dancing masters to carry their art abroad. The first dancer of international fame was Cesare Negri, born in Milan in 1530, who sent his pupils to work in the courts of Flanders, Austria, Bavaria, Spain and Poland. When an Italian princess married into a foreign royal family she took her Italian dancing master with her, so that when Catherine de' Medici was queen mother in France her court included a number of fellow Italians as dancers and writers. Among these was Baldassarino da Belgiojoso who produced a ballet for the queen mother in 1581, *Le Ballet Comique de la Reine*, which was the first ballet where the text, illustrations of the performance, and the music were all published in book form. At this stage ballet was always part of a larger production, with singing and declamation in it, and the concept of ballet with a separate identity on its own did not emerge until the eighteenth century. Of course the mixing of dancing with poetry and song was all part of the attempt to recreate ancient drama, so ballet became involved with the invention of opera, an association which has lasted ever since, and operas

as far apart as Monteverdi's *Orfeo* and Borodin's *Prince Igor* have important ballet episodes in them, while the ritual dances in Sir Michael Tippet's *The Midsummer Marriage* (1955) reflect the very origin of dance.

Professional dancers were always men, as the church condemned women who dared to appear onstage, so the female parts were danced by men in masks and dresses. Women were allowed to dance socially, however, so that they would dance in a private production of a court ballet reserved for courtiers, but would not appear in a public playhouse. It was the same with acting. A queen could act, dance, even sing before the court, but not outside. The court masques under Charles I and the ballets at the French and Italian courts would end in a grand finale where the leading dancers on the stage would come into the audience and lead out members of the court into a general ball. The professional male dancers were brought in to perform comic and acrobatic turns, which it was beneath the dignity of courtiers to perform themselves, but the whole court would join in the formal dances, which were choreographed into elaborate patterns. In the public theatres all the dancers were men, professionals; at court the dancers were amateurs of both sexes, members of the royal family and the aristocracy. But it was the latter who set the tone, and financed the most luxurious performances.

As ballet was part of the attempt to be classical, the costume was predominantly classical too in so far as the Renaissance and the Baroque periods defined such a look. Two leading Italian designers for ballet were Agnolo Bronzino, court painter to Grand Duke Cosimo I de' Medici, who dressed *La Pellegrina* in 1589, and his contemporary Buontalenti who costumed *intermezzi*, the aristocratic entertainments presented during noble wedding ceremonies. They used layers of tunics with high waistlines, which had classical justification, but they

V.A.M   F.614-1936

54 'Two Female Dancers', 1589, by B. Buontalenti. VICTORIA AND ALBERT MUSEUM

The Renaissance version of Roman dress, with tiers of tunics, but smothered in Mannerist decoration. The long skirts and the mules restrict what a female dancer could do.

OPPOSITE PAGE

55 'A Follower of Diana', c 1660, by Henri Gissey. VICTORIA AND ALBERT MUSEUM

The greater freedom and agility of male ballet costume. It is the Roman tunic, much elaborated with cut-out sections, pendants and theatrical tassels. The Baroque taste for ostrich plumes is clear. The mask was a firm tradition for about 200 years. Gissey was designer of the royal festivities for Louis XIV. His instructions to the tailor read 'silver', 'scarlet', 'gold' and 'blue'. The principal ballet tailor in Paris was Jean Baraillon.

departed from accurate reconstruction in the amount of decoration they applied. The contemporary definition of beauty could not be excluded, and the late sixteenth century admired elaborate ornamentation; so they employed scalloped hems, lots of tassels, pendants, puffed sleeves, roundels and animals' faces. The simplicity of a classical outline was broken up into complicated compartments with a multitude of motifs. Every theatre designer wears a pair of spectacles with lenses which can only detect what his period says he ought to see. The ideal may be to be absolutely accurate but the vision is conditioned from birth by the contemporary sight. For beauty to stay fresh it has to change, and that alters what the generations react to. While Buontalenti tried to make his tunics beautiful it was beauty as determined by his age, not the ancient Roman concept of it.

There was one form of ballet costume which male courtiers loved to see, and this was the dress for nymphs. At court such roles could be danced by real women, and nymphs wore short tunics to the mid-calf and boots, which allowed glimpses of legs to escape. As with breeches roles in the next century, courts permitted a degree of licence. The Italians created the look which they defined as all'antica, and when the costume made its first appearance at the French court in 1548 French aristocrats gasped.[1] The lords could justify their admiration in classical terms as the exposure allowed them better to appreciate the limbs on ancient statuary, but au fond it was voyeurism. Neat ankles laced into little boots, a flash of stockings on a shapely calf, and perhaps during a whirling step a glimpse of knees or even a little above, made male spectators drool, for the fashionable farthingale with its stern rigidity did not allow them to have any idea of the shape of a woman's legs, which were concealed behind stout canvas. At this period it was the men who displayed their legs every day by wearing trunkhose and long hose, a costume which allowed for considerable activity. Trunkhose did not impede the legs in any way and for this reason they were adopted by male ballet dancers who retained such garments until the early eighteenth century. Even when male dancers took to kneebreeches, they were not constricted, so male agility in dancing continued. For female dancers at court the problem was the length of skirts and the number of petticoats. Apart from the costumes for nymphs, their ballet gowns remained as long as normal skirts, which restricted to a considerable extent the steps they could perform. High kicks were impossible, apart from being considered improper for a woman, rapid steps meant the lady would fall over her own hemlines, and anything like leaps or spinning in the air were unattainable and the domain of men. Accordingly

the male dancers got the greatest opportunities, whether as amateurs at court, or as professionals in the public playhouse, just as men did in the world outside.

Dominance in ballet now passed to the French court which had greater financial resources than the small Italian states. Louis XIII was an enthusiastic dancer who enjoyed comic roles, so the ballet-comique was devised where the king could clown about in weird disguises. This enthusiasm was inherited by his son Louis XIV, but it took a very different form. Given that king's obsession with royal glory, he was not going to perform comic parts, but demanded court ballets which were lavish, stately and heroic. He of course had the starring part, and no aristocrat dancing alongside the king was allowed to shine. The king was always the centre of attention whatever stage he appeared on. The royal dancing master was Charles-Louis Beauchamp, who was very serious over technique. He set very high standards, and redefined dance steps, giving them the French names they retain to this day. So complex and sophisticated did Beauchamp's ballets become that the amateur courtiers began to opt out. He demanded too great an intensity of application, too many rehearsals, too much ability. In 1671 Louis XIV appointed Beauchamp as Superintendant of the King's Ballets, and they decided to start a ballet school attached to the Académie de Musique. What was unusual about this dancing school, which was intended to supply the court with professionals to relieve the courtiers themselves, was that it took female pupils as well as male. By now actresses had been appearing on the public stage in France for a century, so it could not be argued any longer that they should not dance on the public stage as well, although the Catholic church remained condemnatory. The first ballet in which these professional ballet dancers appeared was Le Triomphe de L'Amour in 1681 where Mlle La Fontaine and Mlle des Martins emerged as the first professional ballerinas. They were to be kept busy appearing at court and at the Paris Opéra, where of course they received their costumes at company expense. Even so they were still inhibited by their dresses with long skirts, by the weight of tinsel and

---

56 'A Female Dancer with Castanets', c 1677, by Jean Berain I. VICTORIA AND ALBERT MUSEUM

Gissey was succeeded in his post by his pupil Berain the elder in 1673. Soon after this the first professional ballerinas were being trained but this made no difference to their type of costume, for the rigid skirt designed by Berain allows no energetic activity.

copper, and even trains, while the Baroque fondness for ostrich plumes crowned their heads with further impediments. An elegant glide and a few gentle turns performed with consummate grace were their limit. Roman artistic theory had an impact on dress for male dancers but not to the extent that it stopped them leaping about. The Roman tunic was introduced from the 1600s as an alternative to trunk hose, and was short enough to leave a man's legs free so there was no inhibition imposed on movement. The first tunics were almost as short as trunk hose but from the 1660s, when knee breeches were becoming established as general wear for men, they descended to knee level to harmonize with the new idea of respectable length. While ancient Roman tunics had been simple it goes without saying that the Baroque theatre dressed them up to glitter, shine, and dazzle.

The first attempt to detach ballet from opera and court spectaculars was made by the English dancing master John Weaver of the Theatre Royal, Drury Lane. He had made a study of dancing in ancient Rome where the mimes had performed without songs or speech, and resolved to introduce this classical precedent into his ballets. He started with *The Loves of Mars and Venus* in 1717 and wrote that it 'was an Attempt in Imitation of the ancient *Pantomimes*, and the first of that kind that has appeared since the Time of the *Roman Emperors*.' There was no singing whatsoever and no declamations. 'Representation and Story was carried on by Dancing, Action and Motion only.'[2] This became Weaver's policy thereafter, producing ballets where the story was told by the dancers in silent gestures, and so ballet, at first a decorative adjunct to opera and plays, became a dramatic work in its own right.

By this time the hoop had made its appearance in the theatre, and as it was worn by actresses and opera singers it also passed to dancers so that they were all the same proportion. The width of hoops was an improvement for female dancers for it freed their legs from layers of petticoats and gave them plenty of space to move about in. But they were still ground length like ordinary fashionable dresses, so what was the point of learning neat footwork if it could not be seen? Eventually one ballerina was bold enough to do something about it. Mlle Camargo made her début as a soloist at the Paris Opéra on 5 May 1726; she was a spirited performer who found long skirts most annoying. She took the brazen step of chopping several inches off her hemlines, thereby shortening her skirts to the bottom of her calves, but because a hoop swings this meant that much more of her legs could be glimpsed as well. It caused a tremendous scandal, and the clergy denounced the innovation as heretical, although Mlle Camargo's supporters, and

needless to say a lot of men spectators, approved of her action, and claimed that short skirts were in the true spirit of the primitive church. The directors of the Opéra were taken completely by surprise and after much debate and agitation eventually conceded that ballerinas could shorten their skirts to the calf, but ruled very firmly that no female dancer could appear in the theatre who was not wearing drawers.[3] This last injunction was necessary because outside court circles few women in the eighteenth century bothered to wear drawers. As skirts reached down to the ground who could tell? Raising the hemlines up on the stage however was a different matter; all the men in the pit were looking upwards, so if Mlle Camargo's hoop should happen to swing upwards when she was near the footlights, a lot more might be revealed than just her ankles. Drawers were a balletic necessity.

The agitation might seem overdone today, but as men were allowed so few glimpses of feminine legs in day-to-day society, the theatre was the only place in town where they might see nice legs in silk stockings, a situation which continued into the Edwardian era. Nowadays the circumstance has changed completely; the men cover their legs up, and it's taken as normal that women should show theirs all the time. Then it was an exception, hence the excitement.

In both London and Paris dancers were dressed with some splendour, which infuriated serious actors, and Mr Chetwood, a prompter at Drury Lane, disapproved. He said dancers should not wear silk vests, silk stockings or fine lace, for everyone who appeared on a stage was a servant of the public, and no servant should outdress his master. 'Dress beyond Station is Pride, and Pride very often brings Self-punishment' he chided, but he went unheeded.[4] Splendour was a theatrical ideal.

Thanks to Mlle Camargo the ballerina increased in fame. Voltaire said she was the first woman to dance like a man; but she was the first woman who *could* dance like a man, because she could lift her feet off the ground. Her shoemaker did well too, for there was no such thing as a ballet shoe at this date. Mlle Camargo danced in ordinary high-heeled shoes, so her performances advertised the handiwork of her supplier.

Her greatest rival was Marie Sallé, who was the same age, both being born in 1710. She made her most important contribution to costume reform in London in 1734 when she appeared in the ballet *Pygmalion* at the Theatre Royal, Covent Garden. She was playing the role of a Greek statue Galatea and correctly observed that ancient Greek statues had not worn hoops. She had come to London to escape from the rigid controls at the Paris Opéra, and Covent Garden allowed her to experiment. She

decided to wear simple muslin, without hoops, and without high heeled shoes, adopting slippers. She looked like a proper statue, and when the statue came to life, she performed most expressively, and won many plaudits. The production was such a success that Covent Garden sent it over to Paris where it was much praised. Marie Sallé returned to London to try another experimental ballet *Bacchus and Ariadne* where she again danced in loose drapery and slippers, and went on to dance in Handel's *Ariadne*, *Ariodante* and *Alcina*. In 1735 she went home to Paris to appear in Rameau's large ballet *Les Indes Galantes*, and she retired in 1740.[5] Nevertheless her success did not cause a costume revolution on the stage. It was too specialized, too particular to one part, a statue. All the fashionable variations on the hoop had not been exhausted yet, and the structure was to see another 40 years of success. Mlle Sallé's idea had been perfect for a statue, but not for real life. Everyone was now so used to women being wide that narrowness was alien.

The most significant work on the nature of ballet appeared in 1760, written by the ballet teacher Jean Georges Noverre, *Lettres sur la Danse*. Noverre, born in 1727, trained under Dupré and made his début as a dancer when 16. At only 20 he became ballet master at the Opéra-Comique in Paris where he presented some sumptuous displays, culminating in *Les Fêtes Chinoises* in 1754, which had chinoiserie sets by François Boucher and costumes designed by

57 'Mademoiselle Camargo Dancing', *c* 1730, by Nicolas Lancret. THE WALLACE COLLECTION, LONDON (*detail*)

Ballet dress for women only became more practical when a famous dancer could impose her will on male tailors and designers. Camargo raised the hem, and abolished heavy headdresses; and while she still wore high-heeled shoes they were lighter in construction than late Baroque ones had been with their block heels.

58 Design for a herald, *c* 1750. P. Lior attrib. VICTORIA AND ALBERT MUSEUM

Fashion affected ballet just as it did the rest of the theatre, so here too the hoop dominated the eighteenth century from 1708 down to the 1780s. This Roman herald with his cuirass and helmet has the same width as a tragic hero like Spranger Barry (see **8**). As with ballerinas some form of undergarment like breeches were compulsory with hoops.

59 Design for a princess in opera-ballet, *c* 1750, by Louis Boquet. VICTORIA AND ALBERT MUSEUM Royal characters in ballet would not wear short skirts, but would perform a graceful glide as became their dignity. The costume has Van Dyck sleeves but otherwise the design is full of Rococo curves.

OPPOSITE PAGE
60 Noverre's ballet *Jason et Medée*, King's Theatre, 1781, by F. Bartolozzi. VICTORIA AND ALBERT MUSEUM
Noverre's *ballet tragique* brought dramatic action into ballet with more determination than before, but his hopes to abolish tall wigs and hoops could not succeed before fashion itself said that such elements ceased to be fashionable. However, his cast wears slippers instead of high-heeled shoes, which allowed for more nimble action.

Louis René Boquet. The production was so highly celebrated that David Garrick, himself married to a dancer, invited Noverre to bring it to London, offering Noverre 350 guineas, and another 150 guineas to go to Boquet to design the costumes. Unfortunately international politics ruined the performances in London, for Britain and France were on the brink of war, and audiences rioted at the sight of French choreography and designs at Drury Lane. Garrick tried to make out that Noverre was Swiss but to no avail, and he lost £4000 on the venture. The one good thing which came out of the disaster was that Noverre was able to see Garrick act:

He was so natural, his expression was so lifelike, his gestures, features and glances were so eloquent and convincing, that he made the action clear even to those who did not understand a word of English.[6]

Noverre was deeply impressed by the range of Garrick's acting, and resolved that ballet ought to be raised to that sublime level. Let ballet act!

In 1760 Noverre was appointed ballet master at the lavish court of the Duke of Wurttemburg, where he tried out his ideas to invent more dramatic ballets which he termed *ballets d'action*. Boquet, appointed costume designer to the Paris Opéra in 1757, went with him. In 1770 Noverre was recruited by Vienna to choreograph for the Court Theatre in the Schönbrunn Palace, and also to act as dancing master to the Empress Maria Theresia and her family, including her daughter the Archduchess Marie Antoinette. Here Noverre concentrated on creating *ballets tragiques*, taking his plots from classical tragedy and interpreting them in passionate mime. In 1772 he presented *Agamemnon*, then *Iphigénie en Tauride*, and in 1773 *Acis et Galathée*, all of them based on classical mythology.[7] Above all he wanted expression:

Children of Terpsichore, renounce *cabrioles*, *entrechats*, and over-complicated steps; abandon grimaces to study sentiments, artless graces and expression, study how to make your gestures noble, never forget that it is the life-blood of dancing; put judgment and sense into your *pas de deux*; let will-power order their course, and good taste preside over all situations.[8]

Where ballet had always been a diversion, a pretty display of talent, Noverre wanted to create a noble art.

When Marie Antoinette became queen of France she wanted Noverre to join her in Paris and in 1775 offered him the top ballet post in the country as ballet master to the Opéra, the Académie Royale de Musique. The resident ballet masters, however, resented this appointment and there was so much in-fighting against Noverre and his new ideas for dramatic ballets that he resigned in 1779, and withdrew into private life. In 1788 sensing the approach of the French Revolution he decided to leave for England, and brought the most famous male dancer of the day with him, Gaetano Vestris. In London Noverre became director of the King's Theatre, which specialized in opera, for the period 1788–93, where Vestris appeared as the star in Noverre's tragedy ballets.

If Noverre was to reform ballet he was soon to understand that ballet costume would have to be reformed too to allow the dancers to perform more dramatically. Looking back on his celebrated *Fêtes Chinôises* he decided the costumes had been wrong.

The dresses killed, so to speak, the production because their colours resembled too closely those of the scenery; everything was splendid, all the colours were brilliant, everything glittered with the same gaudiness; no part was subordinate to another and this uniformity in all details deprived the picture of its effect, because there was no contrast.[9]

It had been a conglomeration of colours and tawdry tinsel with no overall control. Designers in the future ought to avoid such confusion. Do not use blue dresses against a blue set. If the set is rich then the costumes ought to be simple, and vice versa, if the costumes are luxurious the scenery ought to be plain. This was a lesson which Charles Kean had still not learnt in the 1850s.

Noverre himself concluded that costume designers were too arrogant, and seems to have become disenchanted with his once-favoured Boquet.

The costume designer consults no one in regard to his dresses, and often sacrifices the correct costumes of the people of a bygone age to the fashion of the day or at the caprice of a favourite dancer or singer.[10]

Male dancers at the Paris Opéra were still wearing masks for male roles, which struck Noverre as ridiculous and restrictive:

. . . away with those lifeless masks but feeble copies of nature; they hide your features, they stifle, so to speak, your emotions and thus deprive you of the most important means of expression; take off those enormous wigs and those gigantic head-dresses which destroy the true proportions of the head with the body; discard the use of those stiff and cumbersome hoops which detract from the beauties of execution, which disfigure the elegance of your attitudes and mar the beauties of contour which the bust should exhibit in its different positions.[11]

By bust Noverre meant the whole upper part of the body, and he was thinking of the proportions and balance of a classical statue, an approach to be adopted by Sarah Siddons. Change in ballet costume was part of change in theatre dress as a whole.

Noverre's influence had its first success when the Paris Opéra abolished masks in 1773, but his other reforms were followed more slowly. Hoops and tall wigs would not go away until the fashion for them was over.

When Gaetano Vestris appeared in Noverre's *ballet tragique Jason et Medée* at the King's Theatre, Haymarket, London, in March 1781 his ballerinas still had tall wigs and hoops. Where Noverre was more effective was in getting the cast all to wear slippers instead of shoes with high heels. This meant that they could all be more nimble and light on their feet, although the men still had the easiest costumes to operate in. Ballet heroes wore wide skirts just like tragic actors, for a period look affects all aspects of the theatre, but Noverre did manage to start to tame the garment. The skirt on Vestris' costume was broken up into draped sections, which were still wide but which allowed him to kick much higher. It was the triumph of Neo-Classicism in the 1790s which gave Noverre what he wanted, when clothes of classical simplicity, and hence lightness, became acceptable on every stage, and his own approach had been part of that movement. Ballerinas now had the lightest costumes they had ever worn, which caused every theatre manager to check that they were wearing drawers. Slippers or Roman-type sandals became the norm for all dancers and dancing could become much more fluid and airy as a result.

The aim was now for 'ease, purity, delicacy, and lightness' wrote Carlo Blasis in his *Code of Terpsichore* (1830). He stressed dancing on the toes, and for this he required lightweight costumes, Roman tunics or Van Dyck dress for the men, or simple frocks for the girls.[12] Elevation was the new ideal. In 1837 Blasis became director of the Imperial Academy in Milan where he reorganized the ballet school into the pattern still followed today. Pupils were accepted at the age 8 to 12, after passing a medical. They were graded, and promoted according to ability, finally graduating into a career structure at the La Scala Opera or other houses.

The concept of lightness was to be taken to its extreme by the Romantic movement. The increasing definition of women as delicate little things led to ballerinas being expected to appear frail and ethereal, despite their underlying need for iron discipline and endless energy. The preoccupation with ghosts and spirits led to the creation of the *ballet blanc* where every costume was ghostly white. A change in the shape of the fashionable shoe proved a considerable help when square toes

became the vogue from 1830. Square toes can be stood on, so the quest for elevation and lightness had found its instrument. Dancing on the points was discovered, and ballerinas had acquired a technique which ousted the male dancer from his dominating position. Tottering on the toes was seen as the essence of fragile feminity and so it was not taught to males; consequently they could not compete. No matter how far his muscles and his costume allowed him to leap, here was something the male could not do. Audiences flocked to see the new ballerinas specializing in the novel technique and interest in athletic male performances went into a steep decline, to such an extent that male dancers were reduced to supporting roles in ballet for the remainder of the nineteenth century. The star was the ballerina on points; all the man had to do was to hold her up.

The first ballerina to be the Romantic ideal was Marie Taglioni, and when she appeared in *La Sylphide* in Paris in 1832, the Romantic ballet was born. She played an ethereal sylph, so the points technique allowed her to give the impression of

61 Male ballet attitudes from *Code of Terpsichore*, 1830, by Carlo Blasis. THE BRITISH LIBRARY

Neo-Classical rules made ballet costume lighter by discarding ornamentation for white simplicity, which in turn made more lighter movements possible.

62 Female ballet attitudes, from *Code of Terpsichore*, 1830, by Carlo Blasis. THE BRITISH LIBRARY

Neo-Classicism wanted its women to resemble ancient statues, so ancient hairstyles and dresses were promoted. Being light such clothes did allow ballerinas to move more quickly, but their skirts were still long enough to inhibit high kicks.

OPPOSITE PAGE
63 Marie Taglioni in *La Sylphide*, 1832, by Alfred Chalon. VICTORIA AND ALBERT MUSEUM

The ballerina takes over. The square toed shoe allows women to do what male dancers cannot, to dance on their points. The slightly shorter hem on the skirt was not much shorter than Camargo's had been, but being made in much lighter materials like tulle it enabled ballerinas to be agile despite the fact that wide skirts were back in fashion. The classical tutu was born.

RIGHT
64 Marie Taglioni and A. Guerra in *L'Ombre*, Her Majesty's Theatre, 18 June 1840, by J. Bouvier. VICTORIA AND ALBERT MUSEUM

The new concept of feminine fragility so beloved of Romantics was taken to an extreme with Taglioni balancing on rose bushes, an example of trivialization which Noverre would have abhorred. The male dancer now has a liotard which would allow him to be very active, but he was no longer allowed to outshine the ballerina.

floating in the air. Her costume was designed by Eugène Lami who fully appreciated what an insubstantial character should wear, ghostly white, and clouds of trembling silk tulle and net. Fashionable skirts had begun to swell out again, so he kept to that silhouette but retained the shorter hemline now traditional for ballerinas, and thus created the classic tutu, which has been worn in *La Sylphide* ever since. The ballet was acclaimed for its use of points for the non-human characters, thereby stressing their insubstantiality, the white tutu was considered the perfect ballet costume, and the sentimental subject – a beautiful sylph dying when touched by her human lover James – appealed greatly to Romantic minds. The worst costume was for poor James who is supposed to be Scottish, and the one thing French designers cannot get right is Highland dress. When *La Sylphide* was revived in March 1981 by Pierre Lacotte at the Théâtre des Champs Elysées the costume for James resembled a tartan tunic, where shirt and kilt would have been proper, allowing for the fact that the jacket is best left off for ease of dancing.

The sentimentality of Romantic ballet destroyed everything that Noverre had fought for. There were no more ballets of action or tragedy with strong dramatic emphasis; nobility and heroism were ousted by frivolous prettiness. The public was happy to see Taglioni balancing on the top of reinforced rose bushes, the story line was reduced to a shadow, and the ballet became a succession of turns in which different ballerinas showed off their

pointe work. Preoccupation with technique destroyed art, and the idea that ballet could have a serious purpose died.

By the middle of the century ballet was going downhill. While it was still required in operas, the concept of ballet as an independent entity faded, and the stage was reached by the 1880s when ballets were included at music halls as a pretty interval between the comics. The impulse to revive respect for ballet had to come from outside France and England, from the one country where an imperial court still had its court theatre and ballet company, Russia. This fringe of European culture had still kept the pattern of Louis XIV and XV, and the Russian Imperial Ballet, while administered by a highly conservative court bureaucracy, had all the scale and lavish splendour of Baroque court ballets. Catherine the Great had started the Imperial Theatres and the Imperial Ballet School in 1752, but in all its history the Imperial Ballet was very dependent on foreign talent. Its principal teachers were the dancer Christian Johannsson who made his début in 1841 and was still teaching in 1906, Marius Petipa who taught the French technique and schooled both ballerinas and chorus to the same level of ability, and Enrico Cecchetti who excelled in mime and character education. It was Petipa who persuaded Tchaikovsky to compose full-length scores for ballets such as *Swan Lake* and *The Sleeping Beauty*, something serious composers were not doing in Western Europe, preoccupied as they were with operas and symphonies.

65 Anna Pavlova in *Giselle*, Imperial Ballet, St Petersburg, 1903. THE MUSEUM OF LONDON

At the Russian Imperial Ballet the tutu was compulsory but it had grown much wider and contained so much net that Pavlova disliked it.

OPPOSITE PAGE
66 Anna Pavlova in *Giselle*, New York, 1920. THE MUSEUM OF LONDON

When Pavlova had her own company she abandoned the tutu in favour of much simpler costumes which did not impede her movements. She detested the lavish costumes in Diaghilev's Ballets Russes as being too restrictive.

It is likely that the rest of Europe would have known little of these developments but for one man, Sergei Diaghilev. He began as a connoisseur of fine art, not as a balletomane. At first artistic circles in St Petersburg regarded him as a vulgar snob and dandy, the spoilt child of a comfortable provincial background. Diaghilev soon proved to have all the drive and determination of the outsider. By 1898 he had founded an arts journal *The World of Art* and organized exhibitions, and in 1906 took the bold step of mounting an exhibition of Russian art in Paris. This was very successful and Parisians asked him to bring other aspects of art from that unknown country of his, so in 1907 he returned with the bass Chaliapin to sing in Mussorgsky's *Boris Godunov*. The powerful bass had a great impact, and Diaghilev decided to follow this with some Russian ballet. To do so he would have to borrow dancers from the Imperial Ballet which made him wait until the ballet took its summer holiday.

It was May 1909 when Diaghilev next arrived in Paris with his collection, the dancers Anna Pavlova, Karsavina, and the young male Vaslav Nijinski, the choreographer Michel Fokine, and the designers Alexandre Benois and Leon Bakst. The first ballet performed was eighteenth century in taste and dress: *Le Pavillon d'Armide*, with Nijinski in a version of the hooped skirts worn by dancers in the past and draped as Gaetano Vestris' costume had been in 1781, but the other works performed made a much greater impact. The Polovstian Dances from *Prince Igor*, danced in Tartar dress and soft boots, were a sensation after the soft, sentimental ballets Paris was now used to. The vitality, the energy the barbaric drive and pounding rhythm were overwhelmingly exciting and stimulating, while the acrobatic steps of the male dancers were something not seen in French ballet for 80 years. Another sensation was caused by Ida Rubenstein in *Cléopâtre*, with choreography by Fokine and sets and costumes by Bakst, who dressed her in 12 veils which she slowly removed one by one. Bakst loved primary colours and strong colours, so the veils were red, green, orange and indigo, which were a violent, visual shock to a generation accustomed to fashionable tones of pale lavender, sky-blue and softest pink. Strong colours had become regarded as bad taste, but here was Bakst using strident contrasts, peacock blue and bright yellow, shrieking scarlet and lurid pink in an astounding explosion of savage excess. All this was very northern, for in a country like Russia or Sweden where there are long dreary months of wintery grey, people compensate by painting the outsides of buildings orange, yellow, blue or crimson, so Bakst was simply bringing his native tradition with him, and

putting it on the stage; but this was unprecedented in Paris or London where buildings are not so brightly coloured.

Diaghilev fully appreciated the value of sensation, so in 1910 he surpassed the exotic, erotic nature of *Cléopâtre*, with the ballets *The Firebird*, *Les Orientales*, and *Schéhérézade*. The last was set in a harem, with a sultan's wives lolling around in risqué costumes by Bakst, trousers with sections cut out, naked abdomens, and bejewelled bras, the whole topped with ropes of pearls and semi-precious stones. Diaghilev was exploiting sex, and the feeling among the Benois circle back in the 1890s that he was a vulgar showman was proving justified. He knew the value of publicity, and he was not fussy how he got it. This did not please the Imperial Ballet; the directors did not like Diaghilev borrowing its dancers and they disapproved most strongly of the sort of ballets he was putting them in, so it placed a ban on dancers performing for Diaghilev. This act forced Diaghilev to found his own ballet company, Les Ballets Russes, to which he recruited some of the Imperial Ballet's dancers, but he had to find a way to get the Imperial Ballet to sack Nijinski which it was refusing to do. In what was probably an engineered episode Nijinski danced in front of the Czar's family without wearing a jockstrap underneath his tights, which caused imperial outrage and instant dismissal. Such goings-on, and the nature of Bakst's sets and costumes, shocked some of the dancers themselves, most notably the ballerina Anna Pavlova who wrote:

. . . the beauty of the scenes he combines, the splendors [sic] of the setting and the costumes, the charm of the music, exercise so captivating and surprising an effect upon the public, that the dancer's individuality is lost sight of.[13]

To Pavlova the dance was the most important part of ballet and she objected to sets and costumes which were so colourful and spectacular that they reduced the ballerina to a minor role. She left Diaghilev and took residence in London at Ivy House, Hampstead, where she founded a ballet school and organized her own travelling company. She said that her ideal was to make people happy with beauty, enabling them to forget the sadnesses of life. Consequently she concentrated on ballets which were elegant, in good taste, and above all a vessel for brilliant dancing. In this she was continuing the ideal of Romantic ballet, and such creations as *The Swan*, to music by Saint-Saens, and *Dragonfly*, both maintained the emotion and the delicacy of that style. Pavlova became the most famous ballerina in the world thanks to newspapers, photography and film, and because she took ballet all round the world. Founding her company in 1913

she devoted the rest of her life, until she died in 1931, to taking dance to the United States, to South America, to Egypt, India, Japan, and Australia, to bring the beauty of ballet to everybody, and thus embodied in herself the popular image of the prima ballerina.

The changes Pavlova made in ballet costume were for the sake of greater simplicity and easier dancing. Whereas she wore the white tutu when dancing for the Imperial Ballet in *Giselle* in 1903, when she had her own company she replaced this with a much slimmer costume designed by herself which hung in layered leaves of tulle, and which allowed for much higher steps without a quantity of net petticoats getting in the way. Similarly the costume she devised for *Dragonfly* was intended to flutter, so it was a knee-length skirt covered with layers of loose gauze. Above all her costumes were light and liberating, so that she was able to flash across the stage at amazing speed and with astonishing grace and balance. People said she was magical.

Back in Paris a very different policy was underway. Having got Nijinski Diaghilev built him up into the first male ballet star for 80 years, restoring the pre-eminence of the male performer by giving full rein to Nijinski's muscular vitality. In 1911 he gave Nijinski two new ballets designed for him, *Petrushka*, where he was dressed by Benois, and *Le Spectre de la Rose* where Bakst devised the costume. The designs by Benois were perfectly safe, clothing Nijinski as the puppet, but Bakst was more sensational, putting the dancer into a body stocking covered with petal shapes in pink and red. So tight a costume on a male would never have been allowed at the Imperial Ballet, but Diaghilev wanted impact, and publicity, to attract maximum audiences. The costume did cause comment but this was smothered by the admiration for what the costume enabled Nijinski to do, his tremendous leap through the window at the end of the ballet with no breeches or skirts to restrict his spreading legs. Ballet fans were so impressed by his performance they crowded backstage and tore the petals off the costume as mementoes, so every night Madame Stepanova of the wardrobe had to sew new petals on.

In 1912 Nijinski was allowed to choreograph for himself in *L'Après-midi d'un Faune* to Debussy's music. As fauns were classical Nijinski decided to put the ballet in ancient Greece, so Bakst designed

---

67 Anna Pavlova in *The Dragonfly*, New York, *c* 1915. THE MUSEUM OF LONDON

This was the sort of costume Pavlova designed for herself, as insubstantial as possible, for she wanted to move swiftly.

classical dresses for the nymphs with chequered hems, but as fauns were half-human and half-goat Bakst had to devise an appropriate costume. He therefore created another skin-tight outfit, a leotard in piebald brown and white with only a bunch of grapes to conceal the genitals. This was very close to nakedness on stage, the almost complete exposure of human shape from head to toe, and audiences were shocked. However there were other shocks in the production too. In Nijinski's choreography he tried to imitate the angular positions of dancers on ancient Greek vases, which seemed very ugly to audiences used to graceful dancing, and the end of the ballet caused tremendous offence. The faun had been chasing the nymphs but only managed to capture the scarf of one of them, so he took this back to his rock and then laid on it like a lover. This was far too brazen for 1912 and resulted in fierce protests. According to Nijinski's wife Romola, *Le Figaro* denounced the ballet as 'vile movements of erotic bestiality and gestures of heavy shamelessness' and described the faun's costume as an ill-made beast too hideous to behold.

68 Anna Pavlova as the Dying Swan, Buenos Aires, 1928. THE MUSEUM OF LONDON

Pavlova retained the tutu for her most famous solo role, but she shortened it to the knee. The swan costumes, actually made of goose feathers and down, were so fragile they had to be constantly repaired or renewed. One of them still survives, along with Pavlova's *Giselle* costume, her *Russian Dance* costume, and her *Christmas Ballet* costume in the Museum of London.

OPPOSITE PAGE
69 *St Sebastian*, 6 victims 2nd Act, Leon Bakst's design for the ballet with choreography by Fokine, music by Debussy, text by D'Annunzio, Théâtre du Châtelet, Paris, 21 May 1911.
ASHMOLEAN MUSEUM, OXFORD

By the early twentieth century it was possible for designers to reproduce any period anywhere, and Diaghilev's company made its name by its exotic subjects and lavish style. Here Bakst tries Turkish dress in velvet.

The Prefect of Police in Paris was asked to ban the production, but Nijinski found a defender in the sculptor Rodin who announced that Nijinski's art was 'the perfect personification of the ideals of the beauty of the old Greeks'.[14]

The fact that Nijinski married was to change the nature of Les Ballets Russes and made it less Russian. Diaghilev was homosexual, and the loss of Nijinski to a woman made him vicious. He dismissed the dancer and banned anyone in their circle from working with him again. Reacting as if all the Russians had betrayed him he was to bring in Western designers to do his sets and costumes, Picasso, Derain, Marie Laurençin and Matisse. The ballerina Ida Rubenstein left to found her own company, with Bakst designing her clothes which were then made up by Maison Worth.[15] The outbreak of the First World War cut the company off from Russia and both Diaghilev and Pavlova had to recruit English, French and Polish girls for their choruses, although they were given Russian names to begin with. Miss Munnings became Sokolova, and Alicia Marks was renamed Markova. In 1924 Diaghilev engaged his first British *premier danseur* Anton Dolin. It was from these steps that the British Royal Ballet was to emerge, starting as the Vic-Wells Ballet in 1931 under the determined direction of Ninette de Valois.

The Ballets Russes did not bring any one major innovation or reform in ballet costume for amidst all the splendour and sensationalism there was too much of everything. With photography at the artist's hand it was now possible to reproduce anything from any period anywhere, and the result was confusion, not the emergence of a dominant theme or ideal. There was a reaction against skin-tight costumes and Nijinski performed the tennis ballet *Jeu* in trousers. Not until the 1920s made suntans fashionable and bathing costumes became more daring to allow more skin to be burnt, could the theatre follow suit without causing offence. Stockings were still essential in 1910; in 1912 Nijinski got the nymphs in *L'Après-midi d'un Faune* not to wear stockings in good classical accuracy, but this was very much a one-off experiment. The next year, 1913, the chorus in *Le Sacre de Printemps* were back in stockings, although given the prehistoric setting of the ballet bare legs would have been correct, but Nijinski's experiments had upset too many people to be repeated. It took the First World War to unlock the prohibitions, with absent soldiers demanding pin-ups, the silent cinema offering shots of bathing belles, and the postwar craze for sunshine gradually making exposure acceptable. The English stage designer Charles Ricketts saw the Russian Ballet's *Cléopâtre* in August 1918 and considered Bakst's colour scheme hideous, and the clothes a

OPPOSITE PAGE

70 First costume for Pollux in *Hélène de Sparte*, Théâtre du Châtelet, 4 May 1912, by Leon Bakst. ASHMOLEAN MUSEUM, OXFORD

Ancient Greece was equally possible, and in a more correctly Greek version than the Baroque period had attempted. Bakst asks for a single-piece cuirass, and a matt tone for the shield.

ABOVE

71 Alexandre Benois's design for the costume of a dancer brandishing a sword in Stravinsky's opera *Le Rossignol*, Paris Opéra, 1914. ASHMOLEAN MUSEUM, OXFORD

China was also exploited by Diaghilev who produced Stravinsky's opera. There was no culture which he would not touch if he thought it had possibilities. So much exotic extravagance had a tremendous impact but by 1920 opinion was beginning to find it all too overblown.

sorry mixture, apart from Massine 'stark naked save for rather nice bathing drawers, with a huge black spot on his belly'.[16] Such a sight caused some of the girls in the gallery of the theatre to shriek with embarrassment. So much exposure in 1918 was still controversial.

It has often been claimed that the greatest impact on costume by the Ballets Russes was not in theatre but in fashion, causing Parisiennes to dress themselves in Eastern turbans, harem overskirts and quantities of pearls. Such claims are nonsense, for the English Levant Company, trading with Turkey, and the Dutch, English, and French, East India Companies had all been importing pearls, clothes, textiles, furniture and porcelain since the early seventeenth century. There was a craze for things Chinese in the mid-eighteenth century, while there was a vogue for women to wear turbans in the 1770s to 1790s. Many European artists visited the Near East to paint exotic subjects, and pictures of Turkish bazaars or slave girls hung in many Victorian homes. The impact made by Diaghilev's company was primarily in the area of colour, and in the sensational sensuality. Even so, the Fauve art movement was already using strong, raw, colour, and Elinor Glyn was already writing her novels of sexual passion, heroines writhing on bearskins with an Arab sheik or a Russian grand duke, so the bright colour and sensuality would have found their way onto the stage in due course even without a visit from the Ballets Russes. What Diaghilev did was to present the two together at the same time, thus achieving a double impact. He speeded up the appearance of these features on the stage but they would have happened without him. The couturier Paul Poiret had been using kimonos since 1903, took great interest in oriental costume, and was putting Parisiennes into turbans and tunics before the Russians arrived.[17]

72 'Isadora Duncan Dancing', 1908, by Leon Bakst. ASHMOLEAN MUSEUM, OXFORD

The rebel against discipline, ballet schools, and fixed steps, the plump girl from San Francisco who was heavier than any ballerina, went her own way with what Alexander Bland has called a wild momentum. Dancing in Greek tunics, without stockings or shoes, and making the steps up as she went along and felt inspired, she caused a sensation in the smart salons of New York, London and Paris, when she gave her recitals, and started the modern idea of self-expression in experimental ballet, before the Ballets Russes arrived in Paris.

CHAPTER SIX

Spectacle versus Ideas

The contrast between a Charles Kean extravagant spectacular and a Madame Vestris real room set became the leading battlegrounds in the late-nineteenth-century theatre: should the stage be about the past and romantic escapes into history, or should it reflect the problems of the contemporary society? What this meant for costume was, should it be glorious or should it be ordinary? As the theatre was the one place where the ordinary public could see colour, and riches, and golden dresses, when in the smokey, industrial world outside the houses were black with soot and clothes soon became dirty, where horse droppings lay in the street and the Thames stank like an open sewer, why should the theatre deprive the public of romantic spectacle? Some theatre managers refused to lessen the display, and magnificent, enormous productions with hundreds of dresses were still being played during the First World War. They offered glamour to lives which lacked it, while heroic dramas from history made people proud of their country. The late nineteenth century was the time of the height of imperialism in Britain and other countries, so the theatre would please a wide section of society if it presented glamorous pictures of national glory.

Henry Irving was one actor-manager who did so, and was the first actor to be knighted in Britain, for bringing the theatre up to the level demanded by national pride. His first London success came in 1872 as King Charles I in Will's play of that name at the Lyceum Theatre, and Irving did the serious research into history and art that John Philip Kemble, J.R. Planché, and Charles Kean had all called for. He read about the king and had his costumes copied from Van Dyck's portraits with the lace collars, the slashed doublets, the wide breeches, and the boots. Irving showed the same serious approach in 1873 when he played Cardinal Richelieu in Bulwer Lytton's drama, when the future administrator of the Comédie Française Jules

Claretié observed that Irving had a photograph of Champagne's full-length portrait and three studies of the cardinal also from that artist's hand. When Irving acted *Hamlet* in 1874 he kept the costume very simple, just a black tunic edged with beaver fur and black hose, instead of long mourning cloaks and heroic plumes, so that it would allow him to act the role of a young man, an active prince, not give the heavy performance of a middle-aged actor, in heavy clothes. A garment can imprison or release, as all actors can discover.

While the stage was still being attacked by the churches, some priests claiming that all actors lived immoral lives, Irving took the attitude that the theatre could carry a moral message, as the Jesuits had argued two hundred years before. He had the romantic grand manner behind him, and could play with nobility. Tall and lean, he could look more like a cardinal or a king than the over-fed incumbents of those roles in real life. He lacked a beautiful voice, but he could speak beautifully, and Irving attracted back to the theatre the noblemen and the upper middle classes who had turned their backs on the popular melodramas of the 1830s. His performances were noble, and an actor can play an earl or duke with much more nobility than the real thing, so the earls and the dukes came to see. Irving also said it was the theatre's duty to bring colour and beauty to the public, thereby continuing the tradition of Charles Kean that the theatre should offer audiences more wonder than could be seen outside. It was Irving's ambition that the theatre should be accorded the same respect which was given to the other arts, for it was an art in itself, not simply a jumble of other arts. Consequently he was anxious that the most famous painters of the day should be invited to work for the theatre.

In 1892 Irving decided to rival Kean with a mammoth production of Shakespeare's *Henry VIII*. Unlike Kean he called in a Royal Academician to

73 Sir Henry Irving as Charles I in the play by Wills, Lyceum Theatre, 1872, by Bernard Partridge. VICTORIA AND ALBERT MUSEUM

Irving's first London success was regarded as excellently costumed but no recreation of a past look fails to make some mistakes: the shoulders are too square and lack the slope of the 1630s, the collar is not wide enough, the wig is too curled, the slashed sleeves are too hard, the breeches should be fuller at the top, and the boots are too wide and lack butterfly leathers. The line of 1872 shows through, inevitably.

74 Henry Irving as Hamlet, Lyceum Theatre, 1874. British School. VICTORIA AND ALBERT MUSEUM

A roughly sixteenth century version of the Danish prince, but without a codpiece and much too narrow in the shoulders. The slender suited gentleman of 1874 would not wear the broad shouldered coat of the Tudor period, so Hamlet's costume is narrowed down to accord with contemporary taste. By not wearing a plumed hat and long mourning cloak Irving tried to give the prince a more youthful look.

75 Henry Irving as Macbeth, Lyceum Theatre, December 1888, by Bernard Partridge. VICTORIA AND ALBERT MUSEUM

A Viking version of the Scottish king, with a winged helmet such as Wagner was giving to his heroes in *The Ring* cycle. As with Charles Kean there is more Norman than Scottish character in the end result. Designed by Charles Cattermole and made by Auguste et Cie.

76 Ellen Terry as Lady Macbeth, Lyceum Theatre, December 1888. VICTORIA AND ALBERT MUSEUM

Irving's famous leading lady is dressed in thirteenth-century style, having ordered her own gown from her designer Alice Comyns-Carr who wanted to create a soft chain-mail effect. Their dressmaker Mrs Nettleship of 58 Wigmore St came up with a Bohemian yarn in soft green silk and blue tinsel which Mrs Comyns-Carr crocheted to get the effect she wanted. The dress was then sewn with green beetle-wings and bordered at the hem with diamonds and rubies. The long plaits were bound with gold. The result was a new concept of Lady Macbeth, dressed in barbaric splendour. Compare the painting by Sargent on the jacket of this book.

OPPOSITE PAGE
77 Ellen Terry as Ellaline in *The Amber Heart*, Lyceum Theatre, June 1887. VICTORIA AND ALBERT MUSEUM

The reason Ellen Terry appointed Alice Comyns-Carr as her personal designer in 1883 was because she admired her crinkled fabrics, an effect the designer created by cooking clothes in her potato steamer, and because she was a leading figure in the Aesthetic Dress Movement. Mrs Comyns-Carr used Viollet-le-Duc's costume book for reference, and the principal aim of her creations was to look like a Rossetti or Burne-Jones come to life. One barrier to accuracy was Ellen Terry's refusal to wear anything heavy, even if true to period. The lily beside her was the Aesthetic Movement's favourite flower.

oversee the design, Sir Lawrence Alma-Tadema, although Irving already had his own costume designer Seymour Lucas, and his leading lady Ellen Terry was dressed by Mrs Comyns Carr. In fact, given this sub-division of responsibilities, an over-all guiding hand was most advisable. Once again Holbein's portraits of the Tudor court were studied, silks were dyed cardinal red, and scores of sewing machines hummed away over hundreds of Tudor tunics and gowns. A beautiful picture was the result, with all the colour tones worked out to harmonize under Alma-Tadema's direction. There were furs, brocades, silks, velvets and jewels, with Irving as Cardinal Wolsey in appropriate cassock, biretta, cincture, two short capes, and a long train of red corded silk, with red tights underneath. Historical accuracy was all, and Irving was following Charles Kean in this respect most faithfully. When Kean had played the role back in 1855, he had

received an angry letter from a Roman Catholic secretary complaining that his cardinal's costume was incorrect, to which Kean had replied that he had based his costume upon sixteenth-century portraits of cardinals, not nineteenth-century ones.[1] The leading actor-manager now had to be able to reply to criticism by illustrating his superior knowledge of historical facts. The theatre of spectacle could justify its existence by stressing its scholarship and accuracy, even if it did flood the stage with more courtiers and servants than Henry VIII himself had ever possessed. But such gigantic spectacle, portraying the splendours of England's past, appealed greatly to the taste of the current British Empire, for all Europe was now seething with national pride, and the British were proudest of all. Was not their empire the biggest of all? Therefore their theatre had to follow suit, for biggest was best. Of course, once the British

Empire was in decline and Americans started to claim that their biggest was best, the British replied that scale did not guarantee quality, particularly in Texas.

Alma-Tadema was an artist who specialized in classical subjects in the main, not Tudor ones, so in 1896 Irving invited him to design *Cymbeline*, which was set in Britannia during the Roman Empire. Once again, as in the seventeenth and eighteenth centuries the stage would be covered in Roman heroes, but rather more accurately this time, with fewer plumes, and no hoops. Nobody was wearing hoops in 1896, so it was possible to look narrow on the stage; crinolines had been abandoned in 1868.[2] If width had been in fashion, Alma-Tadema would no doubt have been obliged to conform out of regard for modesty and respectability as interpreted by a 'wide' era. Now a narrow look was in vogue, so thinly dressed Romans were possible, but they had to wear tights of course. Modesty still involved being covered up, even if the look was leaner. As for the ancient Britons, they had worn tunics and trousers of sorts, and so presented no problems.

Another artist Irving turned to was Sir Edward Burne-Jones, the Pre-Raphaelite, whom he commissioned to design Carr's *King Arthur* in 1894. Burne-Jones was fascinated by the Arthurian legend. The production opened at the Lyceum on 12 January 1895, and as Mrs Comyns Carr was the playwright's wife she supervised the construction of the costumes. Irving played King Arthur, Ellen Terry was Guinevere, and Johnston Forbes-Robertson portrayed Sir Launcelot. The costumes were armour for the knights, although Burne-Jones's depiction of armour was always more fanciful than mediaeval, and long flowing draperies for the ladies which were closer to Art Nouveau evening gowns than to the late Romano-British period when Arthur was supposed to have lived. The production ran for a hundred performances and was then taken over to the United States. Burne-Jones himself felt that no theatrical enaction could live up to the ideal image of the legend he carried in his mind, but he painted very slender creatures and no actor-manager could promise that all his cast would have the same wistful proportions. Many a costume designer will sigh when he sees the actual bodies his creations have to clothe.

Irving maintained the tradition of Macready in encouraging famous writers to be involved with the theatre, most notably the Poet Laureate Alfred Lord Tennyson. In 1881 he appeared in Tennyson's *The Cup*, and then encouraged the poet to write a play about Archbishop Thomas à Becket. Tennyson wrote it but he died before it was ready for the stage, so it was left to Irving to edit the work and trim it to produce an acting edition. Produced on 6 February 1893, here was another play requiring mediaeval clothes. Irving's own costumes were often tailored by Auguste et Cie, theatrical costumiers of 27 Wellington Street near the Strand, although the designs were usually created by Seymour Lucas, and occasionally by others such as Sir John Gilbert or Charles Cattermole. On this occasion more church vestments were called for, and early mediaeval fashion. Irving was dressed in a purple silk robe, with borders of gold braid decorated with glass jewels, over which was worn a mantle of dark green velvet cut in a lattice pattern over dark green silk, with jewels at the intersections, and a wide border bedecked with gold embroidery, and braid, with more glass jewels, to illustrate the worldly wealth. In Act I Irving wore full ecclesiastical garb with a chasuble of yellow silk damask, decorated with gold braid and glass jewels, a maniple of yellow diapered silk, with a silk fringe, a dalmatic of yellow silk with red velvet stripes, an alb which was cream in the visible parts and grey underneath, and heavily bejewelled apparels of green, red, and silver brocade. The shoes were crimson velvet embroidered with gold flowers. Obviously magnificence was the intention, with the prelate clothed with more glittering splendour than could be seen on the contemporary archbishop of Canterbury. The production was highly successful and Queen Victoria ordered a performance at Windsor Castle.[3] Irving was being true to the ideal that the theatre should be more beautiful and astounding than reality, and that audiences loved.

Although Irving performed in works which often put him into flowing robes, he is known to have gone to a top tailor in London when it came to fitted garments. In 1890 he played Edgar in Merivale's *Ravenswood*, a version of *The Bride of Lammermoor*, in which he wore a black suit designed by Seymour Lucas; to ensure perfect fit it was made by Poole & Sons of 37–39 Savile Row, where no better cut could be found.[4] That was where gentlemen dressed and Irving was proving that actors could be gentlemen too, by his manners and

---

78 Henry Irving as Thomas à Becket in Lord Tennyson's play, Lyceum Theatre, 6 February 1893, by Bernard Partridge. VICTORIA AND ALBERT MUSEUM

This was Irving's simplest costume in the play, for as a star he demanded richness for himself, and in *Macbeth* was so impressed by a crimson velvet cloak Mrs Comyns-Carr had made for Ellen Terry that he commandeered it for himself. The tragic leading man still expected to look more magnificent than anyone else.

his avoidance of any scandals in his private life. His knighthood shows that he succeeded in his aim.

The next major champion of spectacle in the theatre was Sir Herbert Beerbohm Tree (1852–1917). He came from a comfortable family background, was educated as a gentleman, although his private life failed to measure up to that standard; he was determined to rise, hence his taking the name Tree, to the top of which he intended to soar. In 1887 he gained his chance as an actor-manager when he took over the Haymarket Theatre, built by Nash during the Regency period. In 1895 he staged the famous novel *Trilby* in which he played Svengali with greasy locks and snakelike movements, for Tree was a master of make-up and disguise. This production was such a financial success that it enabled Tree to fulfil his greatest dream, a huge new theatre across the road on a site which had known three theatres in its time, starting with Vanbrugh's Queen's Theatre during the reign of Queen Anne in 1705. This spacious edifice, surmounted by a dome, cost Tree £55,000 to erect, but it was the last word in magnificence, with plenty of room for all and excellent acoustics. It opened in 1897, the year of

79 Irving's costume in the Prologue of Tennyson's *Becket*, Lyceum Theatre, 6 February 1893. MUSEUM OF LONDON

The theatrical splendour in purple silk, a gown bordered with gold braid and jewels, and a mantle of green silk with a lattice work covering in dark green velvet, made by Auguste et Cie., theatrical tailors. Many an actor-manager considered it his duty to present such richness.

ABOVE
80 Herbert Beerbohm Tree's production of *Hamlet*, Haymarket Theatre, 1892, by Aiokestier. VICTORIA AND ALBERT MUSEUM

The other champion of theatrical magnificence, Tree, with his towering sets and large casts. It was customary by now to give *Hamlet* a Romanesque setting, but whereas Irving in **74** wore Tudor dress among Norman columns, Tree has got clothes and architecture to agree, by no means a common result when a production often had different designers for costumes and sets.

Queen Victoria's Diamond Jubilee, so the name could only be Her Majesty's. Tree marked the event with a mammoth production of Shakespeare's *Julius Caesar*, deliberately flattering the British Empire by setting it beside the Roman one, as it were. Sir Lawrence Alma-Tadema was still the leading classicist in art, so the design was handed over to him, and as size was no barrier, the result was gigantic sets representing Roman palaces, temples and Senate. As the cast required many Roman senators Alma-Tadema spent many hours ensuring that all the draped togas were correct, as Young and Kemble had striven to achieve at the beginning of that century. Accuracy was still a problem as there was no Roman account of draping to show exactly how it should be done, but he tried to get the effect right.

In 1899 Tree essayed *The Three Musketeers*, with much use of velvet, silk and brocade *à la* Louis XIII period. It might be argued that by this date there was no excuse for making errors in costume for the seventeenth century or similar recent periods in history. After all, there were available a large number of books on costume and photographs of all the corners of the world; however, contemporary style could never be excluded. There was a way of looking at things, dated 1899, which could not be avoided; it affected the way an actor stood, the way he performed, the type of make-up he put on, which made some periods fashionable in modern eyes but which ruled others out, and which subjected the past to a current concept of what mattered in society. Even the designer's medium can give the date away, be it ink and wash, watercolour, oils, or nowadays acrylic paints, as well as the type of paper he was working on; he would design under gas or electric light while an earlier generation designed by candlelight. Moreover a designer dressed in a suit of 1899 while designing clothes of the 1630s, having no idea what it felt like to wear them himself. Clothes affect behaviour but this is one of the most neglected areas in theatre study, and too often a cast rehearses the parts long before it dons the costumes in which the roles have to be performed. Only then and much too late does it occur to the cast that the clothes prevent some of the fluid movements they had prepared. There is a similar disregard for period etiquette, and casts will mill about a royal character with a familiarity impossible in the 1630s. Period formality might slow a production up, but how much a passionate scene will stand out if set against a rigid social pattern, and how much an informal gesture will show if surrounded by formality. A formal bow need not be an empty piece of stage business, for much can be said by the way the bow is made. The way a cloak is thrown can speak

contempt, and the barrier created by a lady's crinoline or hoop makes a touching of hands between man and woman a significant act, as can the removal of a glove so that the hand may be kissed instead of kissing the glove itself. The more a period's restrictions are understood the more vital will be the break-through of a dramatic point. No musketeer should loll about drinking wine when a royal messenger arrives, but he should leap to his feet, remove his hat and bow to the message as if it were the king himself. Correct etiquette, correct management of clothes, can say more than pages of dialogue. Is it enough only to study the text?

Tree's next gargantuan manifestation was *A Midsummer Night's Dream* in 1900, lavish in the extreme with scores of children playing fairies, live rabbits, whole forests and gigantic palaces, but this was not enough and 1906 saw him embarking on Stephan Phillip's *Nero*. Once again Rome was rebuilt onstage, hundreds of togas had to be draped somehow, and the Roman mob became a horde. *The Illustrated London News* for January said that spectacle had reached the limit of resources, but this only stung Tree into mounting *Antony and Cleopatra* that same year with more giant palaces, the gilded barge, and silver robes for the queen. Tree did not take much interest in clothes, but he did read about the period and on discovering that Queen Cleopatra had had five children, stated that his leading lady should be accompanied by the same number. This caused his young Cleopatra, Constance Collier, to protest that it would ruin her image as a sultry temptress of old Nile if she had five brats trailing after her. In the end they compromised with three. Sadly this reflects on Miss Collier's acting range, for it was not enough to wear silver dresses and look attractive. The real Cleopatra was not beautiful, and when she succumbed to the bite of the snake she was not a youthful heroine but a matronly 39, while the ardent Mark Antony was 56. Authenticity was being compromised by legends of young, romantic lovers, who had never been. Tree at 54 was close to the mark, but Miss Collier was much too young.

The year 1910 saw the accession of George V with the coronation planned for 1911, so what did Tree mount to honour these events, what but *Henry VIII*? Spectacle reached its climax. The clothes, after Holbein of course, were designed by Percy Macquoid and made up by B. & J. Simmons, amounting to 92 major outfits, never mind the underlings. There was much use of velvet and brocade, and to audiences everything appeared perfectly accurate, but as they were looking with the eyes of 1910 they could not see that the production bore the mark of 1910. The women, as usual, were close to current fashion, with their skirts narrower than Holbein drew; the black kohl round their eyes

81 Herbert Beerbohm Tree as Richard II, His Majesty's Theatre, 1903. Photograph by N.Y. Floyd, autographed by the actor-manager. VICTORIA AND ALBERT MUSEUM

While Tree wanted a breathtaking picture he was not fussy about the details, so an ermine lined cloak to denote royalty and a gown of some sort would do providing they looked rich. If he had taken the trouble to look at the Wilton Diptych he would have found that the real Richard II had shorter hair, a high waist and wide sleeves. The melodramatic acting manner with uplifted eyes was adopted by the early cinema, and Tree appeared in one film.

82 Costume worn by Constance Benson in *The Taming of the Shrew*, 1901. MUSEUM OF LONDON

Bodice and skirt of dark red velvet painted with old gold tulips, and made by Miss Leicester, court dressmaker of 81 Edgware Road. Often leading actresses were dressed by couturiers or high-class dressmakers instead of theatrical costumiers. In this case the result is an admirable example of Art Nouveau taste, combining a vaguely Elizabethan line with a contemporary pattern, for the theatre had its Art Nouveau period too.

was not Shakespearean, the headdresses were too much a jumble of every possible type, and the slashing was not restrained. In an age when most men wore their hair very short, it was only too obvious that the male cast were all wearing wigs, not Tudor hair. Tree had a historical adviser in G. Ambrose of the College of Heralds who was on constant watch for errors, but Tree was one who would sacrifice accuracy if it got in the way of spectacle. He was not blind to new techniques and in 1915 set off happily to make a film of *Macbeth* in California, where there was no attempt to make it look Scottish, and the clothes were an assemblage of Saxon and Viking styles.[5]

The gargantuan production reached a zenith when the Austrian producer Max Reinhardt expanded right out of the theatre and into town squares, and vast arenas. He disliked the star actor-manager, and favoured the opposite, crowds of actors flowing across space in joint, disciplined mass-movement, instead of individual displays of dramatic talent. His wordless spectacle *Sumurun*, based on 'The Arabian Nights' tales, produced in Berlin, typified his policy as the cast had nothing to say as individuals. It amounted to a large mime in Arab costume, but it attracted sufficient international attention to be brought to London in 1911. Here Reinhardt was very impressed by the great space at the Olympia exhibition complex in Hammersmith Road, and resolved to exploit it to the full. The result was a spectacle entitled *The Miracle*, written by Karl Volmöller with music by Humperdinck, and produced in 1911. It contained a hill, mounted on specially laid rails, which could be run into the arena, and several rostra in the centre mounted on hydraulic jacks, which could be raised and lowered. When a presentation is this large of course the poor costume is reduced in impact and little can be seen except its colour, or whether its fabric is matt or shiny. The period of the piece was mediaeval, and its most famous aspect, so far as high society was concerned, was that Reinhardt engaged Lady Diana Cooper, daughter of the Duke of Rutland, to play the Madonna. She had had a somewhat unconventional upbringing for a ducal offspring, as her mother had been an aesthete who chose to dress her daughter in black velvet most of the time, and launched her as a debutante in grey and beige instead of the traditional white. With this upbringing behind her Lady Diana was perfectly willing to participate in anything so avant garde as Reinhardt's spectacular. She was not required to say anything but to stand there as a statue, with the Madonna's blue veil, a wimple round her throat and a simple dress. In engaging a society lovely Reinhardt was rather betraying his concept of anonymous casts but on the other hand it was good

publicity, and ensured press notices. While Reinhardt has been ranked as the master in rhythmic mass-management, he contributed nothing to costume. A general impression of a period was all he asked for. His large casts provided plenty of work for seamstresses, but no costume principle emerged from his fascination with mechanical effects.

Reinhardt's subject matter was diverse, including Arabia and mediaeval Europe, and this echoes the similar variety already seen in opera, which could also be found in straight theatre and in ballet. Any period anywhere was now general theatrical policy all round. As the poet William Cowper had written long before:

Variety's the very spice of life
That gives it all its flavour.

The Romantic interest in the exotic had grown comprehensive.

In the middle of the nineteenth century, while Wagner was trying to make opera deadly serious, a movement away from grand opera had gathered pace. Frivolous musical pieces were long established from the days when the monopolies on drama held by the English and French royal theatres had limited minor houses to lightweight entertainments, and in the middle of the century such pieces blossomed into operetta. The first master of the art was Jacques Offenbach, who had studied cello at the Paris Conservatoire when aged 14, and grew up into an extremely energetic jack-of-all-theatrical-trades, as composer, conductor, producer, stage-manager, copyist of music parts, and talent-spotter. He began with 'one-acts' in tiny temporary theatres and scored his first big success in 1857 with *Orphée aux Enfers*, which was a satire on the classical legend of Orpheus and Eurydice. Offenbach took another classical story, Helen of Troy, and turned that into a romp called *La Belle Hélène* (1864). This caused much offence among French academics, for hitherto classical legend and history had been treated with immense respect, a pattern established during the Renaissance and Baroque periods. Now here was Offenbach making the gods of Olympus dance to the can-can, but the music was so lively and the tunes so singable, that the general public flocked to the shows. After his essys with ancient Greek dress, Offenbach next chose two contemporary subjects and launched *La Vie Parisienne* in 1866, which did allow for an international range of contemporary dress, as it included South American tourists sampling the delights of crinolined Parisiennes. *La Grande Duchesse de Gerolstein* followed in 1867 and was set in an imaginary but contemporary state. It was the big attraction of Paris in the year of the latest international exhibition, and was visited by several crowned heads. Accordingly the clothes had

to be the very best, and an advertisement for French dressmaking, so the star was costumed in regal splendour by Worth the imperial couturier, even though he was English. He gave the grand duchess ermine cloaks and ball gowns embroidered with her 'national' flowers, much the same as he was supplying to real grand duchesses every day.

Offenbach's operettas were equally successful in London and Vienna, but eventually the Viennese, with their own musical tradition, felt that they ought to respond with their own sort of operetta based on the famous Viennese waltz. Franz Suppé tried his hand at the medium but his music was lively in the Offenbach manner, and it took the waltz king Johann Strauss the younger to produce a Viennese sound. His *Carnival in Rome* allowed for variety of costume, although it received a mixed reception; however, he succeeded triumphantly with *Die Fledermaus* in 1874. While the period was contemporary the plot allowed for a masked ball, so as in his previous work a variety in costume was possible. He did not attain another hit until *The Gipsy Baron* in 1885, which required the costume to be both historical and exotic; it was set in the Austria of Empress Maria Theresia but included Hungarian gipsies, so a wide range of eighteenth-century clothing types was necessary. It was from Hungary that the next master of the Viennese operetta emerged, the bandmaster Franz Lehar. Variety of subject matter appealed to him greatly so his settings ranged from contemporary China, history and imaginary states, all performed in waltz time, whatever the period or place. His most enduring success *The Merry Widow* (1905), which is rarely out of production somewhere, was another Viennese work with a fancy dress party as its centre. While it was set in Paris and required elegant and highly fashionable clothes most of the time, the party-goers included examples of the national costume of the imaginary state from which the heroine came.

83 Costume worn by Sir Johnston Forbes-Robertson in his last appearance as Hamlet, at his farewell in 1913. MUSEUM OF LONDON

A loose tunic of black melton cloth with circular cloak, both appliquéd with black velvet spots, bars and interwoven curves. The black silk tights had padded calves showing that the actor needed some reinforcement in this area. The chain is gilt in a Scandinavian design, and the sword belt is decorated with embossed plaques of dull steel. Strictly speaking as Hamlet is in full mourning for his murdered father his costume should have no decoration except black jet. In the Tudor and Stuart periods mourning meant everything in black including the shirts and underwear.

The Viennese première made the costumes look more Hungarian than anything, possibly as a salute to Lehar himself, but the invention of a national costume from somewhere near the Balkans was a difficult task, for it had to reflect something of that region while trying to suggest something individual at the same time, a sophisticated problem if there ever was one. The Balkans cropped up again, namely Bulgaria, when Oscar Strauss turned Shaw's *Arms and the Man* into *The Chocolate Soldier*, to the fury of the author, in 1908.

In England light opera, as operetta could be termed, followed the Offenbach model to begin with, in the works of Gilbert and Sullivan, but by the turn of the century the musical comedy had emerged, which mixed a sketchy plot with topical sketches and lively songs. The costuming was mainly contemporary, an exercise in frilly glamour, with a bevy of chorus girls to wear it. These choruses were a novelty, and another variation on female exposure on the stage, as they were required to show their legs to increasing degrees. The ideal female form was the result of the distortion of a girl's body by corsets, where any flesh was either pushed upwards to the chest, or downwards to the hips and thighs, producing the hour-glass silhouette but damaging lungs, liver and kidneys, so determined is the imposition of the contemporary fashionable look. The individual girl shall be remade no matter how drastically to accord with the period's image, not with her own (assuming she could think of herself as separate from the current definition of female). Perhaps the most famous chorus girl with this hour-glass shape was Camille Clifford of the retroussé nose and tiny waist.

The first musical comedies were *In Town* (1892) and *The Shop Girl* produced by George Edwardes at his Gaiety Theatre. As the titles suggest they were about boys and girls in the London of the day, while *Floradora* (1899) is a title full of the floral, frivolous, nature of the entertainment. Americans tried the medium with *The Belle of New York* in 1898. Britain responded to that with *The Belle of Mayfair* at the Vaudeville Theatre in 1906, where Camille Clifford got her big opportunity to emerge from the chorus, when she was given the song 'Why They Call Me a Gibson Girl' because she had that figure to perfection. The song was a salute to the American artist Charles Dana Gibson whose drawings of Edwardian beauties with upswept hair and burgeoning bosoms over narrow waists were highly popular on both sides of the Atlantic. As a consequence of that song, written by Leslie Stiles, Miss Clifford was known thereafter as the Gibson Girl.

The first attempts at light opera made in the USA were purely European like their composers, Victor Herbert (Irish), Rudolf Friml (Czech) and Sigmund Romberg (Hungarian) who used the same mixture of settings as European theatre. Friml's *The Vagabond King* was set in the fifteenth century so it required historical costume, and Romberg's *The Student Prince* German costume, and his *Desert Song* Arabic clothes. Any exotic subject was possible except America herself – that had to wait until the jazz age.

Another outcome of the old monopoly on drama in Britain was the music hall. It began in the eighteenth century when taverns would have a large room set aside for an evening of songs, acrobatics, juggling, and dancing. As the urban working class increased in the next century the demand for such entertainments spread. It was the Canterbury Arms tavern in Lambeth which built the first separate theatre for its presentations and during the 1850s many a publican followed this example so that a broad circuit developed, and performers would dash from music hall to music hall, doing several spots in an evening. To be remembered each comedian and singer needed to create a particular identity that was his alone, so clothes, accessories and make-up were all very important, for the performer only had a few minutes onstage in which to make his impact, before the next turn came on. The comedian Grock always carried his fiddle, Scotland's Harry Lauder was never without his kilt and gnarled walking stick, Vesta Tilley the male impersonator was always immaculate in evening dress, Eugene Stratton blacked his face, George Chevalier was always in a costermonger's pearly splendour, Kate Carney would be fluttering with feathers, T.E. Dunville was encased in his skin-tight suit, Harry Tate boasted a ferocious moustache, and Mark Sheridan always combined elegance and artisan practicality with his frock coat and bell-bottomed trousers tied round the knee with string. George Lashwood was as superbly turned out as Beau Brummel. George Robey was known for his heavy eyebrows like two half moons. Little Tich was the exception as his lack of inches was enough in itself to make him memorable. R.G. Knowles was never without a top hat, frock coat and white duck trousers. They would also choose individual material: Harry Champion always sang about food as in 'Boiled Beef and Carrots'; and Marie Lloyd always stressed her Cockney origins and accent with the songs 'My Old Man Said Follow the Van', and 'I'm One of the Ruins that Cromwell Knocked about a Bit'. She went on stage at the Royal Eagle Music Hall in 1885 when she was 15 and never retired until a few days before her death in 1922. She was what they call a trouper. Her clothes were usually glamorous in a cheerfully vulgar way.

There were serious items as well, operatic arias sung by ladies in evening gowns, while the Al-

84 Squire and Marie Bancroft, photograph by
Barrauds, *c* 1885. VICTORIA AND ALBERT MUSEUM

The actor-managers of the Prince of Wales's
Theatre from 1865, and of the Haymarket
Theatre from 1880 till their retirement in 1885,
who produced the realistic drawing room plays
of Tom Robertson. Mrs Bancroft ensured that all
the actresses' costumes were suitable by insisting
that they be made and paid for by her company,
not by personal dressmakers or designers, as
stars were apt to favour.

hambra and the Empire always had balletic interludes between the variety acts. The music hall was
groomed in the West End to be less vulgar and the
London Coliseum proclaimed in 1904 that its turns
were suitable for children. The Palace Theatre was
the scene of the music hall's becoming respectable in
truth when George V ordered a royal command
performance in 1912, which would have been
unthinkable in Queen Victoria's day. However the
music hall with its jokes about mothers-in-laws,
lodgers, milkmen and landlords, its sentimental
songs about mothers and sweethearts or wives,
received a serious challenge from the much slicker
new mixture of glamour and wit, the revue, which
did not rise from the working class but was a West
End creation. Dispensing with plots, the revue was
a lavish spectacular, a series of numbers and chorus
girls, with a few topical sketches, an excuse for
dances, songs and glamorous clothes. The first true
revue *Under the Clock* by Seymour Hicks and Charles
Brookfield opened at the Court Theatre in 1893.
The idea was taken up by the impresarios Albert de
Courville at the London Hippodrome and by André
Charlot at the Alhambra. Where these spectacles
used historical costume it was for a lavish effect,
roughly approximate but in rich fabrics, all glitter
and sparkles. Contemporary dress featured in the
main, with knee-length skirt and frilly petticoats for
the girls and neat lace-up boots which was now
standard dress for the chorus. Female acrobats were
used in their uniform, a corset-tight fitted costume
to the top of the thighs, thick white tights, and
boots. New York followed suit when Florenz
Ziegfeld launched his *Ziegfeld Follies* in 1907, and
later came George White's *Scandals* in 1919. It was
the appearance of ragtime which made the traffic
begin to go the other way. *Hallo Ragtime!* reached
London in 1912, and when the Palace Theatre
started a series of reviews in 1914 *The Passing Show*
many of the songs were American.[6]

Against the contemporary emphasis on lavish,
gargantuan productions the later nineteenth century saw the growth of the Theatre of Ideas, which
was based on the belief that the stage should not be a
fairyland, but that it should be involved with
current problems and questions. It should not offer
escape from those problems, but should participate
in the discussion about them, illustrate them, and
instruct audiences in the wrongs of contemporary
society. The theatre of entertainment had grown so
inflated that the inevitable reaction was a call for
serious theatre which taught. Of course this development took many years, and it was a question of
degrees; what was regarded as serious theatre in the
1860s would be regarded in the 1880s as not being
serious enough. While a Mme Vestris box set was
considered the height of realism in its day, by the end

of the century the avant-garde were saying there should not be any scenery at all. The definition of seriousness was altered throughout the period.

In the 1860s Squire Bancroft and his wife Marie converted an old, unfashionable theatre into the Prince of Wales's Theatre, which they opened on 15 April 1865, and where they mounted what they considered were the most serious productions then:

... we happened to be the persons who brought it into fashion, as it were, as to secure general imitation or adoption, and that care in little things which has since become almost universal; for it was at the old Prince of Wales's Theatre that the example was set of putting every piece on the stage in a realistic way – our stage-rooms became, in fact, such sumptuous apartments that I remember Sir William Fergusson once saying that 'the only drawback to visiting our theatre was that it disgusted him with his own home.'[7]

The playwright involved with the Bancrofts was Thomas William Robertson who supplied them with several serious drawing-room plays. The critic William Archer said that Robertson's true originality 'lay in his knack of placing everyday objects and incidents upon the stage. He dealt in "touches of things common" and enlarged the property list of serious comedy by such objects as milk-cans, tea-kettles and rolling pins.'[8] One can imagine Charles Kean's reaction to the appearance of a common kettle on his stage – replace that object with a flagon of wine in burnished gold, glittering with semi-precious gems! It was with good reason that Robertson's works became known as cup-and-saucer comedies, and they replaced formal wit with easy-going speech straight off the street. In the long run this was not such a good idea for nothing goes out of date so quickly as slang, and a modern audience would laugh at expressions which Robertson intended to be serious. Thus there is a problem in being absolutely true-to-life on the stage, and a more literary dialogue lasts better. In his day however the approach was considered very effective. Robertson's son quoted a critic as saying:

Mr. Robertson stands pre-eminent as the dramatist of this generation. The scene-painter, the carpenter, and the *costumier*, no longer usurp the place of the author and actor. With the aid of only two simple scenes – a boudoir in Mayfair and a humble lodging in Lambeth – Mr. Robertson has succeeded in concentrating an accumulation of incident and satire more interesting and more poignant than might be found in all the sensational dramas of the last half century. The secret of his success is – truth![9]

The play concerned here was *Caste* which the Bancrofts produced in 1867. The contemporary question Robertson examined was class distinction, and the plot concerns a dancer who marries an officer from the aristocracy, and thus moves from Lambeth to Mayfair. The husband is summoned to join his regiment in India, and as his family refuses to recognize or support his wife in his absence she is obliged to retreat to Lambeth with her baby. It works out all right in the end for the officer comes home and the officer's family recognizes his child. Such a production placed few demands on the wardrobe, for everything was 1867. In Act I the heroine's wardrobe would be humble, a shawl, a bonnet and a modest crinoline; in the Mayfair setting she could wear an elegant gown, and for the final scene she would be back in humble clothes again. The hero required a gentleman's outfit to begin with, and then had to change into his regimentals. In *Ours* of 1866 Robertson tackled the Crimean War, but it is extremely unlikely that the cast wore the clothes of 1854–6, for by 1866 these were regarded as decidedly dowdy; they were *démodé* and despised; the ladies would all have worn the flat-fronted crinoline of 1866, not the circular one of the preceding decade. The men's uniforms being a fairly frozen style might be much the same as those of the Crimean period, but their hairstyles and moustaches would show the difference for the mutton chops of the 1850s were being replaced by clean-shaven faces in the 1860s, which looked more youthful, so the young male actors would stick to that rather than age themselves with whiskers. The play began at a country seat in England, where everyone would be wearing elegant attire, and subsequently moves to the Crimea and military huts, where a degree of soiling and wear-and-tear would have to be introduced into the clothes to denote the difficult conditions. The setting for *M.P.* (1870) was among the gentry, so it called for smart contemporary clothes for both sexes, and nothing sensational. Robertson, like a surprising number of playwrights, did not have a clear picture in his mind of exactly what his characters should look like, so his costume directions are few, and the class of the characters is the best clue for the costume designers.

Only slowly did it occur to the playwrights of the Theatre of Ideas that they should be precise in their stage directions regarding the characters. If plays were to be about social problems, then the identity of the characters was very important, for they were supposed to be individuals, not simply conventional heroes or heroines mouthing melodramatic exclamations. Therefore the character's appearance was important too, and if the playwright did not want glamour to be used, then he had to be very clear in his mind as to the precise details of the dress for the characters he was creating. Clothes can say a great deal to an audience. Firstly they identify the wearer's social group, and his or her status in society. Secondly they show if the character has a conventional personality or is given to bold displays of his individuality as he conceives it, for clothes illustrate a state of mind. A suit which was once fine but which has become soiled and worn will indicate that the wearer has undergone a fall in social standing, and conversely a poor character who bursts into finery by the end of the play has obviously improved his cirumstances. Immorality can be seen at one glance if a male and female character are revealed in undress, such as negligées, dressing gowns, smoking jackets or shifts. Lurid clothes betray the vulgar character, while restrained taste defines the lady and gentleman. The cut of a suit declares if the wearer is a clerk or a marquess, the quality of the cloth or silk will say if the lady has a Paris original or is attired in a department store copy. Clothes convey a score of messages, but playwrights only discovered this very gradually, for all their declarations of serious content.

While the Norwegian playwright Henrik Ibsen is highly regarded for his exposures of small town life, and his symbolism, he did not direct what his characters should look like. Thus the designer has to guess that the period of the play is the date when it was written, and that the cast should be dressed according to the suggestion of class given in the setting. *A Doll's House* (1878–9) is set in a flat in Christiana, which suggests middle-class dress of that date with perhaps a touch of Norwegian local colour. *The Pillars of Society* (1875–7) is set in a consul's house in a small coastal town, which again suggests middle class dress but Ibsen does not say so. *Rosmersholm* (1885–6) takes place in an old manor house belonging to a retired minister of the church, so one can assume sober dress, but with Ibsen intelligent guesswork must supply what he fails to define. In Sweden August Strindberg gave more thought to the costume of characters than did Ibsen, but it was not significant. His most famous play is probably *Miss Julie* (1888). In Scene I it is stated that the cook Kurstin has a light cotton dress and a kitchen apron, and the valet Jean wears livery. There is a ballet performed by farm folk in holiday dress with flowers in their hats; but when the heroine Countess Julie enters there is no description of her appearance. As it is midsummer and festivities are taking place, some form of party dress would seem appropriate but Strindberg does not specify whether she is wearing a couture gown, Swedish national dress, or simple evening outfit. As the play develops the cook dons her church clothes; and where it is vital to show that the countess intends to leave, Strindberg indicates that she wears travelling dress, but that is his only indication for this important character, as if he had no clear picture in his mind what she looked like. Similarly in *The Father*, Strindberg's only dress direction is that some army coats are hanging in the cavalry captain's sitting room, one of which is put on the captain after his mind gives way and he has to be strapped into a strait-jacket. As for the period of the play and the family's taste in clothes, nothing is said. An exception to this general approach was his play *The Advent* written in 1899 but set in the 1820s; here Strindberg did give directions to suggest historical garments. The Deemster had 'yellow knee-breeches, blue swallow-tail coat, green hat, etc. The wife has a scarf over her head, a stick, glasses, and a snuff-box.' When shadowy figures emerge from a tomb only the leading one is described, The Other: 'He is very thin and moth-eaten; scant, parted, snuff-brown hair; thin beard, outgrown and worn clothes, without linen, a red woollen scarf wound around his neck'.[10] Here the historical setting forced Strindberg to be more specific, but the occurrence of such directions is irregular.

In Russia Anton Chekhov concerned himself with the *ennui* of provincial society. He was opposed to the melodramatic grand manner of acting to be found in Russian Imperial state theatres and in the rest of Europe, and wanted a much more sensitive, restrained portrayal of the impermanence of life. His first serious plays failed because the actors could not alter their acting style, and it took a new theatre, the Moscow Art Theatre, to evolve a more delicate approach, impressionistic rather than grandiose, which could do Chekhov justice. Like Strindberg he approached costume slowly. *The Seagull* of 1896, set on a country estate, does not state how all the characters should be dressed, and the most important comment on dress is actually given to one of the characters to speak in Act II:

ARKADINA: And then I keep myself as correct-looking as an Englishman. I am always well-groomed, as the saying is, and carefully dressed, with my hair neatly arranged. Do you think I should ever permit myself to leave the house half-dressed, with untidy hair.

This indicates that she maintains metropolitan standards even in the country. In *The Three Sisters* (1901) Chekhov was more or less obliged to indicate some difference between the girls:

Olga, in the regulation blue dress of a teacher at a girls' high school, is walking about correcting exercise books; Masha, in a black dress, with a hat on her knees, sits and reads a book; Irina, in white, stands about, with a thoughtful expression.

but apart from a reminder in Act III that Masha always wears black, and the direction that Natalia

Ivanovna should have a pink dress with a green sash, the only other directions state that the officers should be either in civilian dress or military uniform. In his last play Chekhov at last began to show an awareness of character in dress to a greater degree. *The Cherry Orchard* (1904) was set on another country estate. The character Epikhodov is distinguished by a short jacket and brilliantly polished but squeaky boots, which suggest the awkward man. The old servant Fiers is suitably attired in an old-fashioned livery and tall hat. The ladies Lubov Andreyovna, Anya and Charlotta Ivanovna arrive in travelling clothes, while the adopted daughter is less elegant in a long coat and a kerchief on her head. When Charlotta Ivanovna changes into indoor dress it is a white gown, tightly laced, with a lorgnette hanging at her waist, suggesting something formal about her character. The landowner Simeonov-Pischin wears a long jacket of thin cloth and loose trousers, which make it perfectly clear that he is no man-about-town. Such details all point to the character's nature before he or she says a word, and it is sad that the master of impressionist theatre should discover the impression of clothes only late in life.[11]

It was playwrights in the British Isles who gave the greatest consideration to the appearance of characters in problem plays. After ten years as an actor, when he no doubt learned much about make-up and a character's looks, Arthur Wing Pinero turned author for the stage in 1877. In *The Profligate*, which opened the new Garrick Theatre on 24 April 1889, he tackled an unpleasant subject, marital infidelity, which the commercial theatre avoided. The critics' reaction was that here was a real play at last, which moved the audience and sent them home to ponder, discuss and debate the problem; this was what the serious theatre movement wanted. Pinero defined the characters as follows: the good 'Hugh Murray, a pale, thoughtful, resolute-looking man, of about thirty, plainly dressed'. The rake Lord Dangers was 'a dissipated-looking man of about forty, dressed in the height of fashion.' The profligate himself Dunstan Renshaw was 'a handsome young man with a buoyant self-possessed manner, looking not more than thirty, but with signs of dissolute life in his face; his clothes are fashionable and suggest the bridegroom'. His unfortunate future spouse Leslie Brundenell was 'a sweet looking girl, tastefully but simply dressed.' While the profligate is exposed by the end of the play, it ends with Leslie's decision to forgive him by being his wife not his judge. What Pinero did not examine was the financial status of a wife, for husbands then controlled all the money in the family, including any which the wife brought with her, so for a wife to resolve to forgive an unfaithful husband and remain

with him was often due to economic force, not a question of choice. What Pinero did do was to be precise about the age of his leading characters, to indicate their past and its impact on their physiognomy, and to define the type of clothes of 1889 which should be worn. This was all more detailed than the directions given by Ibsen, Strindberg or Chekhov, and became a regular feature of play texts for the serious theatre in London.

In *The Second Mrs Tanqueray* produced at St James's Theatre on 27 May 1893 Pinero considered the woman with a past. He is precise about the age of his characters, as in Act I; Aubrey Tanqueray is 42, 'handsome, winning in his manner', Frank Mesquith QC MP is 47, 'genial and portly', Gordon Jayne MD is *c* 49, 'soft-speaking and precise, in appearance a type of the prosperous town physician'. The woman herself arrives after the men have left, at 11 p.m. a most shocking hour to call on a widower, in 1893, without a chaperone, showing that she is somewhat unconventional. Paula is described as 'a young woman of about twenty-seven; beautiful, fresh, innocent looking. She is in superb evening dress.' As the play is contemporary Pinero is not obliged to go into great detail as to what evening dress consists of, as this was well known at the time. However he has to specify that much to illustrate the class and manners of the cast. As a lady of 1893 Paula has an evening cloak as well, and wears a flower on her bodice, which Aubrey Tanqueray transfers to his buttonhole, a gesture of intimacy. Act II finds them married, although Tanqueray's daughter by his first wife does not like it. She is a grave girl of about 19, 'dressed simply for walking', while Paula is attired for more expensive pursuits dressed for riding with coat and hat. In Act III Paula is entertaining Lady Orreyed, 'a pretty, affected doll of a woman, with a mincing voice and flaxen hair' and Sir George Orreyed *c* 35, 'with a low forehead, receding, chin and a vacuous expression, with an ominous redness about the nose', which sums that couple up most precisely. Both Paula and Lady Orreyed are in 'sumptuous dinner gowns' which suggests velvet, trimmed with lace, or satin covered with chiffon, embroidered with silk, sequins, and diamenté beads which typified rich dinner gowns at this period, the best examples of which came from Maison Worth in Paris.[12] This elegant life-style is shattered for Paula, when a man with whom she has had a previous relationship arrives at the house, as a friend of the step-daughter, which causes her to commit suicide.

The opposite side of the coin is seen in Pinero's *The Gay Lord Quex* (1899), where the man with a past gets away with it because he has a title, and is a 'gentleman' where the working-class woman Sophy who tries to expose his character is defeated. The editor described it as a comedy of manners where the gentleman remains a gentleman and the good-intentioned working-class woman will always be vulgar.[13] It would be better described as an exposure of the blatant hypocrisy of the upper class, loyal to itself first, before any loyalty to principles or country. Sophy's fiancé Frank Pollit, a palmist, is given a touch of the vulgar, a 'well, if rather showily dressed, young fellow, wearing a frock coat, white waistcoat, and patent-leather boots. He is handsome in a commonplace way.' The patent-leather boots give him away, for a gentleman would have a man-servant to polish his boots daily to a brilliant gloss. The lord of course is impeccable in attire, Lord Quex being 48, 'faultless in dress, in manner debonair and charming.' Of course his smart appearance in frock coat, subdued waistcoat, and burnished top hat, is not the result of his own efforts, but the combined achievement of hair-dresser, tailor, hatter, shoemaker, glover, umbrella maker, shirtmaker, cravat maker, button-hole creator, jeweller, and valet. Clothes declare a person's status, and those of Lord Quex state that he is rich enough to employ a small army of people to turn him out. Quex is engaged to Muriel Eden who is 'prettily dressed' while her mother is an 'ultra-fashionably dressed' woman with shrill and mannered ways, so that Muriel should be in fairly simple day clothes, but Mrs Eden would be overladen with flowers, feather stoles, quantities of lace frothing over her front, and layers of rustling petticoats. Act II presents the Duchess of Strood with whom Quex has had an adulterous affaire, 'a daintily beautiful doll, of about seven-and-thirty, – a poseuse'. Frank Pollit reappears, his lack of taste being illustrated by a tall hat and lemon-coloured gloves. In the duchess's boudoir in Act III Mrs Eden wears a smart dressing jacket, and the duchess changes from her frock into a teagown. Sophy has got into the house as an acting maid, and the duchess gives her a mandarin's robe to use as a dressing gown when doing her hair. It was the established system for mistresses to pass clothes on to the servants, as a right not a favour. While Sophy finds out about Lord Quex and the Duchess of Strood's affair, he outwits her, and his marriage to Muriel Eden goes ahead. Truth is defeated, sins are covered over, and Lord Quex does not commit suicide because his reputation is in danger, unlike Paula Tanqueray. To be found out, not the commission of illegal acts, was regarded as the major mistake among the aristocracy. Mrs Tanqueray was not unfaithful to her husband, her previous relationship lay in the past, but society expected her to die as the only way out of a moral dilemma; Lord Quex, however, being male is allowed to conceal his past. The double standard is obvious.

Perhaps the play which examined clothing psychology most closely was the one which Pinero regarded as his favourite. *The Notorious Mrs Ebbsmith* of 1895, was written, he said, to show that free love will always end in failure. Set in Venice it concerns Lucas, a 'handsome, intellectual looking young man of about twenty eight', who has left his frigid wife to live with the nurse who brought him back to health, Agnes, who was played by Mrs Patrick Campbell. She is presented as a very placid woman: 'Her dress is plain to verge of coarseness'. The affair does not end because love runs out, but because Lucas is the nephew of a duke and his relations bribe and pressurize him to return to his wife. Agnes regards herself as a serious woman, and she and Lucas subscribe to reformist views on marriage, so she considers that her appearance should be serious too. She is appalled when Lucas buys her a gown of silk and lace, but he wants her to look beautiful and to be noticed in society. The Duke of St Olpherts arrives and he tells Agnes that Lucas is not an intellectual but a shallow young man, an epicure, who will flutter from pleasure to pleasure, and does not deserve to be her idol. Agnes responds to this by donning the dress she had rejected. 'She enters, handsomely gowned, her throat and arms bare, the fashion of her hair roughly altered. She appears to be a beautiful woman.' It is as if she is trying to be the woman the epicure would want, and demands to be taken out, looking like the scarlet woman the duke expects her to be. In Act III the duke returns in evening dress and cloak with the family proposition. Lucas should live with his wife, in different parts of the house, so as to maintain the appearance of a successful marriage, and his love Agnes can take up residence discreetly in a suburban villa where he may visit her unofficially. No public relationship between them is allowed, so that Lucas can resume his hope of an official career. This is the family bribe to Lucas; it will help his public advance, if he lives a social lie. Love was not necessarily considered important in a class of arranged marriages and restricted choice. Lucas must seem to be married to a woman of his own social group, whom he can exhibit at ducal receptions, and the fact that he loves a woman of lower rank must be concealed. Lucas accepts that arrangement, Agnes finds it dishonest. When the wife Sybil turns up in Act IV 'beautifully gowned and heavily veiled', Agnes reverts to her severe, serious style 'a rusty, ill-fitting, black stuff dress; her hair is tightly drawn from her brows'. It is her way of showing that she is not what they think. The ducal family wins, Lucas conforms to their lying approach, and a scandalous divorce and an open relationship are avoided.

Here costume is being used very clearly to declare

Top of fur cap.

(Bulgarian Staff Officer)

85 George Bernard Shaw, study of a Bulgarian staff officer's uniform, 1894. VICTORIA AND ALBERT MUSEUM

Shaw did a lot of research into things Bulgarian for the first production of his comedy *Arms and the Man* at the Avenue Theatre in 1894, including drawings of Bulgarian dress and uniforms. He has noted the silver braid and white facings, the seams in the jacket, the type of boot and the top of the fur cap. He was most concerned in matters of costuming.

a person's attitude and conception of herself, with Agnes considering herself the worthy companion of an intelligent young man of advanced ideals, and not a mistress attired in silk and lace, like a doll, pretty to look at but artificial, a painted surface with nothing underneath. To Agnes a glamorous exterior is incompatible with a serious mind, which illustrates the insecurity of her position; she takes an extreme view, for she has not had a proper education and therefore is very concerned to look the part of a serious woman, whereas the woman who had had the benefit of an advanced education would not be afraid to look elegant, having already proved her qualifications. Pinero was justified in being so fond of this play, for it examined Agnes very fully. Her intentions were good, but she was defeated by the dishonest aristocrats she encountered. Pinero was a pioneer in the understanding of the relationship between the look of his characters and their natures.

There is no doubt that the serious playwright who gave most attention to clothes, fabrics, colours, decorations, and character in its visual composition, was George Bernard Shaw. Like many an Irishman before him he had to come to London to find openings for his abilities, and after working as an unsuccessful novelist and then a journalist, saw his first play being produced at the Royalty Theatre in 1892, *Widowers' Houses*. Shaw saw the theatre as a vehicle for the expression of his ideas for social and political reform, and he appreciated that it was important to describe as fully as he could those characters he intended should convey those ideas. Accordingly in *Widowers' Houses* he gave a very full description of the new turn-out of flashy character Lickcheese:

The change in his appearance is dazzling. He is in evening dress, with an overcoat lined throughout with furs presenting all the hues of the tiger. His shirt is fastened at the breast with a single diamond stud. His silk hat is the glossiest black; a handsome gold watch-chain hangs like a garland on his filled-out waistcoat; he has shaved his whiskers and grown a moustache, the ends of which are waxed and pointed. As Sartorius stares speechless at him, he stands, smiling, to be admired, intensely enjoying the effect he is producing.

This tells us everything, and no actor or producer could wish for a better definition of the character, for Shaw describes his looks, his mood, his vanity, while the tigerish hues of the furs indicate a decidedly treacherous aspect. For the designer this was a god-send. There is no doubt whatsoever about what Shaw wanted. He really thought his characters out, considering what made them tick, what they meant in society, and how far their appearance conveyed their natures. He knew that the look and the man are one.

Shaw's next play was *The Philanderer* of 1893 where he conceived that man as a suavely artistic Bohemian:

Leonard Charteris . . . is unconventionally but smartly dressed in a velvet jacket and cashmere trousers. His collar, dyed Wotan blue, is part of his shirt, and turns over a garnet coloured scarf of Indian silk, secured by a turquoise ring. He wears blue socks and leather sandals. The arrangement of his tawny hair, and of his moustaches and short beard, is apparently left to Nature; but he has taken care that Nature shall do him fullest justice.

What a perfect picture this is. The philanderer's tastes and his infatuation with himself are visible the moment the curtain rises on Act I. In pursuing women the philanderer is not making love to them but to himself, but in Act II there enters the New Woman. This was the 1890s term for the serious young woman who was now maintaining that women could follow intellectual subjects, read Ibsen, and undertake athletic pursuits, just as well as the men. Shaw presents her in her club:

She is a pretty girl of eighteen, small and trim, wearing a mountaineering suit of Norfolk jacket and breeches with neat town stockings and shoes. A detachable cloth skirt lies ready to her hand.

This observation is most acute. The New Woman might wear manly tweeds and breeches indoors, but for going outdoors the skirt would have to be put on for the street, for no woman could walk about in breeches in Mayfair. The period was beginning to see the introduction of cycling bloomers, but this was a sporting outfit so it was still improper wear for the centre of town. Shaw was fully aware of the distinction. His great awareness of clothes was part of his interest in reform, for he disliked tight-lacing and restrictive garments, and was an ardent supporter of Dr Jaeger's sanitary woollen clothing in undyed cloth. The Healthy and Artistic Dress Union, founded in 1893, was campaigning for reformed clothing, the end of corsets, the abolition of trousers, and the wearing of wool, and Shaw subscribed to such views. He himself took to wearing kneebreeches in natural wool in both town and country – Dr Jaeger had ruled that trousers were unhealthy as they made the abdomen too warm and the legs too cold, wherefore kneebreeches and stockings would allow for a better distribution of the blood.[14] It was largely Shaw's involvement with this movement which made

him so conscious of clothes onstage and off, and he surpassed other contemporary playwrights in this area.

Shaw set *Arms and the Man* (1894) in Bulgaria; it was not just any period in Bulgaria, but 6 March 1886, and such was his determination to be precise that he descended on a Bulgarian admiral to get detailed information on Bulgarian costume and scenery. William Archer recorded that Shaw was a fanatic for precision.[15] The manservant Nicola is presented in Act II as a proper Bulgarian:

He wears a white Bulgarian costume: jacket with embroidered border, sash, wide knicker bockers, and decorated gaiters. His head is shaved up to the crown, giving him a high Japanese forehead.

The lady of the house Mrs Petkoff looks like a splendid mountain farmer's wife but wishes to appear like a Viennese lady, that city being the nearest centre of fashion for a Bulgarian, so she wears modish teagowns on all occasions. These were the concoctions of lace, silk or chiffon which elegant ladies in high society donned in the afternoon as a relaxation before changing into formal dinner gowns, and they had evolved from the boudoir negligée. Strictly speaking they should only be worn around tea-time, but Mrs Petkoff was being provincial in her misunderstanding of the social rules. Shaw did not specify the heroine's wardrobe in this instance although he wanted it to look 1886, which would have meant a square bustle on a young lady's day gowns.

Another example of Shaw's sensitivity to costume comes in *Man and Superman* of 1901–3. Act I introduces Roebuck Ramsden, a chairman, and alderman, who should be dressed in a highly respectable manner. He possesses four tufts of iron-grey hair, and is attired in a formal black frock coat, a white waistcoat as it is spring, and trousers of that blue-black hue at which the British excel. Ramsden has not yet finished dressing as he is wearing his slippers, but his boots stand ready nearby. The waistcoat is a nice detail, for in the days when professional men always wore dark suits in the city, the only touch of individual frivolity they permitted themselves lay in the cravat and the waistcoat. In the winter months these had to be in sober tones, but come the spring an outburst of restrained colour was allowed, such as white, or cream, or beige. Of course on holiday or when in the country men would wear flannels or tweeds, but in 1901 the rule was very definite – no country clothes in town. The big exception was Shaw himself striding about in his reformed clothes, but Shaw, like that other advocate of kneebreeches Oscar Wilde, was considered to belong to the eccentric fringe, artists you know, not gentlemen. Some considered Shaw a dangerous subversive, for his plays covered such unmentionable subjects as slum landlords, medical morality, prostitution, health, and religion, but Shaw was determined that such subjects should be aired. *Pygamalion* of 1912 was subversive in the sense that it shows that a flower girl can be turned into a lady, but as performed by Sir Herbert Beerbohm Tree as Higgins and Mrs Patrick Campbell as Eliza Doolittle, it was Shaw's first big commercial success. The definition of Eliza was most important for her appearance said everything about her condition. She is discovered selling flowers outside Covent Garden Opera House, a girl aged 18–20.

She wears a little sailor hat of black straw that has long been exposed to the dust and soot of London and has seldom if ever been brushed. Her hair needs washing rather badly: its mousy colour can hardly be natural. She wears a shoddy black coat that reaches nearly to her knees and is shaped to her waist. She has a brown skirt with a coarse apron. Her boots are much the worse for wear. She is no doubt as clean as she can afford to be, but compared to the ladies she is very dirty.

There is the complete picture. One knows before Eliza opens her mouth that she does not have a beautiful accent, and her clothes state her status in society instantly.

Higgins, aged about 40, is immediately identifiable as a superior being. Act II finds him at home:

. . . dressed in a professional-looking black frock-coat, with a white linen collar and black silk tie. He is of the energetic, scientific, type.

With him no more detail is required, for his class will determine how he parts his hair, how much shirt cuff is showing, and the presence of a tie pin, for his appearance is a stock, conventional type for that period. Eliza's transmogrification into a *dame d'élégance* can be seen in Act IV:

Eliza opens the door and is seen on the lighted landing in opera cloak, brilliant evening dress, and diamonds, with fan, flowers, and all accessories.

There cannot be many other accessories as Shaw has given the principal ones, but she would have evening gloves, her dance card and pencil, perhaps an evening reticule, and at this date some sort of bandeau in her hair, while her gown ought to have a train. The splendour is an instant statement of Eliza's elevation. A change of clothes is sufficient to advertise a change of status, from second-hand remnants into a couture gown. No vocal proclamation is necessary, a visual alteration can say all.

Shaw did not trouble himself to provide many descriptions in *Saint Joan* (1924). He does however make Joan's wearing of men's clothes clear, which in her lifetime was considered a sin by the Catholic Church. In Scene 2 she enters the French court 'dressed as a soldier, with her hair bobbed and hanging thickly round her face'. The court laughs at her hair, and Joan retorts, 'I wear it like this because I am a soldier.' She is still in male dress for the trial scene at Rouen, wearing a black page's suit, with chains round her ankles. That was the most important costume matter in the play, so Shaw put it in, but he left the prelates, and the soldiers to look after themselves.

The importance Shaw gave to full descriptions of his characters made a deep impression on a contemporary playwright who was not a part of the Theatre of Ideas, but whose comedies were most successful, Oscar Wilde. In *Lady Windermere's Fan* (1892), and *A Woman of No Importance* (1893), he did not give detailed information on what the cast should look like, but after reading Shaw's *Widowers' Houses* twice, he was so impressed by the flesh and blood which Shaw's descriptions gave to the characters, the sense of an actual presence, that he resolved to do the same in his own plays. This can be seen best in *An Ideal Husband* (1895) where Wilde describes the wicked Mrs Cheveley in full, her make-up and clothes:

. . . tall and rather slight. Lips very thin and highly-coloured, a line of scarlet on a pallid face. Venetian red hair, aquiline nose, and long throat. Rouge accentuates the natural paleness of her complexion. Grey-green eyes that move restlessly. She is in heliotrope, with diamonds. She looks rather like an orchid, and makes great demands on one's curiosity. In all her movements she is extremely graceful. A work of

---

86   Mrs Patrick Campbell as Eliza Doolittle in Shaw's *Pygmalion*, His Majesty's Theatre, 1914. Photograph by Burfort.   VICTORIA AND ALBERT MUSEUM

Shaw directed that Eliza should have a shoddy coat, Mrs Patrick Campbell has begged to differ with a shawl. There is often a battle of wills between actor, author and designer over costume, and Shaw's brilliant definitions of his characters were not always obeyed to the letter. A production is a compromise between wills and so is the costume between ideals, practice, and personal likes and dislikes. It was usual for an actress aged 49 to play a girl of 18, and was regarded as part of her skill. Teenagers had not been invented – the young should know their place.

art, on the whole, but showing the influence of too many schools. (*Act I*)

Exotic, decadent, and dangerous, Mrs Cheveley is next compared to a snake when she changes into another artistic creation:

. . . Lamia-like, she is green and silver. She has a cloak of black satin, lined with dead rose-leaf silk. (*Act III*)

This character's appearance evidently fascinated Wilde, but he did not show such delight in his heroine. Lady Chiltern is described simply as 'a woman of grave Greek beauty, about twenty-seven years of age'. As she is the hostess at a reception which opens the play, she would be in evening dress, as would her husband Sir Robert. 'A man of forty, but looking somewhat younger. Clean-shaven, with finely-cut features, dark-haired and dark-eyed.' Wilde concentrates on the baronet's personality which he sees as being divided into two main streams, the passion and the intellect. His manner is that 'of perfect distinction, with a slight touch of pride', and his head is such that Van Dyck would have liked to paint it. His sister Mabel is described as 'a perfect example of the English type of prettiness, the apple-blossom type. She has all the fragrance and freedom of a flower'.

Several characters in the play get a description. Mrs Marchmont and Lady Basildon have an 'exquisite fragility' that would appeal to Watteau. Lady Markby is 'a pleasant, kindly, popular woman, with grey hair à la marquise and good lace'. The attaché the Vicomte de Nanjac is 'known for his neckties'. Wilde was much more interested in art than Shaw, so the name of yet another painter appears as the cast assembles in Act I:

Love Caversham, an old gentleman of seventy, wearing the riband and star of the Garter. A fine Whig type. Rather like a portrait by Lawrence.

His son is Lord Goring.

Thirty-four, but always says he is younger. A well-bred, expressionless face. He is clever, but would not like to be thought so. A flawless dandy.

This is a character who would like it to be thought that his appearance matters more to him than his contents. Wilde was very fond of showing up the British aristocracy for its concentration on non-intellectual pursuits like huntin', shootin' and fishin', which was no way to survive in an increasingly industrial world, so the period saw several peers in desperate search of American millionairesses or the daughters of wealthy grocers or butchers, when it would have been more sensible to

send the son and heir to learn about business.

Lord Goring is the best dressed man in the play. Act II finds him in day clothes 'dressed in the height of fashion', which means a suit, gloves, cane, boots, and hat. In Act III he is back in evening dress and goes on to discuss his concept of fashion with his butler Phipps.

Enter Lord Goring in evening dress with a buttonhole. He is wearing a silk hat and Inverness cape. White-gloved, he carries a Louis Seize cane. His are all the delicate fopperies of Fashion. [His lordship feels however that his appearance needs a boost.]

LORD GORING: Got a second buttonhole for me, Phipps?
PHIPPS: Yes, my lord.
(Takes his hat, cane, and cape, and presents a new buttonhole on salver.)
LORD GORING: Rather distinguished thing, Phipps. I am the only person of the smallest importance in London at present who wears a buttonhole.
PHIPPS: Yes, my lord. I have observed that.
LORD GORING: (taking out old buttonhole) You see, Phipps, Fashion is what one wears oneself. What is unfashionable is what other people wear.

If it seems strange that Wilde should give most male fashion interest to the second male lead, instead of to the hero Sir Robert Chiltern, it is because Sir Robert's main concern in the play is Mrs Cheveley's attempt to blackmail him, so that for him to display a fondness for taste would detract from the dramatic importance of his principal worry. What is clear however is Wilde's own interest in dress. He had been editor of the ladies' magazine *The Woman's World*, and a member of the Rational Dress Society, founded in 1881, when he had argued that Greek dress was best for women, and cavalier knee-breeches and doublets best for men. Such was his advocacy of dress reform that it is odd that it should not occur to him to put this passion into his plays until after he had read Shaw. What a comedy Wilde could have written about the Aesthetic Dress movement! Perhaps he could not laugh at himself.

There are several references to evening cloaks in Act III as both Lord Caversham and Mrs Cheveley arrive in them, but Wilde is not so interested in the other ladies so much as he is in his villainess. Thus Lady Chiltern is only given 'Enter . . . in walking dress', while Mabel Chiltern enters 'in the most ravishing frock', in Act II, which lacks any suggestion about her particular taste in frocks. Given her floral nature she might well be dressed in something aesthetic and loose, for ladies of the Aesthetic Dress movement loved to bedeck themselves in delicate blooms after the manner of the Pre-Raphaelite school: perhaps as a baronet's sister she is afraid to seem too avant garde in taste.[16] The play terminates with a strong echo of the finale of Pinero's *The Profligate* when Lord Goring tells Lady Chiltern:

Women are not meant to judge us, but to forgive us when we need forgiveness. Pardon, not punishment, is their mission.

There is no question of a divorce because Sir Robert has fallen in his wife's eyes, but a retreat by the wife so that the husband may keep his public pride. In a male-dominated society what mattered most to males was not the respect of women, because women were inferior beings, but the good opinion of other men; the club before the home, the team before the couple.

An Ideal Husband contains Wilde's greatest concentration of character and costume in his plays, for the succeeding work is not so precise. *The Importance of Being Earnest* (1895) has in Act II the direction that Jack shall enter 'dressed in deepest mourning, with crêpe hatband and black gloves' as this is an important fact, a departure from the normal, but nothing is said about the rest of the cast for it is assumed by Wilde that they are normal in their appearance, and representatives of polite society in 1895. Not until Act III is it made clear that the ward Cecily is not so well groomed as the rest of the cast:

LADY BRACKNELL: . . . Come over here, dear. (Cecily goes across.) Pretty child! your dress is sadly simple, and your hair seems almost as Nature might have left it. But we can soon alter all that.

It would have been more helpful if this description of rustic simplicity had been located at Cecily's first entrance in Act II so that producer, actress and reader could have pictured her then.

In Wilde's most exotic play, *Salomé*, where a description of dress in ancient Judaea in the reign of Herod Antipas would be most helpful to designer and producer alike, Wilde evades the subject. He may have thought it too difficult to tackle, but in view of his contacts in the worlds of art and costume he could have found someone to advise him, like Alma-Tadema. Because of its subject matter the play was banned in England as diseased and unhealthy but Sarah Bernhardt performed it in Paris in 1894, and it received a London production in 1905, after attitudes had modified. It was in fact written at about the time when Wilde was becoming aware of Shaw's definition of his characters, and he could have revised *Salomé* as an ideal vehicle for descriptions of costume and nature; but he chose to try Shaw's approach in a new play. Such costume details as *Salomé* contains are more in the spoken words, as part of the poetry, than in the stage directions:[17]

THE CAPPADOCIAN: Is that the Queen Herodias, she who wears a black mitre sewn with pearls, and whose hair is powdered with blue dust?

The appearance of the Prophet Jokanaan is given in the speech of the 1st Soldier: 'He was clothed in camel's hair, and round his loins he had a leathern belt. He was very terrible to look upon.' The text contains descriptions of the rich attire of Greeks, Egyptians and Assyrians, but they do not appear on the stage as members of the cast. Salomé herself carries a fan, but for all her stepfather's preoccupation with her looks, nothing is stated about her attire. When she comes to the famous dance of the seven veils, the veils are brought on by slaves, so she is not wearing them to start with. She does remove her sandals at this point, but that is the only direction. Herod himself has a mantle, later termed a cloak, and is crowned by a garland of roses as he is entertaining, which suggests rose garlands for all the guests too. That is all. From the repeated references to Herod's wealth it follows that his family should be dressed with rich splendour, but it is left to the designer to decide what form this should take.

Salomé offended the censor by its sensuality, Salomé kissing the head of the decapitated Jokanaan, which made this play Wilde's closest to the Theatre of Ideas. It dealt with one of the taboo subjects of the period, sex. In Britain the Lord Chamberlain controlled what could appear on the stage, and banned profanity, improper language, indecency in dress, dancing or gestures, insulting representations of living persons and anything which might cause a breach of the peace or a riot.[18] In addition to the legal position, many theatre managers refused to produce problem plays because they considered them uncommercial. The masses went to the theatre for entertainment and spectacle, they argued, so only a handful of intellectuals would be interested in plays about sordid subjects or social wrongs. Strindberg's dramas about abnormal psychology for example would not draw the crowds in Sweden, so he founded his own little playhouse, the Intima Teatern, in 1907 as the only means to seeing his own works produced; the commercial theatre would not touch them. Such action independent of existing companies and managers was followed by other members of the Theatre of Ideas. In France André Antoine founded his Théâtre Libre in 1887, where he produced Ibsen's *Ghosts*, and in 1897 took over an existing playhouse, renaming it the Théâtre Antoine, to perform non-commercial drama. E. Brieux's play *Les Avariés*, dealing with venereal disease, was banned in Paris, but Antoine allowed

Brieux to read it to an audience at his theatre in 1901, as part of his policy of helping new playwrights, and as a gesture against censorship. His example inspired Otto Brahm to found the Freie Bühne in Germany as a free theatre society, with no permanent building of its own, in order to present controversial works that would not get a hearing elsewhere, such as *Die Familie Selicke*, a picture of the sordid reality of lower middle class life and manners. These events in France and Germany convinced Jack Grein, a dramatic critic, that a similar free theatre should exist in London, so he founded his Independent Theatre in 1891. Bernard Shaw was an early member, for the society was his best hope of seeing one of his serious plays performed. It produced his *Widowers' Houses* in 1892, the first Shaw play to be staged, and in 1896 Ibsen's *Little Eyolf*, where some aesthetic costume was worn, denoting serious dress for a serious play. Actresses like Mrs Patrick Campbell, Janet Achurch and Elizabeth Robins were enthusiastic supporters of this movement, being hungry for plays which gave women an intelligent role to interpret. The Incorporated Stage Society was founded in 1899 by amateur sponsors to promote works of artistic merit which the commercial theatre ignored, and it took over from Grein's Independent Theatre. Its productions used West End theatres on Sundays, which was the only time they were free for private productions, and the society presented over 200 works before it ended at the outbreak of the Second World War in 1939. Shaw benefited here too, and his work about prostitution, *Mrs Warren's Profession*, was given by the Stage Society in 1902. The society could produce banned works because it was a private body playing before its members, and the general public was excluded from the performances. New York followed these developments with the formation of the Washington Square Players in 1914, to produce non-commercial drama, and in 1919 with the establishment of a society called the Theatre Guild, with a membership devoted to new and foreign works which would not be presented by Broadway.

A very different society was founded in London in 1894, William Poel's Elizabethan Stage Society, which was not concerned with new or controversial plays, but with the classics. As an actor-manager Poel was increasingly dissatisfied with the gargantuan productions of Shakespeare presented by Charles Kean and Irving, fearing that the poetry of the text was smothered by the glamour, the colour, the pomp, the crowds of extras, and the elaborate scene changes. Shakespeare had not used scenery at all. His works were first presented on a bare platform, when the actors had only two instruments to employ, the words and the costume, instead of a whole battery of technical tricks including gas, electricity and hydraulics. Beginning with *Twelfth Night* in 1895, Poel tried to get back to the simple staging common in Shakespeare's day, using Elizabethan or Jacobean costume, and not worrying whether *Macbeth* should be done in ancient Scottish, ancient Celtic, old Viking, or any form of antiquarian attire other than the costume common when Shakespeare wrote it, 1606. Here was a new approach to historical accuracy which did not concern itself with the period in which a play was set, but with the time when it was written. Poel was setting himself against a movement which dated back to Aaron Hill in 1731. His influence in simplifying productions of Shakespeare was to be immense, and Shakespeare with little or no scenery has become a regular feature of twentieth-century theatre. Unfortunately Poel's influence on costume has been less significant, for time and time again producers have done Shakespeare's *Antony and Cleopatra* on stage and on film not in Shakespearean dress, but in Roman and ancient Egyptian dress; this was historically wrong in any case because the Ptolemies were a Macedonian dynasty who did not dress in Egyptian clothes except on official occasions. Shakespeare's Cleopatra wore stays, and in order to be true to the text a modern production should wear the clothes of about 1607 with no more than a Jacobean conception of Mediterranean detail or Roman attire. The result would be a mixture of English and foreign, but that is what Shakespeare would have expected.

The question is, where should one place one's loyalty? Is it to the date of the play, to the historical period of the drama, or to a modern interpretation of the aims of the work? No doubt producers of Shakespeare will always debate these points, but when Shakespeare refers to doublets and stays in a Roman play, that should guide the presentation; otherwise ancient clothes alongside Jacobean references to dress will jar, and words and wardrobe will be out of harmony.

CHAPTER SEVEN

Cinematic Extravagance versus Streamlined Simplicity

During the First World War and again during the Depression one traditional aspect of the theatre remained important, which one might term the Theatre of Compensation. It was necessary in Britain and France, for example, to give troops home on leave from the trenches something to cheer them, to entertain them, and to take their minds off the horrors they had witnessed, and it was also essential to give the civilian population something to keep the national spirit up. The musical *Chu Chin Chow* was one production which met this requirement, providing enjoyable tunes, exotic settings, and escape into another age when shells and nerve gas were unknown. The operettas of Franz Lehar were also uplifting, the marches of Sir Edward Elgar stirred national pride, and dancing became an important release for nervous energy with jazzy importations from the USA and the highly sexed tango from Latin America. To the serious theatre reformer such things should not be, but in times of distress frivolity and spectacle can act as a safety valve.

The early silent cinema took over the late Romantic exotic, gigantic spectacular wholesale, together with the melodramatic grand manner of the theatre's acting style, and make-up.[1] A few attempts were made to capture great stars on film before they died. Sarah Bernhardt made a short film about the death of Queen Elizabeth I, but the French star made no attempt to look Elizabethan and instead of a drum farthingale wore a straight gown which unfortunately emphasized her far-from-slender proportions. The rest of the cast were topped by what were obviously cottonwool wigs. Bernhardt's acting consisted of stomping around and throwing her arms in the air, while at the moment of death she fell flat on her face on a pile of cushions. It took time for directors to realize that the flamboyance which looked superb from the back of the stalls in a playhouse would appear overblown and ridiculous when shown close-up and enlarged on a cinema screen, and the evolution of a quieter acting style took twenty years to reach perfection. Dame Nellie Melba was also filmed without sound in London; at the last moment it was decided to include a scene of her in *Lucia di Lammermoor*; so Nathan's received an urgent appeal for one hundred period costumes at Covent Garden Opera House first thing next morning. By now Nathan's wardrobe was big enough to cope with rush orders.

The early Italian cinema was responsible for the introduction of the cinematic epic. The size of a Beerbohm Tree production about Rome was here spread out and expanded even further, and a whole series of epics about ancient Rome was made: *The Fall of Troy* (1911), *The Last Days of Pompeii* (1913), *Quo Vadis* which was to be filmed several times (1913), *Julius Caesar* (1914), *Cabiria* (1912–14), *Hannibal* (1915), and *Mesalina* (1924). Renaissance scholars would have been delighted to see so much interest in Rome, although they would have criticized the sensationalism of the new medium. It says much for the strength of ancient Rome that it can still be revived thus two thousand years later. The glory of the past certainly appealed to Italian Fascists and they encouraged another Roman victory to be filmed, *Scipione L'Africano* (1937), which included Hannibal and his elephants crossing the Alps, Roman and Carthaginian battle fleets, and mighty sets. So much activity in Italy impressed the new American film industry at Hollywood, a site selected because of its reliable Californian sunshine. D. W. Griffiths directed *Intolerance* in 1916 and it had one section in the Italian manner but even bigger, with a cast set of ancient Babylon so large that it had to be filmed from a balloon, so that the cast looked like ants. Biblical history was involved in Roman epics and themes from Jewish history became a regular feature of Hollywood films. Cecil

87 Cinematic glamour. Claudette Colbert in *Zaza*, produced by Albert Lewin, Paramount Pictures, 1938. TV TIMES

Glamour is fashion imposed on all, so this story of the Parisian music hall in the 1890s presents the star as the glamorous ideal of 1938. The hairstyle, the make-up, the angle of the hat, the tulle shoulders, the slender gown, conform to contemporary stereotypes, not those of the 1890s. The film was a remake of a silent version which had starred Gloria Swanson. Hollywood put glamour before accuracy.

B. de Mille's *The Ten Commandments* appeared in 1923, and Austria produced one such in Michael Curtis's *Moon of Israel* (1924), which dealt with the flight of the Jews from Egypt. The principal criticism to be made of these epic features so far as the costuming is concerned is that the classical draped appearance was applied too widely. The difference between Babylonian, Assyrian, Egyptian and Roman dress was not underlined. There was little to distinguish D.W. Griffiths's Babylonian maidens from Roman ones. There was a haphazard approach to begin with, before the Romantic ideal of accurate reproduction became a dominant policy. Once that happened the cinematic publicity would put an emphasis on this point, maintaining as an additional selling point that vast amounts of research had been undertaken for the purposes of this filmatic masterpiece, just as Charles Kean had done in his day. Cecil B. de Mille made this claim a part of his publicity, along with the boast that this was also the biggest film ever made. The tradition of theatrical extravaganza found a safe home in the cinema; when the stage could no longer afford to indulge in such gargantuan productions, the film was able to keep the giant alive.

In France events from French history were taken up as suitable film material. *The Miracle of the Wolves* (1924) was set in the time of Louis XI, the fifteenth century, and where the theatre would have copied period buildings the film was able to use the actual châteaux and city walls surviving from that age. This was something the theatre could not do except in the imagination, to go to the actual spot where the action had actually, or might have, occurred. It was now possible to perform *Hamlet* at Elsinore, although the castle there is in fact much later than the period of the play. Perhaps the most famous French film dealing with national history was Abel Gance's *Napoleon* made in 1925–7 which ran straight into the problem of accurate costuming – Madame Fashion. Of course 1920s taste affected the faces, make-up and hairstyles, but the men's uniforms were reasonably accurate. The difficulty was the women, given that the 1925 definition of beauty in fact dictated how they should look. To be accurate, their dresses should have had the high classical waistlines of Napoleon's day, but in 1925 waists had descended to the hips. Any ideal of accuracy was abandoned at this stage. Faced with two waist levels which were at opposite extremes to each other, Gance compromised and gave the women something which was roughly halfway. It was not at the actual waist, but hung rather unhappily just below, loose, shapeless and laughable. It was neither one thing nor the other, and Gance would have done better to risk the genuine classical line or else stick to the 1925 level. Failure to

do so left the clothes nowhere. One of the best costumed films ever made in France came in the next decade, *La Kermesse Heroïque*. Needless to say the make-up and the actresses' plucked eyebrows shouted that this was a work of the 1930s, but the clothes were well researched and beautifully made. Given that a perfect recreation of the past is not humanly possible, these costumes went some way towards that unobtainable ideal. Not only did they look seventeenth century but they looked smart too, which not every production is able to achieve with its historical reconstructions. The predominant tones for clothes in the seventeenth century among the bourgeoisie were black and white, so in the medium of black and white film the result looked very crisp. Lazare Meerson was the art director responsible for the overall look.

The cinema took over the theatre's variety of subject matter too. In 1924 Fritz Lang in Germany made *Siegfried*, based on the national legends employed by Wagner's operas, with a very big dragon for the hero to kill. The clothes still reflected the Art Nouveau movement as did the patterns, which did not attempt a Saxon or Viking pattern scheme, although the general outline was Saxon. Two years later Lang looked into the future for his subject, and this was to become a repeated theme for film directors, combining as it could highly Romantic adventure stories with monumental sets and rockets of a simplicity advocated by Gordon Craig. *Metropolis* concerns a machine city living under a remote dictatorship, but of course the technology and the cast can only look 1926. The Russians had tried this type of film in 1924 when Protaganov's *Aelita* was made. It told of a Russian who landed on Mars and started a revolution. The sets were Constructivist, resembling huge power stations, but Aelita queen of Mars was simply a leading lady type of 1924, with her waist down where it would be.

The exotic and erotic were taken up by the cinema straight from the stage. If Friml could write a musical called *The Desert Song* the cinema could use that sort of material too. The result was *The Sheik* staring Rudolph Valentino. The theatre's matinée idol was facing a serious challenge from the male film star, although some idols managed to perform in both media, like Ivor Novello. The plot, taken from Elinor Glyn's best selling novel, related how a sheik, who is in fact an English aristocrat by birth, captures an English girl, rapes her and keeps her prisoner until she falls in love with him. At the time it was considered rather absurd by everyone other than Valentino's fans, and Bebe Daniels appeared in a satire called *She's a Sheik* where the heroine captures a man and holds him prisoner until he falls for her. The period was contemporary and the correct costume for exploits in the desert was riding breeches, a costume then very popular among explorers whether mounted or in cars. Another subject where the woman ensnared the man was *Cleopatra*, which Cecil B. de Mille turned into a glamorous vehicle for Claudette Colbert: but 'glamour' means the contemporary look imposed on top of everything.

Cleopatra VII was supposed to be beautiful according to legend if not to fact, and beauty in the 1930s meant false eyelashes, eyebrows plucked or shaven and replaced by drawn pencil lines, flawless complexions, and very neat heads. If the star's complexion should have a spot or two, a hint of veins on the cheeks, or even a sign of wrinkles, it could all be painted out on the negative to produce an impossibly perfect woman who did not exist in real life. When Hollywood photographs are blown up the brush marks can be seen clearly. Where the camera is concerned the subject need not be beautiful in herself for the anonymous plain face with no strong features can be painted and shaded to produce a certain look, and is easier to remould. Accordingly Claudette Colbert was groomed as a more-than-perfect example of 1930s beauty, and her clothes, apart from a historical gesture towards Egyptian headdresses, were typical 1930s bias-cut shimmering lamé evening gowns, with sweeping trains. The promotion of the female star as an impossible ideal which ordinary women could not copy was best seen in Marlene Dietrich, who was filmed through silk screens to give the effect of a scintillating, sparkling, shimmering beauty which could not exist outside the studio. Alas for the young man who fell in love with this artificial creation, for he could not find her like off the screen.

Hollywood became the Dream Machine, which was what the theatre of spectacle had been, but the cinema was able to take the fantasy to a much wider audience and across frontiers. Edith Head designed many of the costume films and Adrian specialized in the gaudy glamour with rhinestones, spangles and sequins, smothering the clothes as much as the Baroque period had done, but without the excuse that an aid to lighting was necessary. There was always a battle between the elegant and the brash in the film studios, with sensational promotion threatening taste, but the great value of the cinema is that it does conserve a record of past styles both good and bad. Above all, where surviving theatre designs, paintings and photographs are static entities, the film records movement and action. It is possible to see how people wore clothes, what unconscious methods of management were necessary to move in those clothes, and how far those garments allowed or prevented motion. Patterns of behaviour are conserved when all the preceding centuries' habits, gestures, and ways have been lost

for ever, but since the 1890s the film has kept a record in motion of each successive generation. Since the advent of sound it has also been able to retain past pronunciation, from the beautiful enunciation required in the 1930s to the grunt of today. Wax cylinders were able to do even better, recording the resounding tones of Mr Gladstone and the equally stentorian voice of Florence Nightingale. The actress Ellen Terry was recorded too, a piece of theatre surviving through the hiss and crackle of the surface.

One important voice in theatre reform rejected both the theatre of spectacle and the theatre of realism, judging the former to be overblown and the latter banal. Edward Gordon Craig, son of the actress Ellen Terry and the architect and stage designer E.W. Godwin, began as an actor in Sir Henry Irving's company at the Lyceum in 1889, but from 1903 he started to do stage design. He considered Irving's productions grossly overdressed and overcrowded, while he found realistic sets with their saucepans and kettles the antithesis of creativity and imagination. He came to have a rather impossible ideal, in which one man controlled the entire theatrical production, writing the play, designing it, producing it, composing the music, training the actors, and inventing machines and lighting as necessary. To date no such superman has emerged, and even the most egotistical actor-manager had to delegate something. He could not sew the costumes and rewire an electrical circuit; there simply is not the rehearsal time for one man to make everything. Nevertheless Craig did have an important impact on stage design, with his advocacy of absolute simplicity. Just as the Neo-Classicists had rejected fussy Rococo styles in favour of monumental solidity, Craig now rejected elaborate Vic-

---

88 Design by Alexandre Benois for the coronation clothes of the Empress Catherine II, for Alexander Korda's film *Catherine the Great*, United Artists, Hollywood, 1934. ASHMOLEAN MUSEUM, OXFORD

Cinematic luxury. Benois copied Lampi's official coronation portrait and his instructions direct that an imperial crown of diamonds and pearls should grace the empress's head. A pectoral of diamonds for the front of her dress, and the cross of the Order of St Andrew, all in diamonds. Mantle of cloth-of-gold embroidered with imperial eagles in black and gold, and lined with ermine. Paniered gown in satin embroidered with imperial eagles in relief in gold. The budgets for films were gigantic compared to those in theatre.

torian taste for simpler shapes and plain geometrical forms. The reaction was predictable, but Craig was one of the first to express it, and his work was seen across Europe; he designed *Venice Preserved* for Berlin in 1905, *Rosmersholm* in Florence in 1906, and *Hamlet* in Moscow in 1912. The set for the last was towering blocks, angular and undecorated, and Craig's concept of costume was always a simple line uncluttered by ornament, clean-cut and pure. His ideals inspired others to follow, notably Harvey Granville-Barker in his presentation of Shakespeare's *The Winter's Tale* at the Savoy Theatre in 1912, where the set, designed by Norman Wilkinson, consisted of square columns with curtains in between, above a row of steps with white as the dominant tone. Unfortunately Granville-Barker commissioned the clothes from another designer, Albert Rutherston, who was not alive to such simplification and turned out a jumble of caftans, turbans, tonnelets, and bootees which owed much to Bakst and the Ballets Russes, and were the exact opposite of what Craig was fighting for. However, the white set for Shakespeare became a feature of advanced productions, and when Norman MacDermott opened his Hampstead Everyman Theatre in 1920 its permanent set for Shakespeare was in ivory.[2]

89 Costume worn by Lillah McCarthy as Viola in *Twelfth Night*, Savoy Theatre, 1912. MUSEUM OF LONDON

Granville Barker's production, designed by Norman Wilkinson, was considered a major step in the simplification of Shakespearian performances. Wilkinson used rich fabrics but kept the silhouette plain. Viola's coat for her embassy to Lady Olivia is in silver-grey brocade trimmed with magenta. Doublet sleeves in black silk slashed and trimmed with green. Red leather belt. Suede gloves trimmed with metal thread and magenta silk. Flat Tudor cap in black velvet with hatband of pearl beads and imitation emerald. It was simpler than Beerbohm Tree's but not exactly poor.

OPPOSITE PAGE
90 Edward Gordon Craig's design for *Electra*, 1913. THE BRITISH LIBRARY

Stark simplicity devoid of ornamentation was advocated by Craig. The costumes are not accurately ancient Greek but long draperies, still with something of an Art Nouveau sweep about them and so long they would be difficult to move in. As the designer Theodore Kommisarzhevsky pointed out the Expressionist Modern Theatre believed in simple stylization.

During the 1920s productions of Shakespeare underwent another change. All the battle for accurate historical costume which had been going on since the eighteenth century was suddenly rejected. Where William Poel put his Shakespeare into Elizabethan and Jacobean dress, the latest idea was to dress Shakespeare in the dress of today. It could be argued that this is what Shakespeare himself would have expected, for if his plays were done in mainly contemporary dress in 1600, the same could apply to 1925. The first off the mark with this policy was Barry Jackson with his Birmingham Repertory Company, who performed *Hamlet* in 1925 in the dress of modern courtiers, with the prince taking his fashion lead from the current Prince of Wales. In 1928 they performed *Macbeth* with the male leads dressed like members of contemporary Scottish regiments, while Lady Macbeth wore the new short skirts and played her sleep walking scene in a dressing gown and fluffy slippers. Other examples of this clothing policy were Michael MacOwan's presentation of *Troilus and Cressida* at the Westminster Theatre in 1938, dressed like contemporary high society, Shakespeare with cocktails, and Tyrone Guthrie's production of *Hamlet* at the Old Vic, also in 1938, which was attired like an elegant contemporary court with ladies in evening gowns with bare shoulders and gentlemen in either uniforms or white tie and tails. The theatre critic J. Agate commented, after seeing a production of *Julius Caesar* at the Embassy Theatre in November 1939 which used modern dress, that he hated this fashion and found the whole thing very precious and self-conscious. The argument was, again, that Shakespeare had seen his plays done in contemporary costume so that modern audiences should expect the same approach in 1939. But were audiences so feeble that they would be put off by the sight of clothes from another period because they were not used to seeing them in the street? Was not the logical development of such an argument that Shakespeare's text would have to put into modern dress, and rewritten in a language redolent of gangsters in New York or Chicago in the manner of Damon Runyon? If audiences did not like historical costume would they not object to historical speech?[3] Such objections won in the long run, for while Shakespeare in modern dress does crop up occasionally, most productions stick to the Romantic policy of clothes of the period of the play. Shakespeare is a national monument so he should be approached with respect, and he should not look ordinary. *Vestir nobilmente*, as L. de' Sommi had insisted back in 1565, is still important for the classics, for the tragedies are not about ordinary folk. One of the principal reasons for going to the theatre is to see something that transcends the mundane and highlights aspects of the human condition, consequently the costume should arguably belong to the same elevated plane. Kean, Irving and Tree all believed they were giving the general public splendour and colour which could not be found outside the playhouse. While a modern director might disagree about bringing beauty forward as his duty to audiences, he does present Shakespeare in an extraordinary manner, knowing full well that the verse is not ordinary so the vesture must match it, no matter how avant garde his production may be. William Archer and James Agate both stated that a great play was one which gave the spectator a special experience,[4] and an experience is not ordinary. It is noticed because it is out of the ordinary and that applies to clothes and language too.

As fashionable clothes in the 1920s and 1930s were simple in outline they accorded with the ideal of simplicity, and the streamlined look was the dominant theme at the Exposition des Arts Décoratifs et Industriels Modernes in Paris in 1925, which promoted rectangular furniture, décors in white or beige, abstract art and textile patterns, and clothes as streamlined as tubular steel. The appearance of simple clothes on the stage was part of a new belief in clean lines for everything, and putting Shakespeare into modern dress was one aspect of this artistic ideal. It represented classical purity after romantic excess, and this attitude was applied to historical recreations as well. A 1930s version of a mediaeval gown flowed as smoothly as a contemporary evening dress, as could be seen in the costumes designed by Theodore Kommisarjhevsky for *King Lear* at Stratford-upon-Avon in 1937 which were simplified in outline, so that the silhouette was plain and streamlined like a racing car. The functional avoids the unnecessary appendage which will reduce efficiency, and this industrial approach informed the stage. Good design now meant reduction to the bare essentials.

Naturally it took time for these artistic ideals to percolate down through society, and a new white or beige Shakespearean production could exist side-by-side with a highly colourful design by Bakst at the next playhouse, for there is always an overlap, and never a sharp division or precise date when one style comes in and another goes out. Strong colour had a big impact on some designers in the West, such as young Claud Lovat Fraser. In 1920 he was asked to design the first production of Gay's *The Beggars' Opera* seen in London for decades, for the Lyric Theatre, Hammersmith. While Hogarth's paintings of the original 1728 production were available, Fraser's budget did not run to a large-scale reconstruction. The sets he made very plain with just a touch of Georgian detail, and because of

91 Claud Lovat Fraser, design for the Tavern Scene, *The Beggar's Opera*, Lyric Theatre, Hammersmith, 1921. THE BRITISH LIBRARY

A streamlined simplicity more elegant than any Georgian tavern would have been, with the cherubs' heads and columns to indicate the period along with the date over the door. Each character is in a strong colour like those of the Ballets Russes, but only one colour each, like crimson, red, lilac and yellow.

92 Design by Claud Lovat Fraser for Lucy Lockit, *The Beggar's Opera*, Lyric Theatre, Hammersmith, 1921. THE BRITISH LIBRARY

The deliberate abandonment of period frills and furbelows for a stripped down version of the past. The costume is entirely in orange, and the hairstyle is strictly 1921. Compare with the original production in **16**.

93 Design by Claud Lovat Fraser for Polly Peacham, *The Beggar's Opera*, Lyric Theatre Hammersmith, 1921. THE BRITISH LIBRARY

Once again the female is dominated by contemporary fashion, short hair, plucked eyebrows, bee-stung lips, even when supposedly being 1728. Dress of rose-pink.

OPPOSITE PAGE

94 Design by Claud Lovat Fraser for Captain Macheath, *The Beggar's Opera*, Lyric Theatre, Hammersmith, 1921. THE BRITISH LIBRARY

Only with male characters is a designer prepared to try to avoid the fashionable stereotype imposed on women. Fraser has kept the redcoat and the black hat trimmed with yellow worn by Macheath in the 1728 production, and he has retained a wig, actually longer than Hogarth painted. Of course the make-up and eyebrows say 1921 but the rest of the costume does try to look period, which Fraser had not done with the female characters to the same degree.

his belief in strong colour he made the costumes much brighter than they had been in 1728. He put Polly Peacham into rose pink and Lucy Lockit into orange, but the red coat for Captain Macheath was the same colour as had been used in the very first production, and Fraser accompanied it with a bright yellow waistcoat, red-heeled shoes, and a black tricorne trimmed with yellow. In the Tavern Scene, Macheath in red stood among ladies in crimson, red, lilac, and yellow. Fraser limited himself to this colour range and there was no blue. He himself wrote that as the play concerned low-class characters there was no need for highly fashionable clothes, so the costume could be 30 years behind the time, or 30 years before. He saw no need to make it exactly 1728, and subjected the female characters in particular not only to strong colour but to the current ideal of simplification.

With the women I have taken greater licence. I have kept faithfully to the outlines of the age, the close-fitting bodice, the flat hoops, the square toed-shoes, but I have taken considerable liberties in the manner in which I have shorn them of ribbons and laces and – for the sake of dramatic simplicity, be it remembered – I have eliminated yards of trimming.[5]

Once again the concept of the female was expressed in terms of the current fashionable ideal, far more so than was applied to the male actors. Lucy Lockit's hairstyle was strictly 1920 with its tight waves, and the absence of decoration on her gown was equally in accordance with the latest definition of smartness for women. Ornamentation was now out of fashion, even when it would have been correct for the period of the play. As so many times before, the current artistic and fashionable vision conditioned any recreation of another age and style. At the time Lovat Fraser's designs were considered the height of elegance, and the revival was a triumphant success, being staged again in 1925. Fraser was regarded as the great hope of British theatre design, but he died in 1921 aged only 31 as his experiences during the First World War had left him with a heart condition. Nevertheless the way he had stylized Georgian décor and costumes to meet 1920s taste became a strong influence on theatre design thereafter, suggesting a period rather than copying it precisely as the Romantics had tried to do.

A new firm of theatrical costumiers opened in London in 1912. It was founded by Morris Berman, a master tailor who had worked for the Czar in St Petersburg but who, possibly foreseeing the disasters ahead in Russia, moved to England, where his son Max ran the new costumiers. Their success was rapid for the firm dressed the two most popular shows during the war, *The Maid of the Mountains* and

THE LYRIC THEATRE
HAMMERSMITH

"THE BEGGARS
OPERA."

Captain Macheath
(Mr Frederick Ranalow.)

Chu Chin Chow. The film industry was just setting up and began to order clothes, a trickle which became a flood after 1919, when Max Berman supplied costumes for films like *Somme, Arras,* and *W. Plan,* which were all about the war itself. In the 1930s the firm became linked with the Alexander Korda organization on a regular basis and costumed many of his productions, including *The Thirty Nine Steps,* and *The Four Feathers.* There were clothes of a futuristic type for *Shape of Things to Come,* contemporary and Edwardian costumes for Jessie Matthews in the film musical *Evergreen,* and more modest schoolmaster's wear for *Goodbye Mr Chips.* Madeleine Carroll, Herbert Marshall, Robert Donat, Rex Harrison, Raymond Massey all passed under Max Berman's hands. In 1932 Berman won an annual order to dress the Crazy Gang's shows at the London Palladium. The firm suffered badly during the Blitz for their premises received a direct hit in 1942 which destroyed all the costume stock apart from some in a warehouse in Lambeth. When Monty Berman, the grandson of Morris, was demobbed from the RAF in 1946 he went about rebuilding the business, and moved into television costuming and international film wardrobes in a big way, with titles like *The African Queen, Moulin Rouge, The Longest Day, Young Winston* to his credit, and at Drury Lane the London production of *My Fair Lady,* to Cecil Beaton's designs.

Meanwhile Nathan's was still doing very well, and in the 1920s it began supplying clothes for revues in quantity. Starting with Beatrice Lillie at the Little Theatre, Nathan's were then engaged by G.B. Cochran to dress his famous revues, which were designed by Gladys Calthrop, Rex Whistler and Oliver Messel. The clothes required were mainly contemporary of course, the 1920s concept of glamour and elegance, with women's waists down at hip level. The chorus were known as Mr Cochran's Young Ladies, and there Anna Neagle, Sarah Churchill and Jessie Matthews first attracted attention. They were groomed, as always, into the period look, short hair, pencil line eyebrows, Cupid's bow lips, for a chorus is standardized and individuality suppressed, by order of the male director who wants the immediate current style, the fashionable stereotype, the latest definition of feminine beauty. Only when a girl is a star can she afford to be different – if she dare.

Among Cochran's stars were the French Alice Delysia, Evelyn Laye, Binnie and Sonnie Hale, John Mills chorus boy, Douglas Byng, Tilly Losch who married an earl, and from the USA the Dolly Sisters. Despite the fact that reformers had disliked the theatre of frivolity it continued to do very well. There was competition in the field for André Charlot's revues were still being produced, featur-

ing the elegant Jack Buchanan showing how to wear an evening suit with style, Jack Hulbert who was less spruce, and that personification of 1930s glamour Gertrude Lawrence. Nathan's started supplying clothes for films in 1912, and then became principal supplier to the Rank Organization for Laurence Olivier's films just after the Second World War, *Henry V,* and *Hamlet,* providing Jacobean and mediaeval costume. A bomb just missed Nathan's so it did not suffer the fate of Berman's, and the firm became involved with espionage, providing agents with very anonymous, unnoticeable clothes without labels. After the war Nathan's and Berman's were regular rivals, even sometimes both contributing to the same production like the film version of *Doctor Zhivago.* When Archie Nathan retired in 1971 an approach was made to Berman's, which was agreed to, and the firms amalgamated as Berman & Nathans in 1972. Their stock had been scattered round London but it was now brought together at Camden Street which houses over one million costumes. The new firm can claim to dress three quarters of British television, many European television companies from Norway to Yugoslavia, American television, and on the same scale film companies. Be it prehistoric furs, Roman armour, mediaeval houppelandes, Tudor doublets, Baroque periwigs, Rococo suits, Romantic revivals, Art Nouveau modes or the latest Punk, Berman & Nathans has got it all.[6]

The American musical began to gain its own identity during these years. Friml's *Rose Marie* retained the exotic formula now translated into Canadian mountains and singing mounties, but in that same year, 1925, came Youman's *No, No, Nanette!* which was more representative of the jazz age. Some composer librettist teams could be as wide in their choice of subject material as the nineteenth century, for Rodgers and Hart produced *The Boys from Syracuse* in 1938 which concerned high jinks in ancient Rome, and then an up-to-the-minute depiction of modern life and night-club types in *Pal Joey* (1940). Those musicals which concerned themselves very closely with American history concentrated on the nineteenth century. Jerome Kern's *Showboat* (1928) set in the South, Rodger's and Hammerstein's *Oklahoma* (1943) and *Carousel* (1945), set in the Mid West and on the coast, reflect the fact that for large slices of the USA there is no written history before the 1840s. As in South Africa the seventeenth century settlements on the coast seem to be overwhelmed by the image and myth of the nineteenth century expansion inland.

The tradition laid down by Pinero and Shaw whereby playwrights gave detailed descriptions of the clothes and ages of their characters was continued by Somerset Maugham, whose plays were increasingly successful from 1904 until 1933, after which he gave up the theatre. In *Lady Frederick* of 1907, set in 1890, he describes Lady Mereston in Act I as a handsome woman of forty, magnificently attired in evening dress. In Act II comes Lady Frederick's dressmaker Madame Claude: 'She is a stout, genteel, person, very splendidly gowned, with a Cockney accent.' Lady Frederick declares that Madame Claude's clothes express her own character, the fullness of her skirt indicating her social virtues, while the frill round the hem suggests her foibles. Lady Frederick is being pursued by a much younger admirer, so in Act III she tries to look her worst in order to dissuade him. 'She wears a kimono, her hair is all dishevelled hanging about her head in a tangled mop. She is not made up and looks haggard and yellow and lined.' She indicates to her beau the number of jars of make-up it requires to turn her into an elegant woman, as well as the assistance of a French maid to do her hair, and does succeed in putting the young man off, after which she accepts an older man. Evidently the young lover was too naive to appreciate that what Lady Frederick looked like was not so important as her character, for that was what he would have to live with. In *Mrs Dot*, set in 1905, Maugham gives little description of the ladies beyond indicating fashionable dress, and concentrates on the looks and ages of the men. Mr Wright is a 'dapper young man, smartly dressed', while 'Gerald is a handsome man of seven or eight and twenty, simple in his manners, carefully dressed but without exaggeration. Freddie is a vivacious boy of two and twenty. Blenkinsop is an old bachelor of five and forty; he is well-preserved and takes a good deal of care of his appearance. He is dressed in the height of fashion.' At this date, Maugham himself was a snappy dresser, but here he makes it clear that for a man to be too concerned about his appearance was displaying an insecurity which a true gentleman would be without. By Act II Freddie is desperately trying to attract a young lady and changes his suits seven times a day; Maugham acutely observes the way the young use clothes in order to be noticed, not having made themselves well-known by other methods, for it takes time for achievement to be recognized.

Maugham's *Our Betters*, a satire on Anglo-American contrasts, opened in New York in 1917 and in London in 1923. Act I introduces Bessie Saunders: 'She is a very pretty American girl, of twenty-two, with fair hair and blue eyes. She is dressed in the latest mode. She wears a hat and gloves, and carries a bag'. The American males however are presented as examples of bad taste. 'Fleming is a nice-looking young American in clothes that were obviously made in New York',

while Thornton Clay is described as stout, bald, effusive, and overdressed. The English characters tell both Americans to get themselves a London tailor without fail. It soon becomes clear that the European ladies present are not much better. There is Lady Grayston, 'a handsome, dashing creature, a woman of thirty-four, with red hair, and a face outrageously painted. She is dressed in a Paris frock, but of greater daring both in colour and cut than a Frenchwoman would bear.' This outrageous creature is joined by the even less gracious Duchesse de Suresnes:

. . . a large, dark woman of forty-five with scarlet lips and painted cheeks, a woman of opulent form, self-assured and outrageously sensual. She suggests a drawing of a Roman Emperor by Aubrey Beardsley. She is gowned with a certain dashing magnificence, and wears a long string of large pearls round her neck.

Maugham describes both women as outrageous in their appearances, and represents them as a sort of caricature which says much of his own sexual bias and fear of women. The next female character, Pearl, is presented as tainted. Having been observed in a compromising situation the night before she decides to behave as nothing had happened.

She is perfectly cool and collected, radiant in a wonderful, audacious gown; she is looking her best and knows it. (*Act III*)

This is a good observation of the best way to outface criticism, by making one's appearance as unruffled and elegant as one can. One more example of a tasteless European is presented when the Duchess sends for Ernest, who thus finds himself in the country when wearing town dress.

He is a little dark man, with large eyes, and long hair, neatly plastered down. He is dressed like a tailor's dummy, in a black coat, white gloves, silk hat, patent leather boots, he is a dancing master and overwhelmingly gentlemanly.

His whole appearance is designed to indicate that he is slick, vulgarly well-dressed, and a self-ingratiating smoothie. His clothes and hair say it all. After beholding this assembly of characters Bessie decides that she would be better off back home in the USA. Evidently Maugham understood the language of clothes very well, and was very acute with the sort of statements about a person that clothes can make.[7]

Other popular playwrights of the day were less devoted to this tradition. Frederick Lonsdale known for his *The Last of Mrs Cheney* (1925), and *Canaries Sometimes Sing* (1929), gives no directions over character and costume. Noel Coward was better in this respect, but his definitions are nevertheless much shorter than the examples set by Pinero and Shaw. Coward's first play to be a West End success was *The Vortex* which opened at the Everyman Theatre, Hampstead, on 25 November 1924. The plot concerned a son who discovered that his mother had young lovers, a sensational subject in 1924, and the press reacted by declaring that while it had a touch of genius the play was about diseased people; Coward was classified as a member of the decadent cocktail set, and a representative of post-war hysteria. The play was contemporary in its setting and the clothes were designed in the fashion of the day, with short skirts for the ladies, by a regular designer for Coward productions, Gladys Calthrop. She also coped with his *Cavalcade* of 1931, which covered the years 1899–1930, so she had to design in the styles of 31 evolving years of dress for some 3700 characters, a mammoth task, requiring both middle class clothes and crowds of working class varieties.

Despite Mrs Calthrop's sterling work, when the budget allowed, Coward liked to commission his theatre wardrobe from the top English couturier in Paris, Captain Molyneux. This happened with *Private Lives* in 1930. The period was contemporary so Molyneux could create up-to-the-minute modes, and ladies in the audience could gaze on the most elegant gowns Paris could offer. In Act I Coward defined the newly wed Sibyl Chase as 'very pretty and blonde, and smartly dressed in travelling clothes'. Her new husband Elyot is also in travelling attire, as they arrive at a hotel on their honeymoon. The other couple in the piece are Victor Prynne and his new wife Amanda. Victor is set at 30–35 in age range, and he too has travelling wear, a light suit. Amanda is presented as a very elegant creature, and as played by Gertrude Lawrence in Molyneux she looked the part fully. Amanda first of all changes into a negligée, but as evening approaches changes again into 'a charmingly simple evening gown, her cloak is flung over her right shoulder'. Molyneux made it of white satin. Sibyl reappears in 'a very pretty evening frock'. Note the distinction: Amanda is gowned and Sibyl is frocked, which makes it clear that the former is dressed and the latter is merely wearing clothes. The two dresses indicate the difference between the two women, Amanda the height of sophistication, Sibyl not in the same class. Amanda and Elyot have been married before, and on this reunion decide to abandon their new mates and go off together. They are found in Paris in Act II, where their clothes make it obvious that they have resumed sexual relations, for Amanda is in pyjamas and Elyot, played by Coward himself, is in a dressing gown. They are confronted by their respective spouses but

depart again in Act III, once more in travelling clothes, which thus illustrate their intention. While Coward did not provide lengthy descriptions of the clothes, he knew that they were important; he wanted the best, for their role was to convey character difference, life-style, and behaviour.[8]

In this period one foreign playwright who seems to have learnt best from Shaw the importance of costume on the stage was the Italian Luigi Pirandello. He gives the same consideration to clothes, age and looks. In *Six Characters in Search of an Author* of 1921 Pirandello provides a full picture of the Father:

. . . a man about 50: hair reddish in colour, thin at the temples; he is not bald however; thick moustaches, falling over his still fresh mouth, which often opens in an empty and uncertain smile. He is fattish, pale, with an especially wide forehead. He has blue, oval-shaped eyes, very clear and piercing. Wears light trousers and a dark jacket.

The Mother is described as always looking crushed and terrified. 'She is dressed in modest black and wears a thick widow's veil of crêpe. When she lifts this, she reveals a wax-like face. She always keeps her eyes downcast.' There are three children. The Step-Daughter who is dashing, beautiful and impudent, and who manages to wear her mourning elegantly. The Boy aged 14 is also in black, and the Child aged about four is in white with a black silk sash. The time was the present 1921, so the costumes were easy to achieve. The rest of the cast were actors and actresses in their ordinary, everyday clothes, who are suddenly confronted by the above group in black, apart from the Father. One other strange character arrives, Madame Pace:

She is a fat, oldish woman with puffy, oxygenated hair. She is rouged and powdered, dressed with a comical elegance in black silk. Round her waist is a long silver chain from which hangs a pair of scissors.

Pirandello was using black to create a mystery about the strange characters. Why are they in mourning? The action buzzes around this mystery, until the stage-manager protests that they are wasting his time. The clothes serve to identify a group, to contrast them with those in ordinary dress, and to suggest a grievous story, even though no one can agree what that fate has been. The clothes state a condition, but do not explain it.

Costume is central to the theme of Pirandello's *Henry IV* of 1922, for the hero likes to live in the past and he expresses this by his dress, not having rebuilt his house in mediaeval manner. Set in the Italy of 1922, the hero, who imitates the emperor

Henry IV of the Holy Roman Empire, hires young men dressed like eleventh-century German knights to represent the emperor's counsellors, while the valets are required to carry halberds and to try to look like guards. In attempt to undo this apparent insanity others arrive with a doctor. When the old servant John enters in modern clothes to inform the knights that the company has arrived, they protest that he is not in period dress. He ushers in the marchioness Donna Matilda Spina:

. . . about 45, still handsome, although there are too patent signs of her attempts to remedy the ravages of time with make-up. Her head is thus rather like a Walkyrie.

She is a widow of several years standing so her clothes should be sober. She has a male companion in Tito Belcredi who is not described, but he should be in a suit of 1922. The doctor Genoni is plump, bald, and has a pointed beard. They are accompanied by the marquess Charles di Nolli who is in deep mourning for his mother, and by Donna Matilda's daughter Frida 19. They are informed that the emperor will not receive them unless they wear period costume, and the knights bring a change of clothes; Donna Matilda receives a mantle and a ducal crown, while Dr Genoni and Belcredi are both put into monks' habits. The emperor then enters, aged about 50.

The hair on the back of his head is already grey; over the temples and forehead it appears blond, owing to its having been tinted in an evident and puerile fashion. On his cheek bones he has two small doll-like dabs of colour, that stand out prominently against the rest of his tragic pallor. He is wearing a penitent's sack over his royal habit.

He is wearing sackcloth as worn by the real emperor Henry IV at Canossa in 1077 where he had to humiliate himself before Pope Gregory VII after a long dispute. The pretended emperor states that the reason he enacts events from the life of the dead emperor is because the pattern and outcome of that existence are known. He prefers to reside in past because the future is certain, whereas as a man in 1922 he would have no idea what would be happening to him in 1923 or thereafter. If his visitors think he is masquerading he retorts that all people masquerade in real life; for example (an obvious reference to the painted marchioness) they pretend that they are younger than they are. There is a lot of truth in that observation, for when there is a cult of youth the elderly try to rejuvenate their appearance. In the 1920s monkeys' glands were supposed to be an aid to prolonged youth, while hair dyes and make-up have long been employed to

improve on nature when nature begins to look veined and wrinkled or grey. Nowadays there is the case of bald men going in for hair transplants to recover the bare dome. All are trying to retain the image of a younger self, but unlike Henry IV they do not go to the extent of trying to *be* someone else.

In Act II the emperor maintains, 'Undressed we don't bother much about who we are. And one's dress is like a phantom that hovers always near one.' The first part of that statement can only apply to occasional nudity. In a society where permanent undress is the normal condition people bother very much about the symbols of their status. In a clothed society the costume can make that statement; in an undressed society ornamentation is employed, either on the skin itself by scars and branding or tattooing, or else by means of the symbols of wealth, beads, copper bangles, ivory teeth and rare shells, or by the symbols of bravery, where young males who have passed certain tests can wear the feathers or fur of particularly dangerous and strong creatures like eagles, jaguars or leopards. In cases of body painting as for a war dance, there is a whole vocabulary of traditional patterns which can only be worn by individuals of the appropriate rank. All human societies express status, so do many animal ones. Pirandello is closer to the mark when he writes that one's dress always hovers near, for that display of status is ever made; it is only the methods and materials which differ.

In Act III the pretended emperor plucks at his pseudo-eleventh century clothes:

This dress which is for me the evident, involuntary caricature of that other continuous, everlasting masquerade, of which we are involuntary puppets, when, without knowing it, we mask ourselves with that which we appear to be.[9]

He can only defy the dress and life style of 1922 by adopting the garments of 1077, but the dilemma is, if all life is masquerade, did not people in 1077 mask themselves with their clothes? He acts as if the past were a pure territory where such things would not be found, but he deceives himself. He may have chosen his identity as Henry IV rather than accepting the one modern society imposed upon him, but he does not ask how many masks the dead emperor had to wear. The past may appear certain, but only to the present, and those in it were participating in the same involuntary masquerade that the hero despises in its contemporary manifestation. He can only caricature the past; he cannot be it. He may choose to be Henry IV, but the real Henry IV did not have that choice, he was born that man. The hero is indulging in a luxury of the selection of identity, of adopting its hairstyle, colouring and clothes, but he assumes a freedom that does not exist. One may assume disguises, but the underlying personality, conditioned by the social group into which one is born, cannot be selected or discarded.

Pirandello is correct in pointing to the masquerading that goes on in life, but that varies in degree. The poor person who dresses as smartly as he can is disguising his poverty, the invalid who uses make-up or a suntanning machine to conceal his pallor is trying to convince others and himself that he is healthier than he is, the upper class person who follows a fashion to look working class, be it the coachman and postillion mode of the Regency, or cowboy jeans in the 1960s, is concealing his financial power; but is this sort of masquerading very damaging? It is surely the masquerade in public life which is most worthy of condemnation – the politician who claims to be a moralist and devoted family man, when he is conducting affairs in private, or the company director who pretends to be a man of integrity in public while accepting bribes and selling trade secrets in private. The amoral masquerade is far worse than any masquerading in dress and appearance, which has a lot to do with compensation.

The Theatre of Ideas of which Pirandello was a worthy member saw the arrival of an American subscriber in the person of Eugene O'Neill. The son of an actor, and a former seaman and journalist, he took English at Harvard in 1914 when he was 26. Thus he had seen something of the rough side of life, and wanted to express humanity under the stress of strong emotions. His *The Hairy Ape* (1922) is set on board a liner, and contrasts the stokers down in the boiler room and the comfortable travellers on the deck and in the staterooms. It was the dirtiest job at sea, shovelling coal onto the fires, and a ship at speed could consume some 20 tons of coal an hour, so the activity was non-stop. O'Neill wrote that the stokers (firemen in American), should look like Neanderthal Man, being short, strong and hairy-chested. This would set casting the play a problem. The period was contemporary so the costume would be 1922, fashionable wear for the passengers, boiler suits for the stokers. In *Desire Under the Elms* produced in 1924, O'Neill turned to farming folk in the 1850s, so the costume was very simple, the plain rough clothing of that period for working people, the corduroy and homespun shirts, when most of the family wardrobe was made by the women. The skirts of dresses should be filled out by petticoats, but there would be no crinolines at this social level, where practical clothing was an essential part of life. In using subjects set among the poor and dimly educated O'Neill was continuing the ideals of the Theatre of Realism, with its ordinary dress and lifelike sets, but he did not restrict himself to realism. *The Fountain* of 1924 was set in the historical past and concerned Ponce de Leon's quest for the Fountain of Youth, but O'Neill did not want it to be staged in a realistic or historical manner. He asked for elaborate masks to convey the character's feelings and inner conflicts and so give them 'a significance beyond themselves', which is how masks had been used in the ancient Greek theatre. O'Neill turned to classical themes in his later works; *Lazarus Laughed* (1928) takes place in ancient Rome, while *Mourning Becomes Electra* tackles the Greek concept of Nemesis, and was staged in 1931. It was O'Neill's concern to examine the human being, and he did not limit himself to any one school or method to say how he should undertake that task, so his costume is realistic and symbolic in turn.[10]

The 1920s considered itself the Machine Age, a period of aeroplanes and motor cars, of magnificent trans-Atlantic liners and express trains, so it was only natural that this admiration for science and machinery should manifest itself onstage. The Constructivist Theatre used sets made of scaffolding, as in a production of G.K. Chesterton's *The Man who Was Thursday*, about anarchists, which the revolutionary regime in Russia considered one of the few Western plays allowable on their stage. It was produced at Moscow's Kamerny Theatre in 1923 by Alex Vesnine with steel scaffolds, lifts, and girders as the set. The Constructivist liked nothing better than to erect a towering structure or giant machine, but this led to the same imbalance already seen in the Romantic period, when actors were reduced to dwarfs by the size of the scenery. Another Russian, Vsevolod Meyerhold, was appointed head of revolutionary theatre in 1920, and he favoured the complete abolition of sets except for the simplest forms. When he designed *The Commander of the Second Army* the set was just a curved wall with a ramp in front and the costumes of course were contemporary Russian military ones. Thus the sets were part of a new ideal but the clothes were realistic, and this mixture was typical of revolutionary theatre, in which the contemporary concept of what a worker looked like dominated.

In England some people felt that the West End drawing-room comedy and the Constructivist policy of international designers were both failing the theatre. Where was the poetry and where was religion? Could not the two combine and flower together? The revival of religious drama in England began in 1928 when Dean George Bell of Canterbury invited the poet John Masefield to write a nativity play, *The Coming of Christ*, which, with music by Gustav Holst and designs by Charles Ricketts, was the first play to be performed inside a cathedral in England since the Reformation. This

caused a sensation and while the seats were free audiences donated £800 as a token of their appreciation and George Bell determined to use this money to commission other religious plays in the future. In 1929 Dean Bell was consecrated Bishop of Chichester in Sussex, and there he appointed Martin Browne as the first Director of Religious Drama in an English see. The Religious Drama Society was founded at the same time, with the new bishop as the first president, to encourage amateur performances at parish level, and to recruit for professional presentations in the future. Bishop Bell maintained his close links with Canterbury which decided to continue to mount religious plays in the way Bell had started. Among the cast in *The Coming of Christ* in 1928 had been Laurence Irving, actor and stage designer, and grandson of the actor Sir Henry Irving. Not surprisingly therefore they collaborated on a revival of Lord Tennyson's *Becket*, in which Sir Henry had triumphed. Bishop Bell placed Laurence Irving in charge of recruiting playwrights willing to write for the church, a task he performed brilliantly, commissioning works from Charles Williams, Dorothy L. Sayers, Christopher Hassal and Christopher Fry. In 1934 Canterbury staged

95 Stella Mary Newton's design for the chorus in the première of T.S. Eliot's *The Rock*, Sadler's Wells Theatre, 1934. STELLA MARY NEWTON

Masks and robes of stiffened hessian create a monumental effect, the colour of stone, to suggest the eternal church, founded on rock.

Laurence Binyon's *The Young King*, and such events in Kent encouraged Exeter Cathedral to commission *The Acts of Saint Peter* in 1933 to celebrate its patron saint on the occasion of the cathedral's 800th anniversary. The new movement was spreading, and it could counter critics of church involvement with the worldly stage, by pointing out that the church in the Middle Ages had supported the mystery plays which were produced every year by the trade guilds, so it was in order for the church in the twentieth century to encourage religious drama again, which could offer a moral lesson to the secular, commercial theatre.

Bishop Bell was most anxious to find an outstanding poet to write church drama, so in December 1930 he invited T.S. Eliot to Chichester to

96 Stella Mary Newton's design for the Plutocrat and the Fascist Blackshirts, in the first production of T.S. Eliot's *The Rock*, Sadler's Wells Theatre, 1934. STELLA MARY NEWTON

Eliot included contemporary threats and dangers in his survey of the history of Christianity in Britain, so Mrs Newton dressed the plutocrat in grey topper, morning coat and grey trousers, with cane and gloves to denote the capitalist gentleman, and the Fascists in their well-known high-necked black shirts with grey trousers.

OPPOSITE PAGE
97 Stella Mary Newton's design for the chorus of women in T.S. Eliot's *Murder in the Cathedral*, 1935. STELLA MARY NEWTON

Two shades of green patterned in red and blue to give the impression of stained glass. Both sexes in Becket's time wore robes patterned with stripes horizontally and other motifs in between.

discuss possibilities with himself and Martin Browne. American-born Eliot had taken British citizenship in 1927 and he had joined the church of England, so the new ecclesiastical movement appealed to him, but four years elapsed before the bishop's hopes coincided with the poet's creative urge. In 1934 Eliot wrote *The Rock*, in response to an appeal from the Bishop of London. The London suburbs were spreading out rapidly and the diocese foresaw the need for 45 new churches to be built in these areas, so it launched an appeal for funds, by staging a celebration of the history of the church in Britain. Lilian Bayliss said they could have her Sadler's Wells Theatre for two weeks, so Eliot set to work, and took as his model that which had inspired the theatre so repeatedly, classical drama, and in particular the choruses used in Greek plays. The work was to have 330 characters, as well as representatives of the decades in history, so who could design for such numbers? In the summer of 1932 Martin Browne had met Stella Mary Pearce at a Scottish drama school. She had been an actress and theatre designer, and now had her own haute couture salon in Barclay Mews, so he turned to her. He wanted something that was more eternal, more

monumental than anything to be seen in the commercial theatre, and Stella Mary Pearce agreed to try. There was no central wardrobe department for the production, the hundreds of historical garments were going to be made by ladies in 30 parishes across London, most of them amateur dressmakers. Miss Pearce coped by giving very precise instructions to each parish group, so that she only needed to pay one visit to inspect the handiwork at each parish base once the construction was underway. She decided every scene should have a different colour, and that the clothes and make-up should be formalized, so she designed all the Danes to be in orange and black with orange faces, the Saxons to be in blue with blue faces, and the craftsmen in white. *The Rock* had a chorus of 16 whom Eliot intended to represent the eternal church, so Miss Pearce dressed them to look like stone, in robes of stiffened hessian draped in a sculptural manner. The set was designed by the painter, mosaicist, and art historian Eric Newton, who used an elongated style reminiscent of Byzantine art, and who also found time to marry Miss Pearce, who thus became Stella Mary Newton, before the play opened. The first night was 28 May

1934 and the critics of *The Observer* and the *New Statesman* agreed that a new era in dramatic literature had begun with Eliot's entry into church drama. After this Laurence Irving and Bishop Bell said Eliot would have to write something for Canterbury. He responded with *Murder in the Cathedral*, which worried Laurence Irving in view of his productions of Tennyson's *Becket* in 1932 and 1933; but Eliot's play proved very different, with the Greek idea of the chorus again prominent.

The performance was to be in the Chapter House at Canterbury Cathedral only 50 yards from the spot where Archbishop Thomas à Becket had been murdered in 1170. This set the designers a problem for the style of the Chapter House was fourteenth century, 200 years later than the event. Laurence Irving designed a permanent set of large screens, reproducing the colours in the building but Stella Mary Newton decided her costumes would have to combat the colour in the place, which was Victorian in date from the last restoration. Accordingly she chose strong colours so that the costumes would stand out against the background, making bright yellow the basic colour for the Tempters. The chorus was onstage all the time, so Mrs Newton

149

98 Stella Mary Newton's design for the monks and the chorus of women in the first production of T.S. Eliot's *Murder in the Cathedral*, Chapter House, Canterbury Cathedral, 1935. STELLA MARY NEWTON

The reality of the production was close to the designer's intentions, but that cannot be guaranteed every time.

OPPOSITE PAGE
99 Stella Mary Newton's design for the First, Second and Third Tempter, in the première of T.S. Eliot's *Murder in the Cathedral*, Chapter House, Canterbury Cathedral, 1935. STELLA MARY NEWTON

Contemporary intrusion to make the characters understandable to a modern audience, as requested by the producer Martin Browne. Although the designer was devoted to historical accuracy, she made this clever compromise.

designed clothes which would give the effect of early stained glass, in two shades of green, decorated with patterns of red and blue, which caused an apparent change of colour and tone every time the chorus of women moved. Their twelfth-century headdresses were also greenish. Professor Tristram had reconstructed the heraldry of the four knights who murdered the archbishop, so Mrs Newton followed his research, putting the four characters into period armour of chain mail with tunics and cloaks over the top, each outfit having the colours of the original coats-of-arms. The priests had Benedictine habits, as did the archbishop. The producer was Martin Browne, and he came up with a very difficult request. At the end of the play the four knights use modern speech to justify their actions, in stark contrast to the poetry of the rest of the tragedy; Browne asked Stella Mary Newton to put something modern into the costumes of the Four Tempters so that the audience could understand their equivalent character types in contemporary society. To three of the Tempers Mrs Newton had given divided skirts, the correct dress for gentlemen in the twelfth century, so she hit on

the idea of making these divided skirts resemble modern trousers. The First Tempter was given the attributes of the man-about-town, with stripes to suggest striped pants, and a top hat cleverly inserted into his mediaeval coronet. The Second Tempter was a politician, so honours and medals were sketched across his chest. The Third Tempter was to resemble a lord from the shires, so he was dressed in diamond checks, which were heraldic in origin, but which now gave the effect of a suit of plus fours, and he was equipped with a rough stick which imitated a golf club. His costume was inspired by the Crecy memorial window in Gloucester Cathedral. The Fourth Tempter was dressed like Becket himself in a Benedictine habit, trying to seduce the archbishop into martyrdom for the false reason of vanity, so his habit bore the palms and crowns of the martyr. Thus the costumes were highly symbolic. The production was lauded to the skies and Eliot's play was declared a classic for the rest of time; but the question was asked, could such a distinguished religious drama transfer to the commercial theatre? In one of the audiences sat Ashley Dukes, producer, playwright, and owner of the Mercury Theatre, at London's Notting Hill Gate, which he had built for his wife Marie Rambert, a former ballerina in the Diaghilev Company who now ran a ballet school. Dukes offered their little auditorium, which only had 136 seats, for a London run. *Murder in the Cathedral* was premiered at Canterbury on 15 June 1935, moved to the Mercury on 1 November 1935, where it ran for seven months and was seen by 20,000 people, and on 30 October 1936 it opened in the West End at the Duchess's Theatre. A poetic religious drama had crossed the divide onto the commercial stage. The set had to be altered for these moves, so at the Mercury Stella Mary Newton designed a simple background of deep blue velvet curtains, with just the church furniture, the archepiscopal throne, the altar and the pulpit, as the stage was very small. At the bigger Duchess Theatre there was room for an architectural set of Norman arches, designed by Frank Napier, which was the correct style for the period of the play.

T.S. Eliot did not write another play until 1939. In the meantime Stella Mary Newton designed other West End productions, with more mediaeval costume for Lionel Hale's *She Passed through Lorraine* which was about Joan of Arc, and *It's Only Yesterday* in 1938; the latter was set in the First World War so she designed the clothes in the 1914–18 styles for the cast and the star Irene Vanbrugh. The last production Mrs Newton designed was John Clement's revival of *Coriolanus* at the Old Vic in 1948, where she did the sets.

The wardrobe departments in West End theatres were still not large, with only a small permanent staff, and when a new play was coming up the wardrobe mistress would engage seamstresses to make the clothes, and then fire them when the work was over. There was a floating population of seamstresses moving from theatre to theatre, as the work became available, while the costume fitter often had her own team of girls who would follow her from job to job. They all needed to live with their ears close to the ground to listen out for the next production that was in the offing.

The impact of fashionable stereotypes still affected actresses, and always will, to such an extent that occasionally an actress might be reluctant or even too alarmed to depart from it. When Dumas's play *The Lady with Camillias* was revived in London, Tallulah Bankhead was invited to star. Now Miss Bankhead was well known as an elegant 1930s type, and she had the very slim hips which were the ideal in that decade. However, the period of the play was of course nineteenth century. Very wide skirts were part of the look of the heroine Camille, so the designer George Sheringham ordered crinolines. Tallulah was horrified. Was she not the epitome of the slim line of the 30s? How could she possibly alter her image? Of course she was not playing Miss Bankhead of the 1930s, she was supposed to be a woman of the previous century; but she would not listen to the designer, and rushed to Stella Mary Newton's couture salon and bought herself a slim gown in oyster. When she put this on for the big party scene and appeared onstage looking narrow when every other woman was wearing a crinoline, the result was ridiculous. Moreover the oyster colour was lost because Sheringham had put the ladies and the set in the cream-yellow range, with the deliberate intention of creating a background against which the heroine would stand out dressed in a sapphire-blue velvet crinoline gown.[7] The producer ordered Miss Bankhead to wear the sapphire blue, and her attempt to remain 1930s was defeated, at least as far as the dress went; her make-up was another matter, so was her hairstyle. Miss Bankhead was not asked to grow her eyebrows to achieve a more natural, nineteenth-century line, but kept her plucked brows.

There is always a limit to how far accuracy will go, and good intentions are always compromised in stage costume and make-up. Many a star will resist if required to change a look with which she is associated in the public mind. Men in the 1930s were no different, and the pencil line moustaches of that decade appeared in many period plays and films where bushier looks would have been correct. The current ideal always intrudes, with the result that everyone looks dated in the publicity photographs as soon as the look has changed, with Brilliantined hairstyles for males replaced by a more natural, ungarnished disorder, in contrast to a period when good grooming was all-important. A period which puts a great emphasis on looking smart, as in the 1930s, will express that attitude on the stage, whereas a more casual decade will not mind how untidy its actors look; they are reflecting the contemporary definition of good style. Of course in time this relaxed look would have become so common, that a return to a more severe, controlled appearance would be inevitable. The pendulum in Western society never stands still.

At the end of 1937 T.S. Eliot told Martin Browne that he did not want to write another historical religious play, as he felt that verse should be spoken by contemporary characters, and not only by people in historical clothes. Over the next two years he worked on *The Family Reunion*, and the result was a modern, verse play but with the theme taken from ancient Greek theatre and religion: the myth of Orestes and the Furies. The play was premiered at London's Westminster Theatre in March 1939, with Michael Redgrave, Helen Hayes and Catherine Lacey in the cast, and John Gielgud and Martin Browne as the co-producers. Now that Eliot was writing for the stage many leading actors were eager to speak his verse and Gielgud was to play *The Family Reunion* several times on radio. The costumes were again by Stella Mary Newton, and as the period of the play was 'today', 1939, she did not have to worry about a period look, or actresses or actors who might stage a revolt against her designs out of a fear of not looking attractive in contemporary terms. Two types of clothes were required, day dress, suits and dresses, and evening dress with black suits for the men and long gowns for the women. Mrs Newton used wool jersey for all the women's costumes, buying a huge roll of undyed jersey, and then dyeing the gowns in the colour range of mauve for Aunt Ivy, brown for Agatha and blue for the character Mary. Decorative touches were kept to the top of the gowns, with the skirts plain, falling in soft folds. The outbreak of the Second World War put a stop to the production; it was 'put to bed' to wait for peacetime, and the costumes were stored away. When the play re-opened after the war it used the same costumes, and as many of the original cast as possible; moreover Mrs Newton had kept that large roll of wool jersey so she was able to make adjustments and alterations in the original material. Such foresight and conservation of fabrics and accessories became essential during the war, when shortages became commonplace. The theatre was given special dispensation by the British government over its fabric allowance, so it did not have to worry about rationing, but nevertheless materials like wool did grow increasingly difficult to get hold of. 'Make-do

and mend' became the motto across the nation, re-use old clothes, make garments out of string, hats out of newspaper, turn old velvet curtains into a gala gown. Silk stockings disappeared, woollen socks became fashionable out of necessity, and anybody who knew an American G.I. would plead for a pair of that American invention, nylons.

The government was well aware that the theatre was necessary for the national morale, both as entertainment and for the eternal value of a speech from Shakespeare, so it founded CEMA, the Council for the Encouragement of Music and the Arts, nowadays known as the Arts Council, to provide funds and organization. People were being evacuated out of the major cities, so Martin Browne decided to found a small professional company, the Pilgrim Players, to continue the work of the Religious Drama Society by commissioning new church drama, and to take its productions all round the country for audiences now far away from a theatre building, and to places which had never had a visit from a company. It had the blessing of CEMA, and the Archbishop of Canterbury, Bishop George Bell of Chichester, Sybil Thorndike and John Gielgud as its patrons, while T.S. Eliot agreed to be both patron and to allow the new company to perform a smaller, travelling version of his *Murder in the Cathedral*. The Pilgrim Players acted that play in Guildford Cathedral, in the Cambridge Arts Theatre, in St Andrew's university, in Durham mining villages and in air-raid shelters. Other plays they did were James Bridie's *Tobias and the Angel*, Obey's *Noah*, and Henri Gheon's *The Way of the Cross*. The last was designed by Stella Mary Newton in 1940, and despite the shortages, she made the clothes from wool, mediaeval gowns, simple in shape and strong in colour. By 1943 however when she designed W.B. Yeats's *The Resurrection* for the Pilgrim Players, she had to make the costumes out of calico, painted to look like something better, now that shortages were more serious.[11]

The religious drama movement was to succeed in its aims, commissioning works that have found a permanent place in modern theatre, notably T.S. Eliot's, and after the war Christopher Fry's. In 1950 Martin Browne took another major step when he produced the first performance in four hundred years of the York Cycle of Mystery Plays, thus reviving mediaeval religious drama. This example was followed by productions of the cycles from other cathedrals and centres, from Lincoln, Chester, Coventry, Wakefield and Cornwall, which all proved that English theatrical genius went back hundreds of years before Shakespeare. Mediaeval costume was thus important. Much research has been undertaken into the presentation of plays in the Middle Ages, when guilds paid for costumes.[12]

100 Stella Mary Newton's design for Catherine Lacey in the premiere of T.S. Eliot's *The Family Reunion*, Westminster Theatre, March 1939.   STELLA MARY NEWTON

T.S. Eliot chose a contemporary subject so the clothes had to be modern but correct for the social class of the characters. Mrs Newton used wool jersey for these dinner gowns. The simpler a dress the longer its elegance lasts.

The foundations of Britain's modern National Theatre were laid during this period. Since the ending of the Stuart dynasty's royal companies there had been no state theatres, although the Lord Chamberlain continued to license playhouses and dramas. The whole approach of the Glorious Revolution in 1688 was that the king's powers should be limited, and the idea of state control was almost an anathema to succeeding generations. While Bulwer Lytton and Sir Henry Irving both favoured the ideal of a national theatre, it was not until the early twentieth century that practical action began. The National Theatre Group was set up by William Archer, Bernard Shaw, Harley Granville Barker and others, and an appeal for money was made at a meeting at the Theatre Royal, Drury Lane in 1908. Over £70,000 was raised, but the outbreak of the First World War put a stop to all the plans. Post-war difficulties postponed matters still further, but by 1938 the accumulated funds of the group had increased to £150,000 so a site was bought in South Kensington, only to have the building of the theatre prevented by the Second World War in 1939. After the war that site was exchanged for one on the South Bank of the Thames, and a foundation stone was laid in 1951. It was agreed that the Old Vic Company should form the basic acting company for the National Theatre, and it was the Old Vic playhouse which was to be the new company home while waiting for the National Theatre building to materialize. The Old Vic was built in 1816 as the Royal Coburg Theatre, became the Royal Victoria in 1833, and was acquired in 1880 by the temperance campaigner Emma Cons who turned it into a coffee music hall offering wholesome entertainment to the working classes. In 1912 her niece Lillian Bayliss took over management, and in 1914 introduced a policy of producing all Shakespeare's plays, which she succeeded in doing by 1923. The Old Vic thus became the London theatre specializing in the national bard, and actors of the stature of Laurence Olivier, John Gielgud, Alec Guiness and Ralph Richardson all forged their reputations with the range of parts Miss Bayliss provided, while Lewis Casson and Sybil Thorndike gave her their support from the very first. The clothing policy was mainly in the Romantic tradition that historical plays should be dressed in period costume of the date of the action, not Poel's ideal that it should always be Shakespearean, although the company did do some productions of Shakespeare in modern dress. In 1963 the Old Vic became the official temporary home of the National Theatre Company, and the National's clothing policy has continued to be Romantic, as has that of the Shakespeare Memorial Theatre at Stratford-upon-Avon, founded in 1879. Directors are ready to do Shakespeare in plastic, Shakespeare in aluminium, Shakespeare in mediaeval dress, Shakespeare in Roman costume, or Shakespeare in outer space, but William Poel's belief that Shakespeare should be costumed as Shakespeare would have expected has still not received the attention it deserves. True, the jumble that existed in 1600 might be beyond the ability of some designers, but knowledge of the period does exist, and costume is the prominent concern, as there was no scenery.

The indefatigable Miss Bayliss was not only the mother of Britain's National Theatre Company, she also was responsible for the birth of the Royal Ballet and the English National Opera. In 1931 she opened Sadler's Wells Theatre in north London as a home for opera, and she also moved her ballet dancers from the Old Vic there too, for operas need dances, a close relationship that has lasted 400 years. These two enterprises went from strength to strength and since the war have won national status. The clothing policy was the same as at the Old Vic, firmly Romantic for the majority of works. Nobody tries to do Verdi's *Aïda* in the 1871 version of ancient Egyptian costume which Verdi himself saw, or Mozart's *Die Zauberflöte* with the mixture of Roman heroic dress, tall wigs and women's hoops which Mozart knew in 1791. To attempt a previous period view of an earlier period is a piece of historical authenticity which the Romantics never ventured upon. No doubt the designer asked to create the costumes for a production of an opera set in 1350 but written in 1850, in the manner of 1850, would reel with shock. He could try 1350 seen with the eyes of 1980, but in 1980 to tackle the 1850 view of 1350 would require layers of sophistication not taught in art colleges. The contemporary policy is the one which rules what is suitable; the modern definition of beauty, the current concept of history, the daily fashion for revivals, the latest argument as to what is ideal, the coeval ability to see, all condition the artistic approach, for producer and designer alike. People are selective in their view of history, and some ages are admired more than others, with the result that periods go in and out of fashion along with everything else. Accordingly the 1850 view of 1350 would only be attempted if this day and age considered 1850 to be the most attractive period in the past, which it does not.

Costume on the stage is ever the slave of the date of the production. Each change in artistic theory results in a change in theatre costume, and when art tries to reform the previous art style, or to reject it, costume follows suit, for it is a part of art. It is one of the ways the latest aesthetic ideal expresses itself, so it is manacled to modernity. The contemporary mentality controls both understanding and appreciation, while advances in knowledge change the awareness of the distinctions between period mentalities, so that the definition of what matters varies. Accordingly each established artistic manner is challenged by the next generation of young artists and designers all eager to proclaim their new theory as the instant cure for the faults of their fathers, and to determine what it is now worthy to know. By such assertion the young identify themselves, and define who and what they are, and what their generation stands for. It follows that they like to look different in clothes and décor, so that they can claim that they are different from their predecessors. This changeability in styles and methods manifests itself in theatre costume as in anything else, and is part of mankind's need for new stimuli. To be a changeless animal or insect, humanity would have to resemble the ant, where each individual lives and dies in an alloted place according to a predetermined function. Human beings are probably unique in their social mobility and freedom from a rigid pattern of life. Consequently they are at liberty to determine their own vision of themselves. While they are not free to choose their own characters, they can select the way in which they shall illustrate themselves, whether it shall be in a straightforward manner or in a masquerade. Humanity can change its plumage, even down to the skin, the hair and even the colour of the eyes, with its paints and dyes, its drugs and lenses. In the wild animals can change according to the season from colour to white, but that is a set pattern repeated with every coming of the winter. Humans may use colour when and how they please, to harmonize with the season or to revolt against it. They display in the same way that animals do but the statement is more sophisticated than in the wild where it suffices for a creature to state its sex and its dominance. This is most obvious in male humans where a variety of ties can proclaim the wearer's

profession, hobby, club, sport, or regiment, although more recently it has been joined by the campaign tee-shirt which can be worn by both sexes. Both garments make statements, and are a part of the language of clothing. As this language exists it is employed by the stage to advertise the characters it presents. While in the crowded street one's individual statement may not be very visible, on a stage it becomes a proclamation. Yet as there are generations, that proclamation may only be peculiar to that generation, for it will be ousted by what the next wave of youth determines as its visual display. There is a look to every age for that is how each era declares itself. Sight is more dominant in the human animal than the sense of smell or touch, so that the visual declaration is the one that will be noticed most by fellow humans.

Of course as humans are predetermined as to the number of arms and legs they have, there is a limit to how far the change of appearance can be carried, but within that limitation much ingenuity is applied to modifying proportion, tone, size and scale, so that each generation can convince itself, that it has discovered a new look for itself, even if it is often only reworking an old theme. So long as the variation seems new to them, the young are happy with this identity, and splash its format over everything else they touch, from motor cars to theatrical costume. Thus there is a period look for everything, and no part of theatre design can escape from this overwhelming inundation, this declaration of identity. Everything on the stage must be subjected by the new aesthetic policy. Costume, hairstyles, make-up, accessories, even the pose, the walk, the stance, and no less the acting manner, all are redefined by the new dominion. Where the intention is to reform, it shall be in the image of the reformer, and no part of theatre costume can escape from that.

Notes to the Text

Chapter One

1 L. de'Sommi, *Quattro Dialoghi in Materia di Rappresentazione Sceniche*, 1565, dialogue no. 3.

2 Ernest Boysse, *Le Théâtre des Jesuites*, 1880, pp. 32–112.

3 *Letters from Liselotte, Elizabeth Charlotte Princess Palatine and Duchess of Orleans*, trans. ed. Maria Kroll, Gollancz, 1970, letter of 16 Dec. 1694.

4 John Nichols, *The Progresses and Public Processions of Queen Elizabeth*, 1823, vol. II, pp. 159–64.

5 John Harris, Stephen Orgel, Roy Strong, *The King's Arcadia: Inigo Jones and the Stuart Court*, Arts Council of Great Britain, 1973, p. 160.

6 Allardyce Nicoll, *A History of English Drama 1660–1900*, Cambridge University Press, 1967, vol. I, p. 72.

7 Leslie Orrery, *A Concise History of Opera*, Thames & Hudson, 1972, pp. 16–19.

8 Nicholas Pevsner, *Academies of Art*, Cambridge University Press, 1940, pp. 84–9.

9 Diana de Marly, 'The Establishment of Roman Dress in Seventeenth Century Portraiture', *Burlington Magazine*, no. 868, vol. CXVII, July 1975, pp. 443–51; Diana de Marly, 'Dress in Baroque Portraiture – The Flight from Fashion', *The Antiquaries Journal*, vol. LX, part 2, 1980, pp. 268–84.

10 C.F. Menestrier, *Des Ballets Anciens et Modernes*, 1682, p. 250.

11 Letter of Katherine Philips to Lady Temple, 24 Jan. 1663/4, quoted in *The London Stage*, p. 74.

12 Samuel Pepys, *Diary*, ed. Latham & Matthews, Bell, 1970, entry for 8 March 1664.

13 Joseph Addison, *The Spectator*, no. 42, Wed. 18 April 1711.

Chapter Two

1 Luigi Riccoboni, *Historical and Critical Account of the Theatres in Europe*, 1741, p. 143.

2 Chappuzeau, *Le Théâtre François*, 1674, Livre III, chap. xxviii.

3 Jules Bonnassies, *La Comédie Française, Histoire Administrative 1658–1757*, 1874, p. 256.

4 Riccoboni, op. cit., p. 152.

5 Menestrier, op. cit., pp. 250–57.

6 Chappuzeau, ibid.

7 *Le Registre de la Grange 1659–1685*, ed. B.E. & G.P. Young, 1947, vol. I, p. 146.

8 A. Jullien, *Histoire du Costume au Théâtre*, 1880, p. 20.

9 Eudore Soulié, *Recherches sur Molière et sa Famille*, 1863, pp. 275–80.

10 *Le Registre de la Grange*, op. cit., vol. I, pp. 133–98; Bonassies, op. cit., p. 257.

11 Despois, *Le Théâtre Français sous Louis XIV*, 1882, pp. 133–4 and note.

12 *The Henslowe Papers*, ed. W. Greg, A.H. Bullen, 1907, Ms. I, 30, and Appendix I pp. 122–3.

13 Diana de Marly, 'The Status of Actors under Charles II of Great Britain: An Examination of the Livery Accounts of the Great Wardrobe', *Theatre Research/Recherches Théâtrales*, vol. XIV, 1980, pp. 45–53.

14 *The Dramatic Records of Sir Henry Herbert, Master of the Revels, 1632–1673*, ed. J.Q. Adams, 1917, Misc. Docs. no. XV, 6 Nov. 1660.

15 Court of Chancery, C24 1070/63; *Intelligence Domestick and Foreign*, 21–25 June 1695.

16 J. Downes, *Roscius Anglicanus*, 1707, passim.

17 Sibyl Rosenfeld, 'The Wardrobes of Lincoln's Inn Fields and Covent Garden', *Theatre Notebook*, vol. V, Oct. 1950–July 1951, pp. 15–19.

18 *George Anne Bellamy, Apology for the Life of,* 1785, vol. I, pp. 51–5, vol. II, pp. 189–90.

19 *The Committee Books of the Theatre Royal Norwich 1768–1825,* ed. D.H. Eshleman, Society for Theatre Research, 1970, Appendix A.

20 Colley Cibber, *Apology for the Life of Mr. Colley Cibber Comedian,* 1740, pp. 185–7.

21 Thomas Betterton, *A History of the English Stage,* 1741, p. 21.

22 Arnold Hare, *George Frederick Cooke, The Actor and the Man,* Society for Theatre Research, 1980, p. 87.

23 G.A. Bellamy, op. cit., II, pp. 191–2.

24 W.R. Chetwood, *A General History of the Stage,* 1749, pp. 22–4.

25 *Drury Lane Journal, Selections from James Winston's Diaries 1819–1827,* ed. A.L. Nelson & G.B. Cross, Society for Theatre Research, 1974, p. 35.

26 Diana de Marly, *Worth, Father of Haute Couture,* Elm Tree, 1980, chap. VIII 'Leading Ladies'.

27 Anthony Vaughan, *Born to Please, Hannah Pritchard, Actress 1711–1768,* Society for Theatre Research, 1979, pp. 84–7.

28 Tate Wilkinson, *Memoirs of His Own Life,* 1791, vol. I, pp. 98–9.

29 Archie Nathan, *Costumes by Nathan,* Newnes, 1966, passim.

30 *The Oxford Companion to the Theatre,* ed. P. Hartnoll, Oxford University Press, 1967, pp. 564–7.

Chapter Three

1 Doran, *Their Majesties' Servants, Annals of the British Stage,* Allen & Co., 1864, vol. II, p. 419.

2 Allardyce Nicoll, op. cit., vol. I, p. 172.

3 Doran, loc. cit.

4 Aaron Hill, *The Plain Dealer,* 12 Oct. 1724, and *The Works,* 1753, vol. I, pp. 89–91.

5 William Cooke, *Memoirs of Charles Macklin, Comedian,* 1804, pp. 90–95.

6 John Evelyn, *Diary,* ed. E.S. de Beer, Oxford University Press, 1959, p. 91, and p. 204.

7 W. Cooke, op. cit., pp. 283–4.

8 *The Statutes of the Realm,* George II, 19, c. 39.

9 Allardyce Nicoll, op. cit., vol. II, p. 414.

10 Donald MacMillan, *Drury Lane Calendar 1747–1776,* Oxford, 1938, p. xxix.

11 Thomas Davies, *Dramatic Miscellanies,* 1784, vol. III, pp. 90–95.

12 *Catalogue of the Library of David Garrick Esq.,* sold by Auction by Mr. Saunders, Wed. 23 April 1823.

13 Georg Lichtenberg, *Lichtenberg's Visits to England as described in his Letters and Diaries,* trans. M.L. Ware & W.H. Quarrell, Oxford, 1938, pp. 21–3.

14 Donald MacMillan, op. cit., note 1.

15 *The Reminiscences of Sarah Kemble Siddons,* ed. W. van Lennep, Cambridge, 1942, p. 19.

16 Ibid, p. 21.

17 G.A. Bellamy, op. cit., vol. II, p. 79.

18 James Boaden, *Memoirs of the Life of John Philip Kemble Esq.,* 1825, vol. I, p. 104.

19 Ibid p. 157.

20 John W. Cole, *The Life and Theatrical Times of Charles Kean FSA,* 1859, vol. I, pp. 107–8.

Chapter Four

1 S. Pepys, *Diary,* loc. cit.

2 J.R. Planché, *Recollections and Reflections,* Tinsley Bros., 1872, vol. I, p. 224.

3 Stella Mary Newton, *Renaissance Theatre Costume and the Sense of the Historic Past,* Rapp & Whiting, André Deutsch, 1973, p. 214.

4 Christopher Murray, *Robert William Elliston, Manager,* Society for Theatre Research, 1975, p. 88.

5 J.R. Planché, *The Costume of Shakespeare's Historical Tragedy King John,* 1823, Preface.

6 J.R. Planché, *History of British Costume,* Charles Knight, 1836, p. 78.

7 Edward Corbould, *The Tournament at Eglinton Castle,* 1840; S. Stevenson & H. Bennett, *Van Dyck in Check Trousers, Fancy Dress in Art and Life 1700–1900,* Scottish National Portrait Gallery, 1978, pp. 105–14.

8 J.W. Cole, op. cit., vol. II, pp. 23–8.

9 Certificates of Election, Society of Antiquaries of London, 1857.

10 James Boaden, op. cit., vol. I, p. 343.

11 Charles E. Pearce, *Mme Vestris and her Times,* Stanley Paul & Co., 1923, passim; Leo Waitzkin, *The Witch of Wych Street, A Study of the Theatrical Reforms of Madame Vestris,* Harvard University Honours Theses in English, no. 6, Harvard University Press, 1933.

12 J.R. Planché, *Recollections,* op. cit., vol. II, p. 22.

13 L. Orrery, op. cit., pp. 141–80.

Chapter Five

1 Stella Mary Newton, op. cit., pp. 204–5.

2 John Weaver, *The History of the Mimes and Pantomimes,* 1728, pp. 45–6.

3 M. Montagu-Nathan, *Mlle Camargo,* British Continental Press, 1932, p. 5.

4 W.R. Chetwood, *A General History of the Stage*, 1749, pp. 26–7.

5 Ifan Fletcher, 'History of Ballet in England 1600–1740', *Bulletin of New York Public Library*, Vol. 63, June 1959, pp. 284–91.

6 Jean Georges Noverre, *Letters on Dancing and Ballets*, trans. Cyril Beaumont, C.W. Beaumont, 1930, p. 82.

7 *Receuil de Programmes de Ballets de M. Noverre Maître de Ballets de la Cour Imperiale et Royale*, Vienna, 1776, passim.

8 Noverre, op. cit., p. 29.

9 Ibid, p. 43.

10 Ibid, p. 62.

11 Ibid, p. 29.

12 Carlo Blasis, *The Code of Terpsichore, The Art of Dancing*, trans. R. Barton, 1830, p. 109.

13 *Pavlova*, ed. Paul Magriel, Henry Holt & Co., New York, 1947, p. 11.

14 Romola Nijinski, *Nijinski*, Victor Gollancz, 1933, pp. 172–6.

15 Charles Spencer, *Leon Bakst*, Academy Editions, 1973, passim.

16 Charles Ricketts, *Self-Portrait*, ed. C. Lewis, Peter Davies, 1939, p. 301.

17 Diana de Marly, *The History of Haute Couture 1850–1950*, Batsford, 1980, pp. 81–97.

Chapter Six

1 *Theatre Notebook*, vol. VI, 1951–2, p. 80.

2 Diana de Marly, *Worth*, op. cit., pp. 91–2.

3 Laurence Irving, *Henry Irving, The Actor and his World*, Faber & Faber 1951, passim.

4 M.R. Holmes, *Stage Costume and Accessories in the London Museum*, HMSO, 1968. Irving's costumes are cat. nos. 18–169.

5 Madeleine Bingham, *The Great Lover, the Life and Art of Herbert Beerbohm Tree*, Hamish Hamilton, 1978, passim.

6 *The Oxford Companion to the Theatre*, op. cit., pp. 664–7.

7 S.B. Bancroft & M. Bancroft, *Mr. & Mrs. Bancroft on and off the Stage*, Richard Bentley & Sons, 1888, vol. II, pp. 393–4.

8 William Archer, *The Theatrical World of 1894*, intr. G.B. Shaw, Walter Scott, 1895, pp. 54–5.

9 *The Principal Dramatic Works of Thomas William Robertson*, intr. by his son, Samuel French, 1889, vol. I, p. x.

10 August Strindberg, *Plays*, trans. E. & W. Oland, Frank Palmer, 1913.

11 *Five Famous Plays of Anton Tchekoff*, trans. J. West & M. Fell, Duckworth, 1939.

12 Diana de Marly, *Worth*, op. cit., pp. 212–17.

13 *The Social Plays of Arthur Wing Pinero*, ed. Clayton Hamilton, E.P. Dutton, New York, 1917.

14 Stella Mary Newton, *Health, Art and Reason, Dress Reformers of the Nineteenth Century*, John Murray, 1974, pp. 136–7.

15 William Archer, op. cit., p. 111.

16 Diana de Marly, *The History of Haute Couture*, op. cit., Chap. IV 'The Revolt against Fashion'.

17 Oscar Wilde, *Plays*, Penguin Books, 1964, with *Salomé* trs. Lord Alfred Douglas.

18 *The Oxford Companion to the Theatre*, op. cit., pp. 247–50.

Chapter Seven

1 *The Oxford Companion to Film*, ed. L.A. Bawden, O.U.P., 1976, and National Film Theatre season programmes.

2 Norman MacDermott, *Everymania, The History of the Everyman Theatre Hampstead 1920–6*, Society for Theatre Research, 1975, p. 51.

3 James Agate, *The Selective Ego*, ed. T. Beaumont, Harrap, 1976, p. 120.

4 Ibid p. 238.

5 John Gay, *The Beggar's Opera*, with scenes and costumes by C. Lovat Fraser, W. Heinemann, 1921.

6 John Gudenian, 'Bermans and Nathans, Costume and the Entertainment World', *Costume*, no. 15, 1981, pp. 60–66.

7 W. Somerset Maugham, *The Collected Plays*, W. Heinemann, 1931.

8 Noel Coward, *Play Parade*, Doubleday, Dorn & Co., New York, 1933.

9 Luigi Pirandello, *Three Plays*, trans. E. Storer, J.M. Dent, 1923.

10 Eugene O'Neill, *Plays*, Boni & Liveright, New York, 1925.

11 Personal discussions with Stella Mary Newton, May–June 1981.

12 Eliot Martin Browne, *The Making of T.S. Eliot's Plays*, Cambridge University Press, 1969, passim.

Bibliography

ADDISON, Joseph, *The Spectator* no. 42, 1711.

AGATE, James, *The Selective Ego*, ed. T. Beaumont, Harrap, 1976.

ARCHER, William, *The Theatrical World of 1894*, intr. G.B. Shaw, Walter Scott, 1895.

BANCROFT, Squire & Marie, *Mr. & Mrs. Bancroft on and off the Stage*, Richard Bentley & Sons, 1888.

BELL, Jasmin, *Anna Pavlova*, HMSO, 1980.

BELLAMY, George Ann, *An Apology for the Life of George Anne Bellamy*, 1785.

BETTERTON, Thomas, *A History of the English Stage*, 1741.

BINGHAM, Madeleine, *The Great Lover, the Life and Art of Herbert Beerbohm Tree*, Hamish Hamilton, 1978.

BLASIS, Carlo, *The Code of Terpsichore, The Art of Dancing*, trans. R. Barton, 1830.

BOADEN, James, *Memoirs of the Life of John Philip Kemble Esq.*, 1825.

BONNASSIES, Jules, *La Comédie Française, Histoire Administrative 1658–1757*, 1874.

BOYSSE, Ernest, *Le Théâtre des Jesuits*, 1880.

BROWNE, Eliot Martin, *The Making of T.S. Eliot's Plays*, Cambridge University Press, 1969.

CHAPPUZEAU, *Le Théâtre François*, 1674.

CHETWOOD, W.R., *A General History of the Stage*, 1749.

CIBBER, Colley, *An Apology for the Life of Mr. Colley Cibber Comedian*, 1740.

CINTHIO, Geraldi, *Discurso sulle Tragedie*, Venice, 1554.

COLE, John, *The Life and Theatrical Times of Charles Kean FSA*, 1859.

COOKE, William, *Memoirs of Charles Macklin Comedian*, 1804.

CORBOULD, Edward, *The Tournament at Eglinton Castle*, 1840.

COWARD, Noel, *Play Parade*, Doubleday, Dorn & Co., New York, 1933.

DAVIES, Thomas, *Dramatic Miscellanies*, 1784.

DE LA GRANGE, *Le Registre de la Grange, 1659–1685*, ed. B.E. & G.P. Young, 1947.

DE MARLY, Diana, 'Dress in Baroque Portraiture – the Flight from Fashion', *The Antiquaries Journal*, vol. I.X, part 2, 1980.

DE MARLY, Diana, 'The Establishment of Roman Dress in Seventeenth Century Portraiture', *The Burlington Magazine* no. 868, vol. CXVII, 1975.

DE MARLY, Diana, 'The Status of Actors under Charles II of Great Britain: An Examination of the Livery Accounts of the Great Wardrobe', *Theatre Research/Recherches Théâtrales*, vol. XIV, 1980.

DE MARLY, Diana, *The History of Haute Couture 1850–1950*, Batsford, 1980.

DE MARLY, Diana, *Worth, Father of Haute Couture*, Elm Tree, 1980.

DE MARLY, Diana, ANDERSON, M., DALLADAY, Roger, and NEWTON, Stella Mary, *The History of the European Theatre*, Visual Publications, 1971.

DEPOIS, *Le Théâtre Français sous Louis XIV*, 1882.

DORAN, *Their Majesties' Servants, Annals of the British Stage*, Allen & Co, 1864.

DOWNES, John, *Roscius Anglicanus*, 1707.

DU FRESNOY, *De Arte Graphica*, trans. John Dryden, 1695.

ELIZABETH CHARLOTTE, *Letters from Liselotte, Elizabeth Charlotte Princess Palatine and Duchess of Orleans*, trans. ed. Maria Kroll, Gollancz, 1970.

Enciclopedia dello Spettacolo, Casa Editrice Le Maschere, Rome, 1954.

ESHLEMAN, Dorothy (ed.), *The Committee Books of the Theatre Royal Norwich 1768–1825*, Society for Theatre Research, 1970.

EVELYN, John, *Diary*, ed. E.S. de Beer, Oxford University Press, 1959.

FLETCHER, Ifan, 'History of Ballet in England 1600–1740', *Bulletin of New York Public Library*, 1959, vol. 63.

GAY, John, *The Beggars' Opera*, intro. by C. Lovat Fraser, W. Heinemann, 1921.

GUDENIAN, John, 'Bermans and Nathans, Costume in the Entertainment World', *Costume*, vol. XV, 1981.

HALL, Lillian, *Catalogue of Dramatic Portraits in the Theatre Collection of the Harvard College Library*, Harvard University Press, 1931.

HARE, Arnold, *George Frederick Cooke, The Actor and the Man*, Society for Theatre Research, 1980.

HENSLOWE, Philip, *The Henslowe Papers*, ed. W. Greg, A.H. Bullen, 1907.

HERBERT, Sir Henry, *The Dramatic Records of Sir Henry Herbert Master of the Revels 1632–1673*, ed. E.Q. Adams, Cornell Studies in English no. 3, New Haven, 1917.

HILL, Aaron, *The Works*, 1753.

HOLMES, M.R., *Stage Costume and Accessories in the London Museum*, HMSO, 1968.

IRVING, Lawrence, *Henry Irving the Actor and his World*, Faber & Faber, 1951.

JEFFERYS, Thomas, *A Collection of the Dresses of Different Nations, Antient and Modern, also of the Principal Characters of the English Stage*, 1757.

JOUVANCY, *Ratio Discendi et Docendi*, 1685.

JULLIAN, A., *Histoire de Costume au Théâtre*, 1880.

KERSLAKE, John, ed. *Catalogue of Theatrical Portraits in London Public Collections*, Society for Theatre Research, 1961.

LENNEP, William van, ed. *The London Stage*, vol. I, Southern Illinois University Press, Carbondale, 1960.

LESURE, François, *Deux Siècles d'Opéra Français*, catalogue de l'Exposition organisée à l'Occasion du Tricentenaire de l'Académie Royale de Musique par la Bibliothèque Nationale, Paris, 1972.

LICHTENBERG, Georg, *Lichtenberg's Visits to England as described in his Letters and Diaries*, trans. Ware and Quarrell, Oxford University Press, 1938.

MACDERMOTT, *Everymania, The History of the Everyman Theatre Hampstead 1920–6*, Society for Theatre Research, 1975.

MACMILLAN, Donald, *Drury Lane Calendar 1747–1776*, Oxford University Press, 1938.

MACREADY, W.C., *Diaries*, ed. W. Toynbee, Chapman & Hall, 1912.

MAGRIEL, Paul, *Pavlova*, Henry Holt & Co., New York, 1947.

MANDER, Raymond, & MITCHENSON, Joe, *Guide to the Maugham Collection of Theatrical Paintings*, National Theatre, 1980.

MAUGHAM, W. Somerset, *The Collected Plays*, W. Heinemann, 1931.

MENESTRIER, C.F., *Des Ballets Anciens et Modernes*, 1682.

MONTAGU-NATHAN, M., *Mlle Camargo*, British Continental Press, 1932.

MURRAY, Christopher, *Robert William Elliston a Theatrical Biography*, Society for Theatre Research, 1975.

NATHAN, Archie, *Costumes by Nathan*, Newnes, 1966.

NEWTON, Stella Mary, *Renaissance Theatre Costume and the Sense of the Historic Past*, Rapp & Whiting/André Deutsch, 1973.

NEWTON, Stella Mary, *Health, Art and Reason, Dress Reformers of the Nineteenth Century*, John Murray, 1974.

NICHOLS, John, *The Progresses and Public Processions of Queen Elizabeth*, 1823.

NICOLL, Allardyce, *A History of English Drama 1660–1900*, vol. I, Cambridge University Press, 1967.

NIJINSKI, Romola, *Nijinski*, Victor Gollancz, 1933.

NOVERRE, Jean Georges, *Letters on Dancing and Ballets*, trans. Cyril Beaumont, C.W. Beaumont, 1930.

NOVERRE, Jean Georges, *Receuil de Programmes de Ballets de M. Noverre Maître de Ballets de la Cour Imperiale et Royale*, Vienna, 1776.

O'NEILL, Eugene, *Plays*, Boni & Liveright, New York, 1925.

ORGEL, Stephen, & STRONG, Roy, *Inigo Jones: The Theatre of the Stuart Court*, Sotheby Parke Bernet, University of California Press, 1973.

ORGEL, Stephen, HARRIS, John, & STRONG, Roy, *The King's Arcadia: Inigo Jones and the Stuart Court*, Arts Council of Great Britain, 1973.

ORRERY, Leslie, *A Concise History of Opera*, Thames & Hudson, 1972.

Oxford Companion to Film, ed. L. A. Bawden, Oxford University Press, 1976.

Oxford Companion to the Theatre, ed. P. Hartnoll, Oxford University Press, 1967.

PEARCE, Charles, *Mme Vestris and her Times*, Stanley Paul & Co., 1923.

PEPYS, Samuel, *Diary*, ed. R. Latham & W. Matthews, Bell, 1970.

PEVSNER, Nicholas, *Academies of Art Past and Present*, Cambridge University Press, 1940.

PINERO, Arthur Wing, *Social Plays*, ed. C. Hamilton, Dutton, New York, 1917.

PIRANDELLO, Luigi, *Three Plays*, trans. E. Storer, J.M. Dent, 1923.

PLANCHÉ, James R., *The Costume of Shakespeare's Historical Tragedy King John*, 1823.

PLANCHÉ, James R., *History of British Costume*, Charles Knight, 1836.

PLANCHÉ, James R., *Recollections and Reflections*, Tinsley Bros., 1872.

READE, Brian, *Catalogue Raisonnée of Ballet Designs*, in the Department of Prints and Drawings at the Victoria and Albert Museum, HMSO, 1967.

RICCOBONI, Luigi, *Historical and Critical Account of the Theatres in Europe*, 1741.

RICKETTS, Charles, *Self-Portrait*, ed. C. Lewis, Peter Davies, 1939.

ROBERTSON, Thomas William, *The Principal Dramatic Works*, Samuel French, 1889.

ROSENFELD, Sibyl, 'The Wardrobes of Lincoln's Inn Fields and Covent Garden', *Theatre Notebook*, vol. V, Oct. 1950–July 1951.

ROSENFELD, Sibyl, *Foreign Theatrical Companies in Great Britain in the 17th and 18th Centuries*, Society for Theatre Research, Pamphlet Series no. 4, 1954–5.

SHAW, George Bernard, *The Complete Plays*, London, 1931.

SIDDONS, Sarah, *Reminiscences*, ed. W. van Lennep, Cambridge University Press, 1942.

SOMMI, Leone d', *Quattro Dialoghi in Materia di Rappresentazione Sceniche*, c 1565.

SOULIÉ, Eudore, *Recherches sur Molière et sa Famille*, 1863.

SPENCER, Charles, *Leon Bakst*, Academy Editions, 1973.

STEVENSON, Sara, & BENNETT, Helen, *Van Dyck in Check Trousers, Fancy Dress in Art and Life 1700–1900*, Scottish National Portrait Gallery, National Museum of Antiquities of Scotland, 1978.

STRINDBERG, August, *Plays*, trans. E. & W. Oland, Frank Palmer, 1913.

TCHEKOFF, Anton, *Five Famous Plays*, trs. J. West & M. Fell, Duckworth, 1939.

VAUGHAN, Anthony, *Born to Please, Hannah Pritchard Actress 1711–1768*, Society for Theatre Research, 1979.

VILLIERS, George, Duke of Buckingham, *The Rehearsal*, 1671.

WAITZKIN, Leo, *The Witch of Wych Street, A Study of the Theatrical Reforms of Madame Vestris*, Harvard University Honours Theses in English no. 6, Harvard University Press, 1933.

WEAVER, John, *The History of the Mimes and Pantomimes*, 1728.

WEBSTER, Mary, *Johan Zoffany 1733–1810*, exhibition catalogue, National Portrait Gallery, 1977.

WILDE, Oscar, *Plays*, Penguin Books, 1964.

WILKINSON, Tate, *Memoirs of his Own Time*, 1795.

WINSTON, James, *Drury Lane Journal, Selections from James Winston's Diaries 1819–1827*, ed. A.L. Nelson & G.B. Cross, Society for Theatre Research, 1974.

Some Theatre Collections in Europe, North America, and Australia

AUSTRALIA
Performing Arts Museum, Victorian Arts Centre, Melbourne.

AUSTRIA
Theatre Collection, National Library, Vienna.

CANADA
Metropolitan Library, Toronto, Theatre Department.

CZECHOSLOVAKIA
Theatre Department, National Museum, Prague. Cesky Krumlov Castle theatre and costume collection.

DENMARK
Teaterhistorisk Museum, Royal Court Theatre, Copenhagen.

FRANCE
Musée de l'Opéra, Paris.
Comédie Française collection, Paris.

GERMANY, EAST
Meiningen Court Theatre.

GERMANY, WEST
Munich Theatre Museum.
Munich Stadtmuseum marionette collection.

HUNGARY
National Theatre, Budapest.

ITALY
La Scala Museum, Milan.

Museo Bucardo, Rome.
Casa Goldoni, Venice.
Meleto Castle, Tuscany, has private theatre and a few eighteenth-century costumes.

NETHERLANDS
Toneel Theatre Museum, Amsterdam.

NORWAY
Theatre Museum, Oslo.

POLAND
Muzeum Teatralne, Teatr Wielki, Warsaw.

ROMANIA
Caragide Theatre Museum, Bucharest.

SWEDEN
Drottningholms Teatermuseum.
Goteborg Theatre Museum.

UNITED KINGDOM
Theatre Museum at Victoria & Albert Museum, London, due to move to Flower Market, Covent Garden, in 1983.
Museum of London theatre costume collection.
Mander & Mitchenson Collection, Beckenham Place, Lewisham, London.
Royal Opera House Covent Garden archives.
Anna Pavlova Museum, Ivy House, Hampstead, London.
British Museum, Department of Prints & Drawings, London.
Society for Theatre Research Library is at present housed at Senate House, London University, until it transfers to the Flower Market, Covent Garden.

Bristol University Theatre Collection, Avon.
Duke of Devonshire's Inigo Jones Collection,
Chatsworth, Derbyshire.

UNITED STATES
California University Theatre Collection,
Berkeley.
Library of Congress, District of Columbia,
Washington.
Motly Design Collection, Illinois University.
Theatre Museum, Boothbay, Maine.
Harvard University Theatre Collection,
Massachusetts.

Billy Rose Collection, New York Public Library.
The Players Collection, New York.
William Seymour Theatre Collection, Princeton
University Library.
Hoblitzelle Theatre Arts Library, Texas
University, Austin, Texas.
Rockefeller Theatre Prints Collection, Yale
University, New Haven.

USSR
Maly Theatre Museum, Leningrad.
Bakhrushin Museum, Moscow.
Bolshoi Theatre Archive, Moscow.

Index